BLOOD ON THE HORNS
The Long Strange Ride
of Michael Jordan's Chicago Bulls

Roland Lazenby

ADDAX
PUBLISHING
GROUP

Lenexa, KS

Published by Addax Publishing Group Inc.
Copyright © 1998 by Roland Lazenby
Designed by Bill Kovarik
Cover Design by Jerry Hirt

Addax Publishing Group Inc.
8643 Hauser Drive
Suite 235
Lenexa, KS 66215

ISBN: 1-886110-59-X

Distributed to the trade by Andrews McMeel Publishing
4520 Main Street
Kansas City, MO 64111

1 3 5 7 9 10 8 6 4 2

Printed in the United States of America

Library of Congress Cataloging-in-Publication Data

Lazenby, Roland.
    Blood on the horns : the long strange ride of Michael Jordan's
Chicago Bulls / by Roland Lazenby.
        p. cm.
    ISBN 1-886110-59-X (hardcover)
        1. Chicago Bulls (Basketball team) 2. Jordan, Michael, 1963- .
3. Jackson, Phil. I. Title.
GV885.52.C45L3916 1998
796.323'64'0977311--dc21
                                                        98-27534
                                                            CIP

"I wanted the Bull to be a true bull, in a bull fight. You know, he's a big and black thing with long horns and red eyes and mean. I wanted a mean looking Bull. Most of the early submissions were of full bodies. The Bull with his head down, that sorta thing. I said, 'I want a face. Gimme a face.' Then they gave me a face that looked real good. Now, I said, 'All we have to do is make his eyes red. I want blood on his nose, or red nostrils, and blood on his horns.' Which they did. They did a beautiful job. That became our symbol."

— *Dick Klein, Chicago Bulls founder, describing his work with designers in 1966 to create the team's logo.*

Preface

A Room with a View

I'm dedicating this book to my father, William Lowry "Hopper" Lazenby, a West Virginia boy with a smooth, two-handed set shot. He was a master of fakes, not just pump fakes and twitches. He faked with his face, his eyes, his arched eyebrows, anything to get you going one way so that he could go the other. He was nicknamed "Hopper" because of basketball, not because he was so good at it— although he was pretty good—but because his older brother, Clyde, was really good. Clyde was an all-stater in West Virginia and earned one of the first basketball scholarships to Virginia Tech back in the 1920s. Anyway, as the story goes, Clyde fell in love and left Tech after about a year to get married, but his nickname "Hopper" stuck. Stuck so well, in fact, that each time another Lazenby came along on the basketball team at Beaver High in Bluefield, West Virginia, he, too, was named "Hopper." In all, there were three "Hopper" Lazenbys, which became a bit confusing in their advancing years.

My older brother, Hampton, was another good player, but I was not. Yet that hasn't prevented me from playing pickup ball with a passion my entire life. I'm 45 now, with aching knees and heels, and still play three or four days a week. I often wonder why I've continued to torture myself by playing lo these many years. I usually answer that question by saying that if you're going to write about a game you should at least have the decency to play it regularly. But deep down I know there's a bigger reason. Because it keeps me close to my father, who died in 1981.

So when Phil Jackson talks about the spiritual side of the game,

I have a decent idea of what he's talking about.

I am telling you this to explain my emotional attachment to the Bulls. There are millions of fans across the globe who have formed their own attachments to the team for their own reasons.

This reason is mine: The Bulls are a special team, made up of special guardians of the game, of which Michael Jordan is certainly one. But the chief guardian is 76-year-old assistant coach Tex Winter, who has spent his professional life developing something he calls the "sideline triangle offense." It's a paradigm for the game that Winter first learned while playing for coach Sam Barry at the University of Southern California. The triangle offense has shown itself to be immensely frustrating and complicated for NBA players trying to learn it. Yet once they learn the triangle offense, what at first seemed complicated makes the game amazingly simple. It is an old-style offense, predicated on the notion of moving the ball, which means that greater players have to share the basketball with lesser players. In short, it means that people like Michael Jordan have to trust people like Dickey Simpkins. It is the essence of teamwork. The triangle, as Tex Winter teaches it, also requires all the players to read the defense and cut to open areas on the floor. As a result, it creates motion in the game, and when the Bulls executed it, those displays of motion could be dazzling.

This, of course, was in distinct contrast to most of the other 28 teams in the NBA, which run those dreadful isolation offenses that the game has evolved to, the kind where one player works near the basket while his four teammates stand on the perimeter waiting for the defense to double-team the ball, which in turn might mean that someone would actually make a pass.

CBS broadcaster Billy Packer, a friend of mine, attended a 1998 playoff game between the Charlotte Hornets and Atlanta Hawks. Disgusted and bored, he got up and left in the third quarter.

Which brings me back to Tex Winter's guardianship. He knows that basketball's past is its future. Apparently not many in the NBA have stopped counting their money long enough to consider that. The Phoenix Suns tried to adopt the triangle offense in October and November 1996. They lost their first dozen games and gave up. "I'm not sure we were really running the triangle," quipped Bulls reserve Joe Kleine, who was on that Phoenix team. "I think maybe we had a square."

The scenario wasn't so laughable for former Bulls assistant Jim

Cleamons, who took over as head coach of the Dallas Mavericks and attempted to install the triangle only to be met with a player revolt. Learning to play the game the right way takes time, time that today's young millionaires don't seem to have.

It's well documented that the Bulls had their own troubles adjusting to the offense in 1990 and 1991. But Winter likes to point out that Jackson's steadfast determination in implementing the triangle with the Bulls was the beginning of his greatness as a head coach. It was also the beginning of the greatness of the Bulls.

In the early days of the game, the old pros used to have a phrase to describe the passing game they ran off the post. They called it "making the ball sing."

The Bulls, of course, have done plenty of that over the past decade. With Jordan's offensive brilliance and Winter's old-style approach, they've thrilled millions of fans. What's better, the Bulls have absolutely overwhelmed their opponents. It has been my delight to watch them beat in the heads of teams running lazily conceived isolation offenses. It has been my dismay that those teams still don't get the message: The Bulls' greatness comes from Michael Jordan's and Scottie Pippen's dedication to playing the game the way it was meant to be played.

In the spring of 1998, Winter was once again nominated for the Naismith Memorial Basketball Hall of Fame after having been passed over several times previously. If they don't elect him this time around, perhaps the nice folks up at the hall should just consider locking the building and throwing away the key.

Which brings me to the reason I wrote this book. The Bulls, on their way to winning a sixth National Basketball Association championship, were caught in a power struggle and about to break up. That was bad because the situation threatened to end the careers of two of the game's greatest guardians, Jordan and Winter, which in turn threatened the game itself.

I wanted to know why.

And this book is an attempt to answer that.

Back when he was forced to ride herd over the Detroit Pistons and all their gnarly egos, coach Chuck Daly used to have a saying: The game is simple, but the people are complicated.

The Pistons, by the way, won two championships and found that they had absolutely exhausted their relationships. It is an incredible testament to the great competitors who have built the

Bulls that they won six and were able to keep going strong despite substantial baggage.

In short, what pushed the Bulls to the brink of a break up?

There was no short answer, but if I had to come up with one, I would say, "The insecurities of general manager Jerry Krause."

Then again, if I had to answer what caused the Bulls to be built into six-time world champions, the answer—right after the words "Michael Jordan and Scottie Pippen"—would be "The insecurities of Jerry Krause."

In reality, they're all responsible for the break up. Jerry Krause. Phil Jackson. Scottie Pippen. Michael Jordan. Jerry Reinsdorf. Tex Winter. Just as they're all responsible for all those sweet, ineffable moments of victory.

That is not a statement that will please Michael Jordan or Scottie Pippen, who loathe Krause. And I am truly sorry to make a statement that displeases Jordan or Pippen, because they are the giant hearts of a great basketball team. But it's true.

Why did they loathe Krause?

Pippen loathed Krause because the general manager had attempted to trade him, something that Pippen considered the severest disrespect.

Jordan also loathed Krause because he had attempted to trade Pippen and had been at odds with Jackson. Both of those things got in the way of the team's ability to compete, and above all, Jordan would brook nothing that interfered with competing.

Thus, as the 1998 season wound to a conclusion, Bulls fans were faced with the power struggle and possible break up of the team. It was a control thing between Krause and the team's two superstars, with Jackson and Winter and Reinsdorf sort of stuck trying to sort things out and move forward. Or something close to that.

Which brings me back to my father's set shot. He used to play in the semi-pro industrial leagues around southern West Virginia back in the late 1930s and '40s. Because I was born later in his life, I never got to see him compete. But I heard tales of how he would lace up that shot, sometimes even when a teammate was wide open under the hoop. I heard that my father once played a game against the Original Celtics, the great barnstorming pro team of that era, and that he was absolutely delighted when Celtics star Davey Banks sat in the stands at midcourt and swished a shot on the first try. I have no idea if these stories are true, but I believe they are, because I used to shoot with my father. He had been badly burned in 1946, before I was born, and could no longer play anything more than h-o-r-s-e or a lightweight one-on-one. We had a 12 by 12 concrete court in the driveway, but he preferred to launch his shots by the giant elm in the side yard, a good 30 feet or more from the hoop. He'd fake one way or another, then pull up and while his eyes grew wide, he'd launch that two-handed set and give a little whoop as it hit, which was sort of his version of talking trash.

His real lesson for me, of course, was that life, just like a good game of h-o-r-s-e, needs wide parameters.

Phil Jackson was talking with me about the power struggle one day when he said something that reminded me of my father. Jackson was talking about how Krause was always trying to establish some sort of control with Pippen and Jordan. "It's all control," the coach said. "It's all wanting to control. I think it's good to have a sense of control, but you have to make your perimeters big. An expansive thing, instead of making it narrow, and then people are bumping into those fences all the time."

The greater the people involved, the greater the parameters, it seems.

From there, I jumped to a naive notion. How about getting all the key figures involved to sit down in a room to discuss the thing? They all had done things to anger and hurt each other. They all had their pain. Why not just talk it out? So I asked Jordan about that one day.

He tilted a questioning eye at me.

"Without blows?" he asked. "There's no way."

"Maybe in a padded room?" I suggested. "Why couldn't it be that simple? Just to talk it out?"

"Even if you put all five of us in one room," he said, "and we tell our pains or whatever, we've proceeded past that. And we had to, to be successful.

"You know what?" he said. "From my perspective, a lot of my pain was over and done with early. And I still pursued my job with the same integrity and determination."

He implied that Krause had not been able to get past his pain, and, in fact, was allowing personal issues to get in the way of winning, which to Jordan was the worst possible sin.

"All the pain and suffering and hurt aside, you still gotta look at what jobs are being done," Jordan said. "If you're gonna sit here and hold grudges, then why should I go through my career.... If I hadn't forgotten that moment, I'd still be giving less than 100 percent, or I'd think of revenge. But I moved forward with the notion of winning."

It was clear that the parameters weren't big enough to allow them to sit down and talk it out.

So this book has become a vastly inferior version of that room. An attempt to get it all out on the table. A room with a view.

For the Bulls.

For their fans.

For my old man.

Roland Lazenby
June 15, 1998

> "You're gonna have to ask yourself, who do you trust?"
> — *The Devil's Advocate*

1/ Power Days, Glitter Nights

No matter where he played, the buildings virtually sparkled for Michael Jordan. Each game, as he stepped onto the floor for introductions, he was greeted by the flashes of a thousand small cameras. The phenomenon was most brilliant at the United Center in Chicago, where the introductions would build to a crescendo of noise and light until Jordan's name was called as the fifth starter, and the arena became a pulsating strobe. Later, at the opening tip, these same lights would again flicker furiously. But they were most maddening during free throws, when Jordan went to the line, and the rows of fans behind the basket would break into a dizzying twinkle, bringing to mind a mirror ball at a junior prom or perhaps the consorting of hyper-charged fireflies on a summer evening.

The fans were regularly reminded that flash cameras were forbidden, that the flashes were unnecessary in the National Basketball Association's fancy, well-lit buildings. But that didn't deter them, and the security staff in every arena seemed to have acquiesced to their thrill at recording the moment.

Asked how he could possibly shoot free throws under the conditions, Jordan replied with an avuncular smile, "I got used to that a long time ago."

Jordan had always been a superstar who understood and accommodated his fans. That was particularly true during the 1997-98 season, as indications grew that it could well be his last in pro basketball. He understood that seemingly everybody wanted an Instamatic record of what appeared to be his final days in the game, even if they were bleary, out-of-focus prints from the upper deck that reduced Jordan and his teammates to hazy apparitions. For the fans, the photo prints were proof that they were there, witnessing his greatness in person. The photographs were something to be tucked in the hope chest as a family heirloom. *Michael was bigger than Babe Ruth*, the grandkids could be told later.

Babe Ruth? Actually, if Jordan was comparable to anyone, it might have well been pro basketball's other truly great competitor, center Bill Russell, who led the Boston Celtics to 11 championships in the 13 seasons between 1957 and 1969. It was Russell's fate to dominate the league during the final ugly days of segregation. There was fan adulation, but there was also hatred. How far did it go? One time somebody broke into Russell's house and defecated in his bed. Good enough reason, it would seem, to be an angry young man.

That was not Jordan's experience, though. Tens of thousands of fans paid homage to him each game night. Hundreds, sometimes thousands, more gathered in the streets. Outside the arenas. Outside his hotels. Hoping to catch a glimpse as Jordan and his teammates exited their bus. Countless others sent him tribute, filling a succession of storage rooms with cards and letters and flowers and gifts and requests.

But the camera lights were by far the warmest measure of his popularity. Each time he made a spectacular play, Michael Jordan's world glittered, a twinkling firmament of adulation that served as a backdrop for his every move.

It was a cold night in mid-March, and the Bulls were back in snowy Chicago to face the New Jersey Nets in the United Center after a rain-soaked, two-game road trip to Texas. Each game was a countdown, with just seventeen appearances remaining on the regular-season schedule. On the surface, there was little to reveal the grip of anxiety quietly tightening around the franchise. But the key figures all sensed the impending showdown over the future of Jordan's career and the future of the team, a showdown that had been building all season. It was a game of chicken, with each side waiting to see who would blink first.

"It's about power," Bulls coach Phil Jackson had explained hoarsely in a private interview at his office in the Berto Center, the team's handsome practice facility in suburban Deerfield, hours before the game. When Jackson began coaching the team in 1989, his hair was black and his face was fresh. The time had not been kind, and neither had this season. His tired eyes were ringed by dark circles, bringing to mind those lines from Townes Van Zandt:

Livin' on the road, my friend,
was gonna keep you free and clean.
Now you wear your skin like iron.
Your breath's as hard as kerosene. . .

Power, indeed. The Bulls were caught in the throes of an internecine struggle for control of the team, with Jackson, Jordan and teammate Scottie Pippen pitted against Jerry Krause, the team's vice president of basketball operations/general manager, who announced before the season began that Jackson would not return as coach in the fall of 1998.

"This is it," Krause had said. "Phil and I know it. We all know it."

In announcing his move, Krause did not identify exactly what had led to Jackson's scheduled departure, but the relationship between the coach and general manager had obviously worn thin, which was not unusual for pro basketball, a small business of big media attention, big salaries and big egos.

Krause's announcement, in turn, prompted Jordan to respond when training camp opened in October that he would retire if Jackson was not retained. "If Phil's not going to be here, I'm certainly not going to be here," Jordan told reporters.

Like that, the short, portly Krause had put himself in the unenviable position of being the man to drive Jordan from the game. At least that was what appeared to be happening. In actuality, the matter involved a tangle of worn relationships. And in time, the future of the team would come down a tug-of-war over the career of Pippen, the star forward who masterfully complemented Jordan during the team's drive to five championships.

In 1991, Pippen made the egregious error of signing a long-term contract with the team, despite being cautioned against such a move even by team officials. As a result, the forward had labored much of the past decade while earning an average of about $3 million a year. While most Americans would be absolutely bug-eyed with delight at such prospects, the NBA had become a fantasy world awash in cash in recent seasons, leaving Pippen to labor for essentially 1991 dollars as he watched dozens of younger, far less accomplished athletes pull in deals worth $10, $15 even $20 million per season.

The problem for the Bulls was that at the close of the 1998 playoffs, Pippen's contract would be up and the going price for his services was forecast to run in the neighborhood of $45 million over three seasons. In the absurdity of NBA dollars, that wasn't a terrible price, except that the Bulls were already paying Jordan approximately $33 million per season.

Where there's money and success and vast public attention, there are usually immensely complicated personality conflicts. Such was the case with Chicago's basketball team. As spring approached, these conflicts had manifested themselves in a nasty little public relations war between the key parties that had created a tangle of illusions for the fans, for the media, for the Bulls themselves.

Despite this uncomfortable checkmate hanging over their heads, the Bulls still managed to work their way through an injury-filled season, and despite early setbacks, found themselves on this night in mid-March with a 47-17 record, the best in the league's Eastern Conference.

Even so, the comfort level was not very high. Heading into the season, Krause had likened the situation to a divorce, and it had that horrible feel to it, with the same air of confusion and mistrust.

Jackson had contended privately for the past few years that Krause employed a "brusque" management style and seemed caught up in the petty trappings of his title. "Jerry wants to be the most powerful person in the organization, and it's hard for him to allow Michael just to be Michael," Jackson said. "Michael doesn't want power. He wants to be one of the players. But he wants a person who's not gonna boss him around or shove him around or squeeze him into corners and do those types of things. That's what it's all about."

In the public's mind, team chairman Jerry Reinsdorf was allied with Krause, his loyal charge. They were known to Bulls fans as "the two Jerrys," the befuddling coalition that had somehow managed to rule the administration of "the Jordan era." As the plot of this story took its twists and turns, the mystery grew, because allowing the break up of this great team appeared to be a colossal business mistake, a miscalculation of gigantic proportions. And Reinsdorf, who had worked his way up from a lower middle-class upbringing in Brooklyn to become a hugely successful real estate/sports entrepreneur, had rarely made big mistakes.

"We've been through this 1,000 times, and nobody can really figure out what the plan is," said Bulls guard Steve Kerr, acknowledging that management's moves had left him and his teammates stumped. "In Chicago, everywhere we go, people are asking us, 'How can they possibly think about breaking this team up?' And frankly, we don't have any answers for that."

Kerr surmised that Reinsdorf, who hadn't been around the team during the season, was getting the same kinds of questions from the Bulls' two dozen minority shareholders, who in turn were being asked questions by family and friends at every cocktail party or family gathering.

"Why," Jordan himself had asked a month earlier, "would you change a coach who has won five championships when he has the respect of his players and certainly the understanding of his players to where they go out and play hard each and every day. Why?

"I think it's more or less a personality conflict, and that has a lot to do with it. It certainly can't be because of (Jackson's) job and what he's done with the players and the respect he's won from the players. His success as a coach is certainly impeccable. I don't think that can be questioned. I think it's more personal than anything."

Actually, the matter was really an issue of Jackson and Jordan trying to take away Krause's power, Reinsdorf implied in a phone conversation from his Arizona home, a winter refuge. "It's Phil who doesn't want to stay on," the team chairman said, adding that in 1996 Jackson had turned down a five-year contract extension.

The suggestion here was that Jackson and Jordan had manipulated the circumstances to make it appear that Krause wanted to break up basketball's most successful team. The public, Reinsdorf said, had "a total misread of what Jerry Krause wants to accomplish, a belief that what Jerry Krause wants to do is dismantle the team. Jerry Krause doesn't want to do that."

Reinsdorf said this privately, yet publicly had been defiantly mum on the issue. He and Krause had suffered a tremendous battering in the press over this issue. He could have spoken publicly to perhaps clear up Jackson's status or at least defend the team's actions, but doing so, he said, would have likely resulted in an even bigger "pissing match," further sullying Reinsdorf's own reputation and that of Jackson's. "We have a great coach," Reinsdorf said. "Why get into it publicly and do something to damage his reputation?"

Yet as a result of their silence, Reinsdorf and Krause, in the public's eyes, appeared tremendously challenged in explaining what they were doing and exactly why they were doing it. What spoke for them was a collection of half-statements and implied motivations from over the past few years.

Clearly, there were practical considerations that drove the owner and his general manager. The Bulls were the most costly team in NBA history with a player payroll for 1997-98 that stretched beyond $60 million, more than twice the league's salary cap. And the Bulls were an aging team. Both Krause and Reinsdorf acknowledged that they wanted to make the transition from the Jordan era to the next team of Bulls without falling into the deep misery of losing, as the Boston Celtics had done in the wake of Larry Bird's retirement in 1992. The Celtics, according to some NBA observers, were so busy honoring the aging Bird and co-stars Kevin McHale and Robert Parish that the team's management failed to plan adequately for the future.

Krause and Reinsdorf said they didn't want to make that same mistake. Instead, it seemed they were making an even bigger one by pushing the wildly popular superstar out the door, the kind of public relations nightmare from which the two Jerrys might never recover.

"They've been saying for three years now they don't want to see this team fall at the end of this run like the Larry Bird Boston Celtics fell," observed a Bulls staff member. "Eventually that's gonna turn around and haunt them. It has and it will. Even if you want to get rid of these guys, you don't say, or you don't insinuate it. You keep your mouth shut from day one."

Krause had often cited the Celtics as his example of a franchise to emulate because of their ability to win 16 league championships while rebuilding a series of teams over three decades. But Pippen said Krause had missed the major point about the Celtics — club president Red Auerbach built his teams on allegiance and mutual respect, the so-called "Celtic Pride." The jersey numbers of the great Celtics were retired, and many of them were allowed to spend their entire careers in Boston.

The Bulls, Pippen said, "just haven't put themselves into a position to be looked at as a franchise like the Lakers, the Boston Celtics, who have had great teams and allowed their great players to finish their careers there."

Celtics players supposedly held great respect, if not love, for Auerbach, Pippen said. "But you won't get any player to say anything good about Krause."

Krause, unfortunately, had made sometimes vague and ambiguous statements, leading to a public interpretation that he so badly wanted to prove that he was a great general manager that he planned to break up a team that had won five championships in seven seasons so that he could start over with new players and establish his own genius.

"I think Krause just wants control," Pippen said in a private interview. "He wants to win a title without Michael. And he wants to win one without Phil. And me. Just to be able to say he's great at what he does."

What Bulls players, team staff members, media representatives and other parties interviewed could not figure out was why Reinsdorf would for even a minute allow Krause to entertain such a notion.

"Both Jerrys egos are large enough to make them think they can do it, despite the obstacles, despite the public opinion," one Bulls employee theorized. "They think they can do it again (win a series of titles) over the next 10 years."

As Phil Jackson noted, Reinsdorf was a "guy who doesn't make bad business deals." That, in turn, led Jackson to speculate that perhaps Reinsdorf was planning to sell the team to a party that would keep Jordan, Pippen and Jackson as the nucleus of the Bulls. "A big corporation," Jackson said when asked about possible purchasers. "A Chicago corporation. It's a possibility. I know there's people out there who would like to see it happen."

Another team official conceded that someday in the next few years Reinsdorf could sell the team, but nothing of that nature was impending, the official said, explaining that "the Bulls are a big part of Jerry's life."

Asked about the situation, Reinsdorf emphasized that his interest was simply winning more championships. "We want to win as many as we can," he said.

Whatever the outcome, the plot was packed with intrigue, pulling the emotional strings of NBA fans everywhere like a soap opera. At every road game in every city, media representatives were peppering Jordan with questions about the team's future. "It's fascinating," Kerr said during a March trip to New York, "to go through this whole thing. It would be better if it were a little less exciting and we could just kind of keep things together. But it's fun to be a part of, regardless of what happens. It's an exciting team to play for."

TEX

Square in the middle of this conflict was the franchise's elder conscience, 76-year-old assistant coach Tex Winter. While it was true that the grind of success and competition had brought an end to the once-close personal ties between Jackson and Krause, it was Winter who had helped hold together their tenuous professional relationship.

Winter brought to the debate the rare perspective of a half century spent in coaching. He had played against Jackie Robinson in junior college and later wound up at Southern Cal, where he was a teammate of Bill Sharman and Alex Hannum playing basketball for the legendary Sam Barry. Only an injury prevented Winter from competing in the 1942 Helsinki Olympics as a pole vaulter. He served in the Navy during World War II, and in the aftermath became one of America's premier college coaches, getting his first head coaching job at Marquette University at age 28. Over his many years in the game, he had devised the Bulls' famed triangle offense and deserved a substantial portion of the credit for the team's success in blending the supremely talented Jordan with the host of role players on the roster.

Furthermore, Winter held a giant regard for Jackson, his immediate boss; a tremendous loyalty to Krause, the longtime friend who had hired him; and a deep and abiding respect for Jordan, whose talent and playing style constantly challenged Winter's deeply held convictions about the game.

"He's been so honest that it's been a blessing for all of us," Jackson said of Winter. "Because he's the one person in the entire organization who can speak his piece. I think Jerry looks to him for balance in a lot of ways. You know, he's the first one to tell Jerry, 'You know, Jerry, you're nothing except the title.' The next minute, he'll tell me, 'What have you coached?' I'll say, 'I coached the CBA championship in Albany.' He'll pop everybody's balloon."

"I feel like sometimes I'm sorta caught in the middle on this thing because I am friends with both Jerry Krause and Phil Jackson," Winter said. "Jerry Krause is our overall boss as far as the franchise is concerned, yet I'm the assistant coach to Phil Jackson. I don't like to get caught in the middle on a lot of the things that might transpire. But a lot of the time I feel like I am. I certainly don't like to be put in that position. But the good thing about it is, Jerry Krause and Phil Jackson have tried to avoid putting me in the box like that. That helps tremendously. Sometimes I put myself in that box because I don't know which way to go, who to support on certain issues and who not to. But I try to be just a mediator more or less."

Surprisingly, despite the circumstances Jackson and Krause "have worked together very well," Winter said, speaking quietly while sitting courtside before a recent game. "One thing, here again, about both of them, they're smart enough to know that the team comes first, the organization comes first. As a consequence, neither one is going to intentionally do anything to hurt the organization, especially the team."

Asked if he had discussed the situation with Krause and Jackson, Winter said, "I try to stay away from that, because I don't want to feel like I'm in the middle on the thing. On the other hand, there's times that I'm with Phil, and we do talk about the relationship somewhat. And there's times that I'm with Jerry and certain things come up. What I try to do, as best I can, is to take the middle-of-the-road view on the thing and try to help each maybe understand what the other is doing and the reasoning for it."

Winter admitted the circumstances had become complicated and frustrating at times, but he pointed out that "both of them have a great deal of respect for me, and I have a great deal of respect for both of them. They know that the only thing I'm interested in seeing is that the Bulls be as good a basketball team as we can possibly be."

Like most Bulls fans, Winter held on to the hope that a reconciliation could occur. "I think it's possible," he said, pointing out that Jerry Reinsdorf had a sign in his office that said "Nothing is cut in stone."

"That pretty much in itself explains Jerry Reinsdorf's philosophy," Winter said. "In the final analysis, he's the guy who will make the decision on what does transpire with this franchise."

Bulls guard Ron Harper, however, figured the conflict had been overheated too long, leaving too many scorched relationships. "There will never be peace here," he said, sitting in the locker room before the New Jersey tip off. "There will never be peace. There's always gong to be a bad feel for guys. This is it. There ain't no tomorrow."

The Bulls' game on this Monday night against New Jersey was their fifth in nine days, and it showed. In the first quarter, Chicago's Toni Kukoc fired a pass underneath to Pippen, who flipped up a reverse that missed badly. A few minutes later, Pippen penetrated and dropped a pass off to Kukoc, who wasn't looking. The ball bounced off his arm, and the Nets scooped it up and headed the other way.

In another sequence, Jordan rose up for a slam dunk and found instead the back of the rim. The crowd emitted a tremendous groan as the ball soared high and out of bounds. Later Jordan was fouled on a putback, the shot missed, and he made only one of two free throws, allowing the Nets to hope that they might be able to do a little business against the Bulls on this night, much as the woeful Dallas Mavericks had done two games ago in Texas with a surprising win.

The crowd offered up another huge groan and an ohh! or two late in the quarter when Jordan moved for yet another dunk only to be greeted by New Jersey's David Vaughn, who stuffed Jordan's shot, a move that left even Vaughn blinking in surprise. This was the same David Vaughn who had been acquired briefly by the Bulls in February, only to be released a few days later.

With 52.4 seconds to go in the first period, Steve Kerr replaced Jordan, who came to the bench tiredly chewing his gum and took a seat as his teammates patted his rump and the crowd applauded. As the noise settled, a fan shouted, "We love you, Michael!"

Yes, they did. Someone was calling Jordan's name at seemingly every interval. If the fans weren't yelling, they were flashing those infernal Instamatics.

Despite this slow start on a tired evening, Jordan was in the midst of yet another spectacular season, thrilling crowds everywhere with extraordinary performances. Even at age 35 when the athletic skills of most players begin to show dramatic erosion, he was once again leading the league in scoring, averaging better than 28 points a game, and although he had come to rely on his excellent jump shot in recent seasons, Jordan could still display the leaping ability, body control and confounding athleticism that amazed spectators and drove television ratings. Remarkably, he'd shown that he was still capable of taking over virtually any game while scoring 40 or more points, a skill level that the vast majority of his younger opponents would never come close to displaying.

"Can Michael play any better?" longtime Bulls photographer Bill Smith asked one night before a game. "Is this 1987? How can he walk away? I have a hard time accepting it."

His thoughts echoed the sentiments of many fans. The better Jordan played, the greater the longing for him to stay in the game. "If you're winning, why ruin a good thing?" asked Tina Martinez, a longtime Bulls fan waiting in the Berto Center parking lot in hopes of getting players to sign her basketball after a recent practice. "I mean, if they lost the championship I could understand it. But they're not. If they got a good team why ruin it?"

Jackson admitted the situation left him uneasy. "The only downside of this whole thing, in my mind's eye, is the fact that if Michael Jordan's not ready to retire, we're taking one of the greatest players, or heroes, that we've had in our society and limiting what he can do," the coach said. "We're deprived of seeing someone extremely special go out the way he wants to go out, in the style he wants to go out, because we've never seen someone of his age with the superstar status that he's had. I don't know of another sports hero in our history who has been able to play at this level at this age. Michael has just destroyed the concepts of what we think of as normal, of what a man his age should be able to do.

"So that's the only downside in this whole thing," Jackson concluded. "Jerry Reinsdorf and I have a good relationship. Jerry Krause and I understand each other. We may not have as close a relationship as we used to, but we understand each other. I know he's got a direction he wants to follow, and he knows I've got some things on my agenda."

Jordan had led the Bulls to five championships over the past seven seasons, and it seemed a good bet that the team could claim yet another title in June. Most important, he had done all of this with a high-flying style and charisma that had made it possible for the league to rake in billion after billion in television rights revenue, ticket sales and merchandise licensing fees from across the globe.

What Jordan's presence had meant to the NBA, to his team and to the struggling city of Chicago was almost beyond description. Before he arrived in 1984, the Bulls were a sorry franchise considering the possibility of relocating to another city. They had a terrible practice facility and played in decrepit Chicago Stadium before embarrassingly meager crowds. The roster was riddled with cocaine abusers, and winning half of the season's 82 games seemed an impossibility. In the middle of Jordan's rookie season, the team, which had lost money throughout its two decades of operation, was sold for a mere $16 million, and most of the money was immediately turned over to a Wisconsin businessman who had won a judgment against the team's owners.

Selling the team was a move the former owners would come to rue because Jordan's arrival in the city as a rookie ignited an unprecedented interest in pro basketball and a swift transformation of the Bulls and the league. Fourteen years later the Bulls were arguably the most successful professional sports franchise in the world, worth $350 million or more. A sign of this success was the streak of more than 500 consecutive home sellouts, the longest in the NBA, dating back to 1988.

The Stadium, long a landmark on Madison Street, was razed to make way in 1994 for the United Center, the fancy new $175 million building just across the street that the Bulls shared with the National Hockey League's Chicago Blackhawks. The early sales of tickets and corporate suites at the building had gone so well over the building's first four seasons that a substantial portion of the Bulls' debt for the construction had already been retired. However, the spring of 1998 had brought the first signs that Jordan's threatened departure could have a dramatic effect on the team's revenues and perhaps even its long-term value.

If Jordan left the team, how fitting it would be if no fans showed up for the opening of the 1998-99 season, Pippen said. "That would send them a message."

"But they're all right," he said of the team's financial standing. "They got the place sold out."

Actually, that wasn't entirely true. One problem in particular was the renewing of the lucrative skybox contracts by corporate clients. One third of the Bulls' skybox leases were up for renewal. Anticipating perhaps a messy end to the Jordan era at the end of the 1998 season, the team abruptly moved up its schedule for renewing those contracts from the summer to spring.

The team's corporate clients, however, were reportedly reluctant to renew until they knew the team's position on the return of Jackson, Jordan and Pippen. A sign of the difficulty was the fact that the team soon offered a 15 percent discount enticing customers to renew.

"The best timing would have been last year for the boxes," said Jackson, pointing out that if the franchise had made a transition to new players, a new coach and a post-Jordan era in 1997 it could have been better for business, because fans and corporate clients would have been able to see just what kind of team the Bulls would put on the floor in the wake of the Jordan years.

"The people buying the skyboxes are in it for a longer haul," observed Terry Armour, who covered the team for the *Chicago Tribune*. "They want to know, and they have to know, down the stretch who the hell is gonna be here."

The Bulls, however, had won the 1997 title, and immediately afterward Jordan issued a public appeal to keep the team together for yet another year and yet another run at a championship. Reinsdorf was said to have been annoyed by that plea, not so much because the key players and coaches were retained, but because Jordan had usurped Reinsdorf's opportunity to make the gesture.

The situation made it appear that Reinsdorf was bowing to the out-pouring of public opinion, something he detested, not out of a dis-regard for the public, but because his experience had taught him that the popular move in the business of sports could also be the fallible one.

"Michael chose to make his statement the night we won the championship," Reinsdorf said in a private interview for this book. "I was just annoyed that he made it that night. That should have been a night of celebration, not a night of campaigning for the next year."

Despite the irritation and the cost, Reinsdorf knew the popular move was the only move. He re-signed Jordan, Jackson and team-mate Dennis Rodman to one-year contracts worth nearly $50 million with the stated goal of winning a sixth Bulls championship.

Nevertheless, the season had brought a terrible public relations climate for both Krause and Reinsdorf, neither of whom possessed strong public relations skills. Behind the scenes they sought the counsel of public relations consultants to devise ways to improve their battered images. Reinsdorf's answer, obviously, was to wait in hopes that the situation would answer itself.

"Both Jerrys are their own worst enemies," a team source con-ceded. Reinsdorf often refused to play public relations games, and Krause, for all his success as a scout, had a record of one disastrous encounter after another in the public arena.

"(Krause) doesn't have a lot of them (public relations skills)," Jackson said. "Jerry Reinsdorf knows this. They've really tried to monitor this man. They've tried to become spin experts in a lot of ways. They've got a strategy, and they've got people they've hired that they pay a lot of money to manufacture a good spin on the Bulls. I want to see the Bulls have success in many ways. But every time they keep kicking themselves or stubbing their toe by doing these kinds of things to the community."

Indeed, the marvel was that not only could Jordan continue per-forming at a championship level, but he could do so while waging a battle for control of the team. "Michael is such a professional, such a player first, that he puts it in the background," Kerr said. "Michael doesn't mess around. He plays."

Yet Jordan could display world-class public relations skills to rival his athletic abilities. And he was obviously using them subtly and effec-tively to counter Krause's efforts to fire Jackson. "He's obviously a PR machine with all of his endorsements," Steve Kerr said of Jordan, who earned tens of millions off the court endorsing products. "His image is obviously very important to him. And I think, in one regard, that means that he doesn't want to look like the guy who's trying to take over the organization. . . He's very savvy."

Asked if Jordan presented an awesome opponent for Krause and Reinsdorf, Kerr smiled and said, "I think it's safe to assume Michael has the majority of support from Bulls fans on this whole issue."

"He'll never lose," agreed the *Tribune's* Terry Armour. "He is so revered in Chicago, around the world, in the NBA, there's no way Michael could lose. At the end of last year, when he was at the podium, he pissed Jerry Reinsdorf off when he said, 'I want everybody back.' You know Jerry Reinsdorf and Jerry Krause are saying, 'Damn, Michael does this, and there's no way we can look good on this.' Michael has built Chicago into the sports town that it is. Michael will never lose a PR showdown."

Just as he faked out opponents with his flashy post moves in the pivot, Jordan had shown an ability to get Krause leaping at the wrong time. In February, while the team was in Utah on a West Coast road trip, Krause made headlines in Chicago by telling *Chicago Tribune* columnist Fred Mitchell that this was definitely Jackson's last season with the team.

It was a gigantic mistake, said Armour. "When we were in Utah that's when Krause said, 'We'd love to have Michael back, but if Michael wants Phil back, it's just not gonna happen.' On that road trip, every stop we went to, somebody in a different city said, 'Hey, Michael, is this your last year?' He'd say, 'Oh yeah, it could be. If Phil's not coming back, I'm not coming back. So I'm treating it like it's my last one.' I think Krause just got fed up with reading it and said, 'OK, I'm gonna strike now and I'm gonna say, 'You know we want Michael back, but he's not coming back under Phil.' Krause did that just to kind of start the public relations thing."

Bulls fans recoiled at Krause's insistence, which only strengthened Jordan's standing. It was as if Jordan and Krause were playing poker and Krause had unwittingly flashed his cards. "He's bluffing them, and Michael's bluffed them before," Armour said. "Hell, Michael's the consummate poker player, too. He knows what to do. He knows how to play all kinds of games with these guys.

"I think he's having fun with it. He likes to make Krause — I don't know if it's so much a Reinsdorf thing — but he likes to make Krause sweat."

After Krause's comments opened the door for Jordan to blast

management to a global media gathering at the All Star Weekend in New York in February, Reinsdorf wisely called for a moratorium on publicly discussing the issue. It was the best move he could make, short of trying to explain the tangled conflicts.

"All talk about retirements, replacements or rosters changes are premature," the chairman said in a statement released by the team. "This management brought this coach and these players back this season to try to win a sixth NBA championship. With half the season and the playoffs still ahead, that should be everyone's total focus. That's my focus. Period."

The personality conflicts aside, perhaps the most difficult challenge facing the Bulls was the mind-boggling economics of the NBA itself. In fact, the league's owners had just voted to tear up the collective bargaining agreement negotiated just two summers ago, meaning they had to renegotiate a new agreement with the players association. Facing re-signing young, unproven free-agent stars to long-term guaranteed contracts in excess of $120 million, the league's owners decided they needed to rework their labor agreement. As proof of this, the owners had suggested that as many as 17 teams could lose money in 1998, despite the fact that the league's annual revenues, driven by Jordan's stardom, had ballooned to better than $2 billion.

With a veteran roster, the Bulls had been able to avoid the gamble of huge, long-term contracts for unproven young players. Instead, Reinsdorf had agreed to spend nearly $70 million on player and coaches salaries in hopes of winning a sixth title in 1998. But the future of the franchise was not mortgaged. "I'm pretty sure they're still making money, though not as much," Jordan said of the circumstances.

Reinsdorf conceded that the Bulls remained profitable despite the gigantic payroll, an indication of just how much the team had raked in during the seasons when Jordan and Pippen both earned less than $4 million. Yet, even if Jackson and Jordan and Pippen and Krause worked out their differences, the real pinch would come with the 1998-99 balance sheet. With Jordan, Pippen, center Luc Longley, forward Dennis Rodman and several other key players as free agents, keeping the team together would require a payroll bloated to $80 million or more. This would not be the happiest of circumstances for the Bulls' secondary owners, some of whom were said to be clamoring for a dividend check.

To say the least, the financial pressures on Reinsdorf seemed substantial. "At some point," said the *Tribune's* Terry Armour, "the investors are asking Reinsdorf, 'What the hell is going on?' There's a lot of pressure from all angles to keep this thing going, but eventually it's gonna dissolve. It's gonna dissolve. Their thing is to make it as painless and as inexpensive as possible."

The timing, however, was not favorable. July 1, 1998, loomed as the date that the Bulls would supposedly have to secure a retirement letter from Jordan. If they didn't, his $33-35 million contract for 1997-98 would count against the team's salary cap, thus making it virtually impossible for the Bulls to sign new free agent talent. With that scenario, the team faced the terrible prospect of having to renounce the greatest player of all time. "I'm not gonna wish bad things on people," Jordan said when asked about the circumstances. "For the sake of the fans in Chicago, I hope they don't pay the price. But if it happens, then they will. But I don't want to wish bad things on the public, the people in Chicago."

The circumstances left a bad air hanging about the club, but the players continued to make light of it. They talked daily about theirs being a team capable of shrugging off controversy and going about its winning ways. "There's more bullshit flying around this team than a dairy in a tornado," said center Luc Longley, an Australian. "There's always something going on. Dennis is always doing his thing, or something's going on. Michael's retiring, or Jerry's making noise. We've had more controversy or circumstance around this team in the last three years, so we've had a lot of practice at putting things out of our minds."

But as the spring unfolded, the Bulls were beginning to understand that conflict had eaten its way into the cracks of a team that over the two previous seasons had shown an incredibly strong chemistry. Jackson had constantly preached against divisiveness, yet even he felt it. The coach said that Krause used certain players to keep him informed of the team's inner workings. "He has guys on the team that he kinda has in his pocket who will rat on me in certain situations," Jackson said.

Were the circumstances breeding a paranoia in the minds of Krause and Jackson and Reinsdorf? Kerr seemed shocked when an interviewer suggested that someone on the team would be funneling information to Krause, as Jackson had suggested. All of the players feel a tremendous loyalty to Jackson, Kerr said.

"Phil is a player's coach very definitely," Tex Winter agreed. "It's very obvious that the players love him. Any time that you can get a superstar like Michael Jordan going to bat for the head coach the way he has, even to the extent to say that he's not going to play anymore unless he plays for Phil, you're not gonna find that very often. That's a wonderful relationship. It's an indication of how Phil has cultivated that relationship. Phil has a tremendous relationship with most of the players. Some of them probably like him better than others. That's just natural. But he likes some players better than others. That's human nature. Coaches do that."

"What's happened over the last couple of years," observed team trainer Chip Schaefer, "is that the Bulls have become a house divided, and you were either Jerry's guy or Phil's guy, whether you wanted to be or not. I think it was a situation where Phil had his coaches, Jerry had his scouts. Jerry had his secretary, Phil had his. As much as I get along with and work well with Al Vermeil (the team's strength and conditioning coach), as Jerry and Phil kind of fell out there was this perception that Al was Jerry's guy and I was Phil's guy. Sometimes what I think happens, because they're being combative, they draw people close to them, whether you want to be or not. There were times on issues that Phil pulled me to him when in fact I may well have wanted to remain neutral on that issue. I'm trying to remain neutral, like Switzerland, and I just can't. I'm getting pulled to one side or the other and it's really difficult."

Despite their allegiance to Jackson and Jordan and the success that brought, many Bulls players felt some loyalty to Krause, or at least a respect for his position and the power he held over them. After all, it was he who had brought them there, rescued them from the Clippers and the Warriors and other points of exile around the NBA to come to Chicago to play a role as an extra in Michael Jordan's Traveling All Star Revue.

At the close of the season, all but Ron Harper, Toni Kukoc, Keith Booth and Randy Brown would be free agents. And it was Krause who would decide whether they were offered a contract to return.

Understandably, most players didn't want to discuss the circumstances. "I refuse to answer on the grounds that I'm a free agent this summer," Longley said when asked about the issue.

The bad blood between Jackson and Krause had made for uneasy circumstances, Toni Kukoc said. "I don't know how that thing's gonna end up. But I think it's not good for our team."

It was Krause who campaigned long and hard to lure Kukoc to Chicago from Europe. But Kukoc said, "I think more of Phil than I do Jerry. But it does bother me a little bit. Playing for a team like this, I was always focused on the team. I pretty much have a good relationship with everybody in the organization." Under the circumstances, that wasn't always easy, Kukoc acknowledged.

The idea that somebody on the roster was viewed as a spy for Krause was particularly troubling to reserve center/forward Bill Wennington. "I'm nobody's boy," he said.

What worried Wennington was that he'd never been the kind of player to do a lot of smooching up to coaches. A Canadian, Wennington had been taught that players were players and coaches were coaches and that it was wrong for a player to initiate a personal relationship to improve his standing on the team. As a result, Wennington wasn't as close to the coaches as some teammates who put an effort into such a relationship. In the past that was never much of an issue. But with Jackson and Krause at odds, Wennington began to wonder. He sometimes noticed unusual patterns to his playing time; it seemed that his minutes on the court came in strange intervals.

Was that because Wennington was suspected of being a Krause stooge? It was a question that Wennington had pondered. But he decided it was a question better off left alone.

Before the season, he had been set to sign a two-year free agent contract with the Indiana Pacers, playing with two of his college teammates at St. John's, Chris Mullin and Mark Jackson. It would have been a good situation playing for new Pacers coach Larry Bird, but Wennington's agent had given the Bulls a courtesy call before the Indiana deal was signed. Suddenly, Wennington found himself back in Chicago on a one-year deal. Now, with his playing time diminished, he wondered about his prospects for next year.

He wasn't alone in that regard. Virtually all the players and coaches wondered about next season. Would the situation eventually affect the team's playoff chances?

Rodman, in one of his rare utterances, pronounced that it wouldn't. "We have a lot of turmoil on this team," he said. "but when we get on the court everything is fine."

"We talk about it," Steve Kerr admitted. "But the nice thing is, we don't let it affect our play."

In a strange way, the circumstances, the sense of being besieged by management, could have a positive effect on the Bulls performance,

Kerr said. "Maybe it gives us all an edge. I think that's a possibility sub-consciously. We certainly don't talk about it. We don't say, 'Let's go do it for us.' But maybe it does give us an edge."

The undermanned Nets were playing fiercely on this night, and the Bulls were all thumbs. Pippen and Kerr missed shots. Burrell made a bad pass. Backup center Joe Kleine threw his massive body on the floor for a loose ball, but then he made a bad pass, and the Nets were headed the other way.

Jordan returned to the game with roughly six and half minutes left in the second period and New Jersey holding a 29-28 lead. Moments later, the Nets moved up 33-30, and their confidence was tangible. They squatted low in their defensive stances, with the notion that they could take this one.

Kukoc, however, hit a trey with three minutes left in the half, and from that a glimmer of life sparked in his weary teammates. Chicago forged a 37-35 halftime lead and seemed poised to take over in the third.

Jordan began the period hunkered down on defense, facing New Jersey's Kerry Kittles. The Bulls star was obviously struggling offensively, but Jordan had never shown qualms about turning to the game's lesser arts. After all, as he often pointed out, "Our offense sells tickets, but our defense wins games."

Kukoc flicked a slick behind-the-back pass to Rodman for an easy two. Moments later, Chicago's ball movement produced anoth-er Kukoc trey that put the Bulls up, 42-37, then up two more when Harper scored on a fast break run by Pippen. Earlier in the season, when Pippen was out with a foot injury, the Bulls got no transition buckets, but after his return those baskets came in sweet bunches, usually off of his excellent defense.

Jordan knifed inside for a jam to push the score to 46-37. Then the Bulls worked the offensive boards, another of their staples, for a Kukoc putback. From there, their defense owned the period. When Harper hit two free throws to make it 51-39, the look in the Nets' eyes was all but extinguished.

Phil Jackson called this scenario "cracking the case," when the Bulls' defense kept the pressure up until the opponent folded under the impossibilities. A Pippen trey boosted the lead to 54-41 with five minutes to go in third. The Nets had made just three for of their 12 shots from the floor for the period, and that was when they get a shot. For the most part, Pippen and company were feeding off New Jersey's passing lanes, nibbling away at the opposition's hope until there was none at all.

From there, every Bulls play established its own aesthetic. Jordan rose up in the midst of a triple team and zipped a pass to Rodman underneath. Another easy two.

Moments later, Rodman collected his eleventh rebound, a retrieval of a missed Jordan free throw and drew the delight of the crowd as well as a foul. Then Pippen's defensive presence forced yet another turnover, and the ensuing break produced two Kukoc free throws and a 60-43 lead. The Nets were completely marooned in doubt. Even when they got a shot they missed. Finally, point guard Sam Cassell could only smile at his team's ineptitude in the face of Chicago's half-court pressure. Mercifully, the period ended, 67-45. The Bulls had outscored Nets 30-10.

Jordan opened the fourth period at the free throw line, and the building was afire with cameras, yet another in a season of Kodak moments. With just under eight minutes left, Jordan laced in a jumper to give him 17, and Jackson decided that was enough. Still riding the emotion of the onslaught, the crowd loudly showered appreciation on Jordan and Rodman coming off the floor.

On the bench, Rodman bummed a stick of gum from a reporter on press row, popped it in his mouth and waited out the conclusion to a game that had become an agonizing parade of fouls and free throws. As he did, the house organ piped out, "If you're happy and you know it clap your hands."

Meanwhile, some dweeb a dozen rows back in the end zone was yelling, "Jordan, can I have your Gatorade towel?"

Jordan didn't hear him. Arms folded, he stretched back in his seat and chomped his gum during a time out. Jordan gazed around the arena, taking in every detail of the evening show as a Bulls promotions crew used an air gun to fire balled-up T shirts into the crowd's upper deck. By waving their arms to call for noise, the crew had various sections of the arena performing like trained animals. Obviously savoring the moment with a smile, Jordan took his time surveying the 21,000 happy faces packed in around him.

"I was just enjoying the moment," he said later, "just enjoying the fun."

Yes, he acknowledged that he was in a high stakes game of poker with the remains of his career on the table. He would love to play another year, or three, he said, but that's only if Jackson remained coach.

"I don't know what the date is that Michael should leave the game," Jackson said. "He may leave this year and go happily into retirement. He may have second thoughts this summer and decide he's not through playing and come back and play. That doesn't matter.

"I've encouraged him to play until he feels he's played it out. I think it's real important for him to do that. That shouldn't be a decision based on whether I coach or not. It should be based on whether he can play or not."

Jordan was asked if he knew about the unhappy end to the career of Laker great Jerry West, who got into a nasty fight in 1974 with Jack Kent Cooke, then the Lakers' owner. West had wanted to play another season or two and easily could have, but he retired abruptly during training camp in 1974. "No one ever had to pay me to play basketball," West said in an interview 20 years later, the bitterness obvious in his voice. "But Mr. Cooke's manipulation made me not want to play for him. My relationship with Mr. Cooke was acrimonious because the negotiations were a game to him. I knew that. It was very frustrating."

Jordan had often made a similar comment, that he would play the game even if there was no pay.

"I never knew that," Jordan said upon hearing how West's career ended, how the Laker great remained bitter decades later. "Will I have the same feelings?" Jordan asked. "Is that what you're asking me? I can't say that. It hasn't ended yet. Hopefully, it doesn't come to that."

Pippen, too, badly wanted to remain a Bull but saw little chance of that happening.

"I don't think public opinion is gonna rule it," he said. "But it would be great to keep this team together. No one wants to turn and walk away. We've had too much satisfaction. We're having too much fun to sort of throw it all in the wash. But that's how they're going to run their ball club, and there's nothing that we as players can do but turn the other cheek and go the other way."

"Lose? I don't lose. I win. That's my job. That's what I do."
— *The Devil's Advocate*

2/ "Let's Go, Millionaires"

Perhaps the most amazing thing about Michael Jordan's Chicago Bulls was that they didn't come apart sooner. After all, the NBA is a horrific grind of a business. It is a competitive environment that routinely churns out high-priced failures and burned-out relationships.

The Bulls, however, had been nothing if not sinewy over their decade of glory. Jackson, for example, had more tenure at his current post than any other coach in the league, except for Utah's Jerry Sloan. And Krause had been the team's chief basketball executive since 1985. The reason they hadn't parted sooner was probably because they'd been too busy giving their all to the demanding Jordan, the most unique taskmaster in the history of the game. Without question, it was his competitive fury, his presence, that drove the entire franchise. It reached from the lowliest employee to the organization's board room.

"As fine a coach as Phil is, so much of it is just this unbelievable trickle down from Michael Jordan," said Chip Schaefer, the Bulls' trainer since 1990. "As much as has been said and written about him athletically, it still hasn't been enough. People are sick of realizing it, but it's like, 'No, no. Do you really realize what this guy is? Do you really realize what this guy is? I don't think you do.'"

Tex Winter recalled the fall of 1985 when he first joined the team and began observing Jordan up close. The first thing he felt was intimidation, Winter said. Never mind that he was 63 at the time and owner of one of the best coaching reputations in America. Never mind that Jordan was a mere 22-year-old heading into his second professional season.

"I was in such awe of Michael that I was hesitant about even talking with him," Winter recalled. "I watched him a great deal and learned a great deal about watching him and his mannerisms. But it took a couple of years before I felt comfortable even visiting with Michael a whole lot."

Likewise, Jackson recalled the anxiety he felt upon taking over as head coach in 1989 and the strong urge he felt to please Jordan with his preparation and approach. It wasn't the kind of anxiety that kept him awake at nights, Jackson says. But it was intimidating.

One of Jordan's traits was a biting sense of humor that he used to chide teammates and staff members who didn't seem diligent enough in rising to his stringent competitive standards. And when the sense of humor didn't seem to work, Jordan never hesitated to singe them with his anger.

"He really thoroughly enjoys himself and enjoys his teammates," Winter said of Jordan. "He pokes an awful lot of fun at them, even to the point sometimes that he can get pretty vicious, even to the point that he's insulting and ridicules them. But they seem to accept that because he does it in sort of a humorous manner. They come back at him. And he doesn't mind. The trouble is, they don't have the ammunition he has. And that makes a big difference. He loves that, and they know that he loves that. He gets a big charge for some reason out of belittling people and putting them down. I think he does it because he feels it challenges him to be better."

"I can be hard when I want to be," Jordan acknowledged when asked about the matter, adding that his sense of humor was one of his main tools in coping with the rigors of a season and the playoffs. "It would drive me crazy if I didn't have it."

In his 52 seasons of coaching pro and college basketball, Winter said he'd never been around a personality as complicated as Jordan's.

"Personality-wise, he's a study. He really is," Winter said. "I'm really sorry that I ... I guess I don't have the intelligence to grasp a lot of things that makes Michael tick, that make him what he is. I think I analyze him pretty good, but he is a mystery man in an awful lot of ways, and I think he always will be, maybe even to himself."

Without question, Jordan possessed tremendous personal charm, wit, and intelligence to accompany his legendary athletic skills. But it was the competitive drive that set him apart. Chicago sports broadcaster Jim Rose gained rare insight to this once when he played in a charity basketball game with Jordan against several other NBA stars. Rose had covered the team since Jordan's early seasons and knew of his competitive demands, so the broadcaster had literally spent weeks practicing for the game. And he was a good amateur player, but during the game he missed an open layup, which sparked Jordan's fury.

"You're not black enough," Jordan supposedly barked at Rose, deeply offending the broadcaster, so much so that Rose immediately fired the ball at Jordan. There I was, the broadcaster thought later, trying to take Michael Jordan's head off with the ball!

Jordan himself was chagrined that he made the remark and later apologized. But the incident was revealing to Rose in that it showed just how badly Jordan wanted to win at everything, how intuitive he was in knowing which buttons to push to get through emotionally to his teammates.

"He did it all in good fun," Rose said. "Michael doesn't like to lose at all. I missed the layup. I got mad and threw the ball at him and stormed off the court. Michael doesn't have a mean bone in his body. He's a wonderful person, but there are some times when his competitiveness takes over."

Steve Kerr remembered gaining a similar insight upon Jordan's return to the game in 1995 after spending most of two seasons attempting to play professional baseball. Upon his return, Jordan had found a Bulls team with many new faces, most of whom had no idea what it took to win a championship. "I had heard stuff about him," Kerr said, "but I hadn't experienced it first-hand. I was surprised how he just took control of the entire team's emotional level and challenged every single player in practice to improve and never let up on anybody."

Jordan's approach was a revelation that left Kerr thinking, "Maybe this is what it takes to win a championship. This guy's been through it. He's won three of them. If this is what it takes, then it's well worth it."

"I remember very vividly the year he came back and played in the spring," Schaefer recalled. "There were rumors for weeks about his coming back. I frequently go and have dinner with various players. I have a nice relationship with a lot of these guys. I was having dinner with Larry Krystkowiak and Luc Longley and Steve Kerr, guys who hadn't played with Michael before. These guys were so excited about the prospects of playing with him, like kids almost in how they felt about it. I remember sitting there and listening to those guys and thinking, 'Boy, you have no idea how hard it is playing with him.' Guys were so excited about playing with him, but they had no idea how hard it was going to be."

"His personality raised the level of our practices each day, which in turn made us that much better," Kerr said.

Yet it also led to a fight between Kerr and Jordan that next fall in training camp. "It was a case of practice getting out of hand," Kerr recalled, "just a lot of trash-talking and their team was just abusing us. It was during training camp. Michael was coming off the come-back when he hadn't played that well in the (1995) playoffs, at least as far as his standards were concerned. He was out to prove a point and get his game back in order. So every practice was like a war. And it just spilled over one day."

It was the first and only fistfight in Kerr's life. "We were bark-ing at each other, and it got out of hand," Kerr said. "He threw a forearm at me, so I threw one back at him, and he kind of attacked me from there.

"He was just letting us know how they were kicking our ass. I knew they were kicking our ass. He didn't have to tell me about it. Why wouldn't that piss me off? It's natural. Other guys were pissed off too. He just happened to be guarding me at the time."

Since their fisticuffs the two have had a great relationship, Kerr said.

"That attitude," Jackson said of Jordan, "that tremendous com-petitiveness, sometimes makes it tough to be a teammate, because you see that tremendous competitiveness is gonna eat you up every-where. It's gonna eat you up playing golf with him next week, play-ing cards with him next month. That attitude of arrogance is gonna be there. It's not always the best for personal connections and friend-ship. But it certainly makes for greatness."

"I suspect that Bird was the same way," Schaefer said, "and I know from observing countless Laker practices during my time at Loyola Marymount that Magic was a bitch at practice. You drop one of his passes, you miss a layup, you miss an assignment on defense, man, if eyes could kill, that's the way it was."

Former Bulls guard John Paxson, a broadcaster with the team, agreed. "Michael is easily the most demanding athlete I've been around," Paxson said, reflecting on his days on the team. "I don't want any of that to sound like there's something wrong with that, because there's not. But if you showed weakness around him, he'd run you off. He was always challenging you in little ways. The thing you had to do with Michael Jordan is you had to gain his confidence as a player. You had to do something that gave him some trust in you as a player. He was hard on teammates as far as demanding you play hard, you execute. So there had to come some point where you did something on the floor to earn his trust. That was the hardest thing for new guys coming in, and some guys couldn't deal with it."

"He took Steve Colter right out of here," Krause said of Jordan. "Blew him right out of here. Colter couldn't handle Michael and was gone. Dennis Hopson couldn't handle Michael. I made a trade figuring Colter was strong enough, but he wasn't."

The fact that Jordan chased some would-be teammates off "may be good a good thing," Kerr said. "You've got to kind of weed out the people who can't really help out. And Michael has a way of finding those guys, finding weaknesses.

"Obviously we all have weaknesses," Kerr added and laughed, "except for Michael. And what he does, he forces us to fight and be competitive, to fight through those weaknesses and not accept them, to work on them, and to improve ourselves."

Make no mistake, though. What Jordan did was pure challenge.

"There's not a whole lot of encouragement," Kerr conceded. Scott Burrell, new to the Bulls in 1997-98, could certainly confirm that. At 6-6, Burrell was gifted with the kind of athleticism that made him an outstanding high school quarterback in football. He was also a good enough pitcher to get drafted by the majors. But for five seasons he'd made his living in the NBA after a solid college career at the University of Connecticut. Despite his size, Burrell had the ability to get down and guard quick, small guards in the NBA, a facet that Jerry Krause loved. The Bulls general manager had tried for years to work a trade for Burrell but wasn't able to do so until the 1997 offseason when Chicago traded forward Dickey Simpkins to the Golden State Warriors to get Burrell.

The only knock against Burrell was that his NBA career had been plagued by a series of serious injuries. But as soon as he arrived in Chicago, he discovered that the Bulls' extensive training and weightlifting program would go a long way toward keeping him healthy. He also discovered a level of intensity among Chicago's players in doing the training work needed to remain supremely competitive. It was obvious that Jordan's drive was infusing the whole roster.

Yet, like many players who come to the Bulls, Burrell spent his first months with the team struggling to get a grasp of the complicated triangle offense. As a result, Burrell also found himself coming face to face with Jordan's competitive fury.

Early in the season, Burrell was late for practice because he had been helping guard Randy Brown with some personal chores. When Burrell finally arrived, Jordan glared at him, a team staff member confided. "Michael told him, 'You get your ass here. Don't you ever be late again. We don't come to practice late. You're out there hanging with Randy Brown. You can't do that shit. Randy can handle it.

You can't. You get your ass here on time.' He lit him up. Michael was serious as could be. Michael knows everything that's going on."

It might be the way some players would talk to a rookie but not a veteran of five NBA seasons, which left Burrell unsure of exactly how to respond. What's worse, Jordan's treatment wasn't just an occasional confrontation. It also included what seemed to Burrell like constant teasing and humiliation, even during the tonk games Jordan, Pippen, Burrell, Harper and Brown would play on the team plane. To the surprise of his teammates and the Bulls' staff, Burrell began going right back at Jordan, something that few people dared to do. Some teammates tried to tell him it was better just to take the tongue lashing quietly and hope that Jordan turned his attention elsewhere.

"Scott Burrell would stand right in the fire, right in the middle of it, ride it along, try to stick up and try to hang in there," a Bulls insider observed. "He was not gonna be defeated."

It wasn't easy. On another occasion, when Burrell struggled with his play, Jordan told him, "We're gonna trade your sorry ass back to Golden State for Dickey Simpkins."

The words stung and added tremendous pressure to Burrell, but he was even more determined not to back down. "I look at it as motivation to make me a better player," he said, admitting that five months into the season he still wasn't sure how to take Jordan's words. "But I don't really know what it is. I can't control what he says. I can't do anything about it. Whatever he says, I use it to motivate me."

"I've been challenged before," Burrell said, "but not on an everyday basis like this."

Still, Burrell said he figured that if Jordan was intent on having him traded, "he'd have done it by now."

For his part, Jordan smiled when asked about Burrell. "I'm about to give up on him," Jordan said, then quickly added, "I'm just kidding."

Burrell was like any other talented player trying to find a role in Chicago's championship chemistry, Jordan said. "They have to find out about themselves. They have to come to our level. We have high expectations around here. We have certain things we have to go through, and certain dedication you have to give. To be a part of this team, you have to submit to that. And I'm the one who gives them a lot of shit to make sure they meet up to that standard.

"We all reap the benefits from it. He'll be happy that he did it once we win the championship, because he'll understand it then."

Asked about the stridence of Burrell's introduction, Jordan said, "Sometimes I have to beat it in his head. He's a good kid, though."

"I don't know why he does it," the 26-year-old Burrell said, "whether he's trying to make me a better person or what. I haven't known him long enough to try to get close to him."

"What Michael wants to do is toughen him up," said one long-time Bulls employee. "And Scott has a little confidence thing."

"He's toughening up Scott," agreed another Bulls insider. "He's giving him some thick skin and building up his game, building up his game mentally."

"That's what it is, mental," Jordan said. "You gotta force them to think. This team is not a physical team. We don't have physical advantages. We have mental advantages, and I think that's what you try to force him to utilize, his brain more than his muscle."

What Jordan had to teach his new teammates couldn't be learned in a finishing school. Instead, it was a process of hard knocks, and Jordan was only happy to apply them.

"That's going through the fucking stages of being on a losing team to a championship team," Jordan explained, his voice turning harsh. He, of course, learned these lessons over the seven years he was trying to lift Chicago to a championship level. The Detroit Pistons, better known as the Motor City Bad Boys, took quite a delight in dealing out their own brand of meanness. There was, after all, the enduring image of Jordan sobbing on the back of the team bus in 1990 after the Pistons had issued the Bulls a physical whipping in the Eastern Conference finals for the second straight year.

In those earlier years, Jordan was an emerging leader, and while he perhaps showed more patience with his teammates, there was no question his motivational touches even then were often brilliant. The result was that the Bulls became very good, and it seemed that Jordan had learned just how to keep them there. Chip Schaefer recalled that in 1993 the team was in the middle of a disastrous West Coast road trip and had arrived in Denver having lost two of the previous three games. "There are times that we travel the morning after games," Schaefer recalled. "Generally those are times where the guys have gone out after a game and had a few drinks or whatever and gotten in late. And we'll fly the next morning to the next city. Sometimes we'll have a day off, and sometimes we'll have a practice scheduled. A lot of times there's a mood with this team where Phil will give the guys a day off because they need it. For some reason, Phil went ahead and had practice that day. We were in Denver at McNichols Arena, and guys were just bitching and moaning about practice. Just a real negative attitude. Michael's just sort of sitting there as I was taping him. Horace Grant was there bitching, and Scottie and B.J. Armstrong were complaining. Michael is always the last guy to get taped, and after I finished he's there lacing up his shoes, soaking it up as these guys around him are bitching about having to practice. He finished lacing and sat up and said, 'Let's go, millionaires.' It was simple, sort of innocuous comment, but he said a lot in those three words. He was telling them that we had just lost a couple of games and it was time to go to work."

And that, as well-paid athletes, they had an obligation to work hard.

"With Michael," said former teammate Horace Grant, "it was always mental."

There was little question that Jordan was far more strident in his relationships with his teammates after his return from retirement in 1995. The team, after all, was rebuilt while Jordan was away from the game, meaning that when he returned he found himself working with a group who had no real idea how to win a championship.

"A lot of these guys have come from programs who have never experienced the stages of being a champion," Jordan said of his rough approach with new teammates. "I'm just speeding up the process."

With Burrell, it seemed to be working.

By March, he had mustered the courage to challenge Jordan in a game of one on one, something that Kerr had never considered attempting. "Scott is stupid," he said, laughing. "I'm not stupid."

Burrell even had a chance to win, with the score tied at six all. Burrell had the ball, but Ron Harper, an interested sideline observer, called Burrell for traveling. The ball went over to Jordan, who promptly went to the rack for a slam and a 7-6 win.

Michael ended up getting the last shot to win, but Scott Burrell was talking trash right in Michael's face," said one witness. "Michael hit the winning shot and pranced off."

A few days later, Burrell was able to secure a rematch. But Jordan won easily. "Michael just walked off," said a Bulls employee, "and Scott was like, 'C'mon, let's go back out there and finish this!' Then Michael finally said, 'You just want to play so you can go tell your kids when they grow up that you beat Michael Jordan once. What am I gonna tell my kids? I beat Scott Burrell? Big deal. They'll slap the hell out of me.'"

Burrell laughed at the retelling of the story and pointed out that he had a little better luck playing cards against Jordan, the only problem there being "it doesn't matter if he wins or loses, his bank account doesn't go any lower."

On the court, Burrell had begun to get the hang of the Bulls' offense and had found the proper places to get and hit his shot. Just before the New Jersey game, in a big matchup against Miami, he passed up a three-pointer and instead zipped the ball to Jordan for a jam.

"Jordan went right up to Burrell," a team employee observed, "and pointed at him, gave him a pop that said, 'That's my boy. That's why I've been working on you the last five months.' That's what's amazing about a guy like Michael. He'll work on you and work on you and work on you and challenge you. But it's all with a reward. He toughens you up and the team wins and everybody's happy.

"He's got balls of steel and no conscience," the Bulls insider said of Jordan. "Michael thinks he can win with just him and four little sisters of the poor. But the little sisters of the poor have to be tough and have confidence."

"I don't mind that at all," Krause said when asked of Jordan's approach with Burrell. "I like that. One thing about Scott Burrell, I knew he was strong. 'Cause I knew Scott from years back. I'm proud of that trade."

Where there seemed to be light at the end of the tunnel for Burrell, there was none of that for Toni Kukoc and Luc Longley, who had been consistent Jordan targets since his return to the team in 1995. "With Toni and Luc, it's very pointed criticism of their games," Kerr said, "because he sees a lot of potential in them that hasn't been tapped."

Jordan's criticism can be tough, Longley admitted. "But he does let up. He's gotten better about it as he's gotten to know me. He understands what different guys can tolerate, respond to. It was heavier early on. But he knows me better now, knows what I can and can't do. I don't get tired of it at all. It's part of the dynamic of this team."

Kukoc, though, said it wouldn't bother him in the least if Jordan decided to embark on a period of extended silence.

"Sometimes, those things you can take hard right away, when you hear things right away," the Croatian forward said. "They might not always be pleasant and good to hear."

When the language was too harsh, Kukoc said he'd wait to calm down, then go tell Jordan that it was too much. And Jordan was always willing to listen. "He has no problem talking about things, discussing things," Kukoc said. "I wouldn't give it back to him. I'm not that kind of person that can go kind of hard. I'm gonna wait five or ten minutes, and try to talk to him about things."

"It's another way he has of challenging himself," Tex Winter theorized, pointing out that if Jordan was so hard on his teammates it allowed him little room for personal letdowns.

Steve Kerr agreed, pointing out that "if you look at his past, it's filled with moments of sort of created challenges for himself to raise his level. The Van Gundy thing (in 1997 when Jordan took a routine comment by New York coach Jeff Van Gundy and turned it into his motivation for scorching the Knicks in a regular-season game) was relatively innocent, yet Michael turned it into armageddon or something. There's no question he finds ways to motivate himself."

"Michael has made up his mind that he's going to enjoy his time of playing basketball," Tex Winter said. "I think he made his mind up a long time ago. He enjoys playing, and he wants to keep it fun and loose. And that's what he attempts to do. His methods sometimes in my mind are questionable. But if that's what it takes for him to enjoy himself and to challenge himself, then so be it."

"The thing that amazes me," Kerr said after a moment's thought, "is that the standards he has set are so unbelievably high that it's almost unfair that he has to maintain them. It's incredible. Every arena that we go into all season long, he's expected to get 40 points. He loves it. That's the amazing thing about him. The combination of incredible talent, work ethic, basketball skills and competitiveness. It's just an unbelievable combination."

Kerr also agreed with Winter: Jordan was a quite complicated piece of work. "Most of us are pretty straight forward and easy to figure out," Kerr said. "He's not easy to figure out at times."

Jordan acknowledged that, as Paxson had said, he sometimes had come down so hard that he'd run people off. "You have a better understanding for me as a leader if you have the same motivation, the same understanding for what we're trying to achieve, and what it takes to get there," Jordan explained. "Now, if you and I don't get along, certainly you won't understand the dedication it takes to win. So if I run 'em off, I don't run 'em off with the intention of running 'em off. I run 'em off with the intention of having them understand what it takes to be a champion, what it takes to dedicate yourself to winning.

"I'm not hard every single day. I mean there are days where you have to relax and let the tension flow or ease. But for the most part, when you have to focus, you have to focus. As a leader, that's what I have to do.

"And I'm not by myself. Pip does the same, and Phil does the same. But I do it more consistently, I guess, because I've been here the longest. I feel obligated to make sure that we maintain the same type of expectations, the same level."

Jordan did admit that his status and standing in pro basketball allowed him to do things that perhaps no other player — probably even no coach — could get away with. "You don't want to do it in a way that they misinterpret the relationship," he said. "It's nothing personal. I love all my teammates. I would do anything. I would extend myself to make sure they're successful. But they have to do the same. They have to have a better understanding of what it takes."

Perhaps, no one had suffered more of Jordan's verbal torment over the years than Krause. Yet, like some players, the general manager seemed determined to stand up to the superstar. Krause had even been known to caution the new players he brought to the team not to cave in under Jordan's verbal fusillades, not to "defer" to Jordan because that could mean losing the star's respect.

At the start of this season, in fact, Krause risked a Jordan chastisement by telling reporters that players and coaches alone don't win championships, "organizations do." In another setting, Krause's comment could have been well taken. Yes, organizations did win championships, but the flip side of the argument was that Jordan's demanding nature was the engine driving the franchise. He set the standard. No one involved in the organization wanted to let him down, wanted to fail him, and that extended from the lowliest marketing assistant to his teammates to Krause himself.

As a result, the Bulls were the best of many things. They were the best coached, with a staff that worked intense hours, figuring out opponents and how to break them down. The team also featured the league's best management from a personnel standpoint. The scouting was thorough and likewise intense and continued to add a steady flow of auxiliary talent around Jordan, of which Burrell was a sound example.

The claim that the Bulls were the best marketed team in the NBA was no stretch, either. Game nights were a delight in the Windy City, taking on the feel of well-staged, superbly acted theatre. The central plot always involved Jordan's and his teammates' magical performances, around which the team's marketing staff added the proper dashes of comedic relief and fan participation.

Yes, it could easily be argued that the end result of Jordan's demanding, inspiring nature was the total package that was the Bulls.

Not surprisingly, Jerry Reinsdorf was not enamored of the idea of Jordan motivating Krause. "Jerry Krause has gotten the best out of Jerry Krause," the chairman said. That perhaps was true. But it was Jordan who had demanded it of him. Demanded it of them all.

3/ On the Bus

It was on the team bus during the 1997 playoffs that Michael Jordan killed Jerry Krause. Absolutely killed him.

As it turned out, the situation was just one of several sequences that ensured the '97 playoffs would long be remembered in Bulls lore for their strangeness. For example, there was the great Gatorade switchup during Game 4 of the Finals against the Utah Jazz. A team assistant got confused and served the players Gator Lode instead of Gatorade. "That's something you drink after the game," longtime Bulls equipment manager John Ligmanowski said of the Gator Lode. "It's a high carbohydrate drink. So they each had the equivalent to 20 baked potatoes during the game. It slowed 'em down a little bit.

"Dennis and Michael and Scottie, they all had stomach aches," Ligmanowski added. "They were drinking Gator Lode instead of Gatorade. Dennis had to run off the floor to go to the bathroom. Scottie was laying down, and Michael asked to be taken out of the game. And he never asks that, or very rarely."

Trying to figure out what was going on, trainer Chip Schaefer discovered the mistake late in the game and was furious. But by then it was too late. The "baked potatoes" had begun to weigh heavily on the Bulls' bellies.

"We were in control of the game," Schaefer recalled, "and late in the game one guy after another starts complaining about cramping and upset stomachs and stuff. I'm wracking my brain trying to figure out what was going on. The Jazz happened to be a Coca Cola or Powerade team. In his misplaced loyalty, the ball boy tried to smuggle Gatorade onto the floor in a gym bag and picked up the wrong cans. It's a dense, thick drink. It's almost syrupy. The ball boy, in his loyalty to the Quaker Oats Company and Gatorade, didn't want to use Powerade, so he was pouring Gator Lode into cups for them to drink. Of course, the guys come off the floor and gulp down whatever people are giving them. These guys were knocking back thousands of calories of Gator Lode. It was too late to do anything about it."

Still, the Bulls had managed to take a five-point lead with about two and a half minutes remaining in the game when the Jazz surged past them, outscoring Chicago 13-2 to win 78-73, tying the series at two-all.

"Never, ever, ever had I heard Michael ask to come out of a game before," Schaefer said. "Dennis, Michael and Scottie all had upset stomachs. We later won the title anyway, so we can look back on it and laugh. But it would have been terrible if that caused a swing in the series momentum."

Needless to say, Gator Lode was not a problem for Game 5. "We got that straightened out," Ligmanowski said.

Instead, Jordan's health was the worry. He had to overcome a nasty virus, but did so in true Jordanian fashion, driving the Bulls to victory in Game 5 and a 3-2 lead in the best-of-seven series. The action then returned to Chicago for Game 6, where Jordan's offense and Steve Kerr's late jumper helped drive the Bulls to their fifth championship. It was another of those sweet title nights in Chicago, where the spray of champagne mixed with the humidity and the swirl of humanity to create an intoxicating steam in the Bulls' jam-packed locker room. But the celebratory moment ended badly, with Jordan leaving the United Center in a state of fury. Somebody had stolen more than $100,000 worth of his jewelry, including his wedding ring, a watch and a necklace, apparently during the revelry of the celebration.

It was not a pretty sight.

But then again, the entire '97 playoff run, as beautiful as it was, had been marked by little pockets of ugliness. Especially whenever Jordan killed Krause, which usually happened on the team bus after a road playoff win.

Team staff members figure it was the alcohol that made Jordan do it. In the first half hour after a game, Jordan and various team-mates would pound down five or six beers and often fire up a cigar. It's not unusual for pro basketball players to drink beer after games. They've been doing it for decades. It helped them replace the body fluids they've sweated away. Jordan certainly wasn't wasted when he killed Krause. But he was buzzed enough to turn loose his wicked sense of humor. Some Bulls said Jordan ought to register his sense of humor as a weapon. It was that lethal.

For years, Jordan had sat at the back of the bus after games, zinging teammates and anybody in range with his laserlike wit. He liked to hit the usual targets. Jordan would zap Kukoc for his showing in the 1992 Olympics, or for his defense, or for that European forgetfulness when it comes to deodorant. Or there was Ligmanowski, an easy target for his weight.

Ligmanowski would have liked to come back at Jordan, but it was hard to do. Sometimes the team's longtime equipment man just took aim at Pippen.

"If it gets real bad," Ligmanowski said, "I get on 'em about nose jokes. Like last year in the playoffs (against Miami) when Scottie got hit in the head and he had that big knot on his head. I told him, 'You scared the hell out of me. I thought you were growing two noses.' He got a little hot about that. They get on me about my weight and stuff sometimes. If you're gonna dish it out, you gotta be able to take it."

Jordan used the humor to police the roster, Ligmanowski said. "If he doesn't feel somebody's doing their job, or sucking it up to go play, he'll say something. He'll get a dig in and let them know how he feels."

"I don't take things too seriously," Jordan said. "I take them serious enough. I'm able to laugh at myself before I laugh at anybody else. And that's important. I can laugh at myself. But then I can be hard."

He was particularly hard on Krause during the '97 playoffs.

"That was ugly," said one observer. "As ugly as it gets."

"Jerry Krause! Jerry Krause!" Jordan would yell from the back of the bus. "Hey, Jerry Krause, let's go fishin'. (Krause had taken up fishing over the past few years.)

"Hey, Jerry Krause, let's go fish. It's B. Y. O. P. Bring Your Own Pole. Don't worry. If we don't catch anything, you can just eat the bait yourself."

The back seats of the bus, where most of the players sat, exploded in laughter at these darts, while at the front of the bus, where team staff members rode, people bit their lips, some of them frowning at the discomfort of a player belittling the team's vice president and general manager. Jackson, who was never the target of Jordan's impishness, seemed to smile with his eyes.

"Those guys would get a few beers in 'em back there, and then they'd start in on him," a Bulls staff member said.

"Phil sometimes sits there and says nothing," said another Bulls employee. "You're Phil Jackson and your boss is being hammered by one of the players. At least say something. Phil does not stick up for him in any of those situations. It's just like school kids, like school kids ganging up on somebody."

"I don't know in retrospect what Phil could have done," Chip Schaefer said. "It's not like he would have turned and said, 'That's enough, Michael.'"

Krause, for the most part, endured Jordan's 1997 assaults in silence. Occasionally when the barrage got especially heavy, Krause would turn to whoever was sitting nearby and say, "The mouth from North Carolina is at it again."

"Maybe it's a defense mechanism as far as Jerry is concerned," Tex Winter said of Krause's silence. "But it doesn't seem to bother him that much. I think he's got a pretty thick skin."

"Brad Sellers, now he was a good draft pick," Jordan would be yelling from the back.

One of the major barrages landed during the NBA Finals in Utah, as the bus struggled up the steep drive to the Park City resort where the team stayed. "We were reduced to like 25 miles per hour in these buses because we'd have to climb up over this big summit to get to Park City," Chip Schaefer said. "You can make it from Salt Lake to Park City in a car in 30 minutes. But these buses were just terrible, and were reduced to like 25 miles per hour and the cars were just buzzing past us. It just sort of created this situation where it went on and on."

"Hey, Jerry Krause, this bus went faster yesterday without your fat ass on it!" Jordan would yell, followed by the team's laugh track.

"Krause doesn't have much to go back at Michael with. He calls him Baldy or something silly like that," a Bulls employee observed. "When those guys are having their beers and they're back there smoking their cigars and they're buzzed over a victory, if Jerry said anything back to them he'd just be feeding the fire. They would just come back with something worse. That's the way they are."

"They'll have a couple of beers after a game," Schaefer said. "I don't think anybody is abusive about it. They drink their Gatorade and Gator Lode, and they like beer, too. Teasing is a cruel thing. It's cruel when it's done on a playground with 6-year-olds and 10-year-olds and 15-year-olds, and it's cruel with adults, too. Have I heard comments before and cracked a smile? Probably. But I've also heard comments before and wished in my heart that he would just be quiet and leave him alone."

Center Luc Longley admitted that while Jordan's barbs made

the players laugh, the moment could also be uncomfortable, especially if you were the butt of Jordan's jokes. "They're a little bit tense at times. But for the most part, they're pretty funny," Longley said.

Jordan could be wicked, the center added. "He's on a pedestal, at least as far as he's concerned. Well, that's the wrong way to put it. But he's in a position where he can crack on people fairly securely. But people crack back at him, and he handles that just as well. It's usually not a mean thing."

"I think there's always been a tension there," Bill Wennington said. "For whatever reason, Michael just always gets on Jerry. Whenever Jerry's around he's gonna get on him, especially if it's a team function where all the players are around. Michael's gonna get on him. And the bus is a closed area, so there's nowhere for anyone to go. So you just gotta sit there."

"He's very smart," Chip Schaefer said of Jordan. "The worst thing you can do is try to come back at him. If you don't, it'll fizzle out. Like if he starts making fun of you, you don't want to turn back around and say, 'Who you talking to, Baldy?' Then you've elevated it to his level. You're better off just laughing it off and hoping it will move on to somebody else maybe."

"Michael's ability puts him in a position where he feels he can go out there and do that," Wennington said. "As far as what he does with the team, he's a great basketball player, and he's our team leader. And team leaders can zing anyone. It's a totem pole, and he's high man on the totem pole right now, so everyone under him's gotta take it. What you gotta do — at least what I do — is just take your lumps. If you start to zing him back, no one's gonna side with me. They're all gonna side with him, cause no one wants him zingin' them. So it'll be 12 against one. So you just take your two minutes of lumps. I've seen guys fire back, and it backfires. Scott Burrell starts firin' back, and then instead of just your five minutes of torture, you've got a whole hour of it.

"He'll ride anyone," Wennington added. "They'll get in the mood, and they'll just start pickin' on someone, and that's it. But you gotta be careful 'cause every now and then, he'll zing someone and you laugh a little too loud, and he'll turn around and look at you like, 'Let's go for you!'"

Steve Kerr said Jordan's jabs were a lot easier to take after a win, but he also had comments after losses. "He's cracking on people all the time," Kerr said. "Those are fun moments. Those are moments that really last in the memory. He said some incredibly funny things. I think what makes them kind of special is that it's just us on the bus. It's just the team. They're kind of intimate moments because they're right after an emotional game, one way or another. The guys get going on the back of the bus, and it's very entertaining."

Kerr said there was no question that Jordan was extra hard on Krause. Asked if Krause took it well, Kerr just smiled and raised his eyebrows.

"Michael is a very funny comedian," guard Ron Harper said. "He keeps everybody loose. When it's very tense, when there are tight ballgames, he keeps you very very loose. He has an ability to say things that you don't expect. He scores from the back of the bus a lot. He gets on Jerry Krause a lot."

Asked if Krause took the ribbing well, Harper laughed and said. "He don't have a choice, does he?"

"I think Jerry has the ability to maybe recognize Michael for what he is," Tex Winter said. "He knows that Michael has the personality that likes to challenge people and belittle people and berate people. I think he just accepts that. He really doesn't have much choice, as great a basketball player as Michael is. And Jerry's the first to tell you that. Everybody recognizes how valuable Michael is to this ball club."

Asked if the conflict added to Krause's frustrations in dealing with the team, Winter replied, "I'm sure it does. I'm sure it does."

Did Jordan cross the line with Krause? "I guess maybe that there isn't even a line because he crosses it so often," Winter said, adding that the situation was an obvious byproduct of the mingling of "the personalities, their egos."

"Michael can be as stubborn as Jerry," pointed out another longtime team staff member. "They're both incredibly stubborn. But that's what makes people successful."

"In Jerry's case, and Michael's too, they sort of avoid each other as much as they can," Winter said. "But there are times when they've got to face off with each other and talk about things because that's part of the running of a franchise and being the superstar on a franchise.

"It's unfortunate that Michael has not had a little bit better relationship with Krause," Winter added. "I'm not gonna take sides on it, but I will say this, Jerry is the general manager. Then again, because Michael is involved in a lot of the negotiations and dealings with him, it's a give-and-take proposition. It's too bad that they can't kinda find a middle ground there. But for some reason, Michael's had sort of this resentment, and it's a shame."

Another Bulls employee with insight into the relationship said that Krause would never believe it but Jackson had actually asked Jordan to ease up on the general manager. Jordan supposedly replied that he knew he shouldn't go so hard, "but sometimes I just can't help myself."

"I think they've visited about it," Winter agreed. "Phil has talked to Michael about trying to accept authority a little bit more as it's handed down from Jerry. I think Phil has helped a little bit in that regard. But on the other hand, sometimes I feel like he doesn't help as much as he maybe should, to be honest with you."

Winter said that he'd told Jackson he needed to do more to ease the situation. Jackson's response was that getting between the players and Krause was a question of "balance."

"Just trying to keep an even balance all the time," Jackson said. "Trying to present his point of view, where it makes sense, then trying to play an even field. If I present the prejudiced side, I'm unrealistic or not truthful. . . . Jerry's felt like I've been disloyal to him in certain situations. He brought this up to me at one point, and I said, 'Jerry, I've only been fair. I've gotten these players to comply with so many things that I think are fairly done and we've kept them moving in the right way. But if I hadn't been honest and they couldn't read the honesty, then we wouldn't have been successful. And you know I don't have anything against you being in this job."

Jackson and Jordan had discussed the internal friction. "We've sat down and talked about it a couple of times, and I've asked him to really curtail it," the coach said. "It makes it really uncomfortable for everybody else. And he says, 'Sometimes I think it's good for the team.'

"I said, 'Why?' And that was his excuse. He's taking up for Scottie. He's taking up for the team. He's airing some things for the team, and he thinks, 'If all these guys have to take this much, I'm gonna give them back a little bit.'"

"If anything, it was a frustration," Jordan said when asked about the moments. "It wasn't really in cahoots with what was happening with Scottie. I mean that was all a part of it, yes. But I didn't really do it for him.

"I did it for myself. I don't think we, as an organ..." he started to say organization and paused, "we as a team, should always have to walk around on our toes with the GM following us everywhere we went. So we didn't feel like we had freedom. It's like your father overlooking your shoulder all the time. So sometimes I just felt compelled to vent frustration towards Jerry, which was probably uncalled for. But I was really trying to get him away from the team, so we could be ourselves, in a sense, and do our job without having someone looking over our shoulders.

"A lot of it was just fun," Jordan said. "It wasn't anything derogatory towards him. It was all in jest. He laughed at it, and sometimes he would reply."

In the past, Jackson had suggested that Krause not travel with the team because he was "brusque" and "sets the players on edge with his presence." Jackson supposedly brought up Krause's travel with the team during his contract renewal talks in 1996. Essentially, Krause only traveled with the team during the preseason, during the team's first West Coast road trip each November and during the playoffs. At other times, the general manager was usually off scouting college talent for each season's draft.

"Jerry felt like any exclusion or any intrusion into that territory, which is his territory, is an effort to keep him from trying to do his job," Jackson said of the issue. "I suggested a number of ways around that. Flying in the plane, then taking a private car to the games with scouts, with people who are necessary to ride on the bus at game time. Taking a private carrier back to the hotel afterwards. Flying commercially. Doing things like that to keep his distance. But he says, 'I don't get a feel for the team and what the team's all about.' Well, it's obvious that since 1991 Jerry really hasn't had a feel for the mood of the team. Basically, he knows how to run the show and how it goes. It's a pretty smooth operation."

"I think that Jerry feels like as general manager he should be able to make the decisions as to whether he's going to be on the bus or not," Winter said. "That is one of the sore spots as far as Phil and the players are concerned. Maybe as a coach, Phil in this case feels that the general manager shouldn't be on the bus early in the year. I think Phil has said on occasion that he doesn't think other general managers do that. And Jerry says he thinks they do.

"So what do you do?" Winter said with a laugh. "If Jerry wants to be on the bus, I think that's his prerogative. Unfortunately, if the players do respond negatively, or a player even, particularly of Michael Jordan's status, responds negatively to it, well then it's something that maybe Jerry should take into consideration and maybe say, 'Well, it's not that important to me.'" .

Most general managers don't hover around their teams, Jordan said. "That was our whole argument from day one," he said, pointing out that Jackson has tried for three years to get Krause to relent.

"That shows you how much power he has," Jordan said of Jackson. "We don't want to feel like we're under a microscope the whole time while we're working. That's very important. I think that helps the team grow."

"That's Michael's opinion," Krause said. "That's not mine. Obviously Michael hasn't been able to push me away. For good reason.

"But I came here out of baseball," the GM added. "All baseball general managers travel with their teams. That's very normal. . . . I find that to be effective at what I do, I have to see players on the road, OK? I don't have to visit with them every day or talk to 'em. But I have to watch 'em on the road, because I judge our team a lot by what goes on on the road, OK?"

Krause admitted that he was one of the first, if not the first, GM in pro basketball to travel so closely with his team. Today, he said, many other GMs now travel regularly with their teams. Krause pointed out that he traveled with the team only until early January each season, then went off to scout college games to find new talent. "But you know how I feel about it?" he said. "It really doesn't matter. When somebody criticizes me for that, I say, 'Wait a minute. I've got to do my job the way I know how to do it. That's the way I know how to do my job. If a player can't handle me being on the team bus, he shouldn't be on that bus.' Michael can handle it. He handles it fine. It doesn't bother his play."

Krause acknowledged that his investigative nature (which had led to his nickname "the Sleuth") was part of the reason Jackson and the players didn't want him traveling with him, because he might collect information about their personal lives on the road. Since he arrived on the job in 1985 and found the roster populated with partiers, the general manager had made it his business to be aware of off-court activities. He had talked frequently of trading guard Sedale Threatt in 1988 out of fear that his liking for a good time off the court might influence younger Bulls players.

Asked if it was a question of maintaining a proper distance from the team, Krause said, "Michael is the only player I've known who's come up with that. Part of that is that there's other things involved, too. A player can have a lot more freedom if I'm not around, in the sense that you can do what you want to do and not be worried about whether I'm walking the hall. I'm coming up late or something. I'm not talking about Michael. I'm talking about anybody. But the point being that on the road I don't eat with the players; I don't play cards with 'em; I don't do any of that stuff with 'em. I never have. I do my job the way I see fit, and I resent the fact that people say I shouldn't be doing this because Michael says it. I say, 'Well, wait a minute now. It ain't been too bad, what I've done.' I resent. . . . I shouldn't say resent. What's more, if I'm gonna do my job, I'm gonna do my job my way."

"He likes to see the players and how they react in certain situations," Jackson said. "There have been some situations that have set the players on edge. Michael is always the last one in the bathroom. It's kind of a pecking order between the taping table and the bathroom. With him going in the bathroom, and Jerry's still in there in the players' locker room in the bathroom using the toilet when Michael's getting ready for the game and he's the last one in there."

It sounded immensely loony, that the ultimate superstar of the NBA and his general manager were at odds over a little potty time. But the situation was more complicated than that. Like many great athletes, Jordan was a prisoner of his superstitions. The Lakers' Jerry West wouldn't wear green as a player because the team lost so many times to the Celtics. Beyond that, he had an involved list of superstitions. West would travel by the same exact route each game night to the Forum, where before tipoff he went through an elaborate ritual that even included positioning torn gum wrappers around his locker.

While perhaps not so intricate, Jordan had his own ritual. "He's a routine guy," Chip Schaefer said. "He's the last guy to get taped, then he gets the game notes and goes in the bathroom before Phil talks. He comes out, he stretches, he snaps his warm-up bottoms on the same way every time. He stands in the same place for the National Anthem, right behind me or in front of me depending on which way we're facing. He's the last guy to get the resin on his hands before they go onto the floor. He gives two pats of the hand in front of Johnny Kerr, our broadcaster. It's very much a routine thing, from the Carolina practice shorts underneath his Bulls shorts to all the things. He's like that."

The Bulls had emphasized meditation in recent seasons, and Jordan used the time before each game to clear his mind. Jordan was a master of concentration, and the purpose of this pre-game time was to fix that focus. In a world that constantly besieged him for his time and attention, his pre-game moments were his time to be alone, unless, of course, Krause was there. No one else on the team would have dared to invade Jordan's solitude, but Krause seemed oblivious to it, Jackson said.

The GM said that the bathroom incidents were rare, that Jackson's even bringing them up was an outrage. "That's Phil,"

Krause said. "Phil's the ultimate narcissist. He tries to make himself look big by making other people look small."

Jackson said the bathroom conflict was just one of many smaller conflicts between the star and general manager that had added up over the years into a big one. "It's with those type of things, where Jerry doesn't know boundaries," the coach said. "That's really what irritates the players almost more than anything, even more than the way he has dealt with the team, the trading and not trading of players, the rumors and everything else. Just his intrusion into the society where he doesn't belong. He just shows a lack of the idea of boundaries as to where to the players stop and management begins. Those are the things you don't like to bring up, but these are the things that just alienate Jerry from the team, his behavior."

In 1995 Jackson used the word "brusque" to describe Krause, and it set off many of the fireworks that burned in their relationship three years later. "I used that word one time, and he called me into his office," Jackson said of Krause. "I told him when he brought me in his office, 'That's about as nice a word as I can use, Jerry.' Jerry doesn't have a good idea, or doesn't know what his presence does to people. He's not aware of it. Other people are aware of his presence. It's just a lack of an idea what his image or his presence brings to the table, which is also a space in which he doesn't have boundary definitions.

"I talked to Jerry when I took the job. I talked to Jerry in subsequent years about this really being a problem," Jackson added. "One of the things that's a great measure of an individual is how he treats people when he has nothing to benefit by it. Jerry comes up failing all the time in that territory. This is one of the things we talk about. What is important in life and what isn't. So Jerry has sort of run to the end of the rope with the guys."

Still, there were longtime Bulls employees who had the utmost regard for Jackson and Jordan yet maintained a loyalty to Krause. They respected the general manager for the difficult stances he had taken over the years in pursuing the vision that he and Reinsdorf had for the team. The problem, said several of these employees, was that Krause seemed to harbor an unrealistic urge to "be one of the guys."

"He can't be one of the guys," said an employee who thought highly of Krause. "It's hard to be on the bus and around these guys all the time. And then he's got to decide on their livelihoods and their contracts? I think he'd get a lot more respect if he weren't around the players all the time. He can see them during the holidays, at the Christmas party, even talk to them once in a while if he has something to say, but otherwise he should stay away. He can watch them from afar to evaluate the team. They don't even have to know he's there.

"If they have a problem, they should be able to go see him and respect him, instead of giving him shit on the team bus or avoiding him."

"Hopefully we've done some right things around here," Krause said. "What we've tried to do is just be straight. I think what's gone wrong, from a public standpoint, with Jerry's reluctance to talk and my reluctance to talk publicly, a lot of things have gotten misunderstood. We've tried to take the high road all the time, and guys are going the low road on us."

Clinging to his optimism, Winter hoped time would cure the situation. "A lot of times I don't think these youngsters have enough respect for the position an individual holds," the assistant coach said. "In a way, it's sort of immaturity on their part. They'll grow out of it as they grow older."

The question that immediately came to mind was, would they grow older as Bulls?

"I bet," Jackson said in late March 1998, "if everything was said and done and we won the championship and minds were changed with everybody in the organization, and Reinsdorf said, 'This team has to come back,' it would be difficult to get the players to do that."

ANCIENT INJURIES

The friction between Krause and Jordan had evidenced itself in many ways over the 13 years since Reinsdorf took over the team. They boiled to something of an emotional head in early November 1994, when Jordan had "retired" for the first time and the team held "A Salute To Michael," a ceremony to retire Jordan's number 23 jersey in the United Center. It was night the team unveiled a bronze statue of Jordan in action, called "The Spirit," just outside the building.

The event quickly became something of a nightmare for the Bulls' staff. The trouble, it seemed, began when NBA Entertainment took control of the event away from the Bulls to make it into a nationally broadcast program for Turner Network Television. As first envisioned, the "retirement" was to be a night of intimacy and warmth involving Jordan, his coaches and teammates, and the fans.

Instead, NBA Entertainment turned it into a dimly conceived TV special in which every line was scripted. Rather than a memorable evening with the Chicago crowd that had followed Jordan's every jump stop on his rise to greatness, the session unfolded as a vapid showcase of television business connections.

Instead of a circle of friends, there was a "cast," including broadcaster Larry King and actors Craig T. Nelson, Kelsey Grammer, Sinbad, George Wendt, Woody Harrelson and Robert Smigel, all of whom had little or no real connection with Jordan and the Bulls. The show moved from one hollow segment to another. The script writers had effectively removed any emotion from the format, except for odd moments when the crowd grew impatient with the awkward silliness of this staged event.

Sadly, the only impromptu moment of the evening was one of profound embarrassment, especially for Krause. When he and Jerry Reinsdorf were introduced, the crowd of 21,000 booed lustily. "C'mon, now," Jordan chastised the fans. "Both Jerrys are good guys."

It was an uncomfortable moment, but not unprecedented. At virtually every rally or celebration of the Bulls three straight championship seasons from 1991 to 1993, Krause had been the target of merciless booing from Chicago crowds. Never mind that by just about all accounts his personnel moves factored heavily into their success, the fans took a special delight in deriding him.

This night, however, was perhaps the worst for Thelma, Krause's wife of many years. She began crying, and Krause himself grew furious. For years, he had ignored the booing and hardened himself to the fans. "I learned long ago that when we won, Michael would get the credit," Krause has explained, "and when we lost I would get the blame. I knew that. It was something I accepted."

But this was different. The booing had finally gotten to his wife, and she was openly weeping. "One of the really sad moments that I've seen before," Chip Schaefer said, "was at the retirement function for Michael at the United Center when Jerry was roundly booed, and Michael had to say, 'Don't be hard on him.' I could see from where I was sitting Thelma Krause just broken down in tears over it. That was really sad, really sad. I felt genuine pity for him and his family at that moment. Here was a night supposed to be a celebration for one of the great athletes in the history of the world. Here's this guy being treated that way."

Later, Dean Smith, who coached Jordan at the University of North Carolina and remained one of his mentors, sought to console

Thelma Krause. Smith pointed out that it was nice of Jordan to speak up for Krause. The comment sparked the pent-up anger and emotion in the GM's wife, and she told Smith in clear terms what she thought of Jordan's effort. It was too little, too late, she said angrily. Then she proceeded to give Smith a piece of her mind.

Smith and Jordan had often been at odds with Krause over the years, particularly when it came to the Bulls' personnel decisions regarding University of North Carolina players. Both Jordan and Smith had lobbied long and hard to get Krause to draft Joe Wolf in the first round of the 1987 draft, and their efforts had created a tension-filled draft day dilemma for Krause. But then Reinsdorf told the general manager to "go with his gut" because his instincts on personnel had served the franchise well. So Krause selected Horace Grant, who developed into a key player in the Bulls' first three championships. Wolf, meanwhile, went on to become an underachieving career role player. After the draft, Krause recalled, "Dean Smith called me and ripped my rear end, literally. 'How could you do that, you dumbell?' Literally. And Michael said, 'What the hell? You took that dummy!?!' And for years that's what he called Horace, dummy. To his face. Dummy. Right to his face. Unbelievable."

So Thelma Krause had no compunction about telling Dean Smith off that night. Krause himself didn't seem to mind it too much either.

THE SLEUTH

The nature of Krause's conflict was readily apparent. There was the NBA, the domain of giants, and there was Jerry Krause, all of, say, 5-5 and 220 pounds. It was an incongruity that seemingly escaped no one, least of all Krause himself, who had been known to refer to himself in the third person as "the little sonofabitch."

Could it be any other way?

If you were 5-5 and you wanted to rule in the land of giants, you had to be willing to battle every day. You had to climb up on whatever stack of metaphors you could find and stare down a roster of Goliaths, huge men with huge egos. Approach it any other way and you could very quickly wind up serving as somebody's mascot. You could wind up getting your head rubbed for good luck or picking up towels in the locker room. Krause knew this, because he'd been there.

He wasn't entirely alone, of course. There were a smattering of undersized coaches working the league, led by Cleveland's Mike Fratello and Philadelphia's Larry Brown. Plus, pro basketball seemed to have found a role for a number of tiny ballhawks from Spud Webb to Muggsy Bogues. Before them, there was little Barney Sedran, the guy who could lace up those long jump shots in the days before the hoops even had backboards. Barney, by the way, is a Hall of Famer.

They all were admired for their chutzpa.

All, perhaps, except Krause.

Then again his circumstances were singular. He didn't have Muggsy's speed or Spud's springs or Fratello's Napoleonic persona. Before he was the Bulls' general manager he was a baseball and basketball scout and before that he was a charting assistant and team manager, a stats and towels guy. While he did play baseball in high school, he was a third-string catcher, the type of guy who found his niche warming up pitchers and was happy to have it. The kind with the attitude that, "I may be the warm-up catcher, but I'm gonna be the best warm-up catcher in the city."

That desperation to overcome his physical liabilities seemed to drive Krause to an athletic fanaticism. Games absorbed his life. Even if he couldn't play them, he wanted to be around them. The son of a Russian jewish immigrant, he grew up in Chicago, and in media interviews over the years, he recalled being a distinct minority in his own neighborhood, where he was called "kike" and "sheeny." After those interviews some people who knew Krause at the time came forward to question if he hadn't perhaps overstated the circumstances. Regardless, one of the beacons on his landscape was Jim Smilgoff, the legendary baseball coach at Taft High School.

Not only was Smilgoff a mean, tough competitor, he was Jewish. Needless to say, Jerry Krause worshiped him. When Krause's family moved to another neighborhood, Krause recalled that he decided to ride his bike eight miles each way each day so he could continue at Taft playing for Smilgoff, never mind that he would never be more than a warm-up catcher.

It so happened that Krause had a high school teammate who was a good enough pitcher to attract pro scouts, including a short, portly bird dog for the New York Yankees named Freddie Hasselman, who quizzed the warm-up catcher about the prospect. It was then that Krause discovered being a warm-up catcher was a good way to get to know the big-league scouts, who would hang around the batting cage quizzing him on the strength of the pitcher's arm and other issues.

The exchange led to a friendship between Krause and Hasselman, who was portly and had never played the game. Krause wondered how someone like that could be a scout, and Hasselman passed along this secret: "You don't have to be a chicken to smell a rotten egg."

It would prove to be the revelation of revelations for Jerry Krause. He later attended Bradley University and worked his way into a spot as the student assistant to Braves basketball coach Chuck Orsborn. His duties were to chart offensive and defensive plays, and that proved to be a major training ground for his scouting days. He also managed to hang on with Bradley's baseball team, where his relationship with Hasselman grew.

After college, he found his way into a series of scouting jobs for a variety of pro and semi-pro teams. It was a hard life, 280 nights on the road each year for roughly $100 a week, but Krause consumed it with relish. Later, he would joke about naming his unwritten autobiography *One Million National Anthems.* Wherever they played a game, he tried to be there, hanging out in the locker room, talking to coaches, watching and charting players. He wore a snap-brim hat and a raincoat and was obsessively secretive, so they began calling him "Sleuth."

He even wandered way up to the University of North Dakota in the 1960s to meet a young coach named Bill Fitch and to scout a rawboned forward named Phil Jackson. "He's not what you would consider an athlete," Jackson pointed out in 1995, "and even back then, 30 years ago, he was an unusual fellow to be out there scouting a basketball player.

"But Jerry has done whatever it took to get to the top and hold his position. That's why he has such a great knowledge of the game, from A to Z. He did whatever it took, from going and getting the sandwiches and coffee, to whatever, just to keep hanging around the game and learning. And he's always been able to pick out talent. He was down there at Kansas State when Tex Winter coached there in the '60s, hanging out with Tex the way he would later hang out with Bighouse Gaines at Winston-Salem State. He's always had an eye for people who are dedicated to what they do."

Nobody ever outworked him. Krause smugly operated by his "two cocktail rule." While other scouts were having two cocktails, he was down the road, seeing another game, searching for that great undiscovered talent to send up to the big leagues.

One of his first big scores was a scouting gig with the old Baltimore Bullets. He said he advised the Bullets to draft a fine young small college player named Jerry Sloan and later pushed to his bosses in Baltimore to select Earl "The Pearl" Monroe, out of little Winston-Salem State.

Those early successes, however, didn't buy Krause any seniority. The scouting circuit was a hard road in those days, and Krause soon left the Bullets to join the Bulls in the late 1960s shortly after they had entered the league as an expansion team. But a poor relationship with Bulls coach Dick Motta meant that Krause had to move on after a couple of seasons in Chicago. The next stop was another expansion team, the Phoenix Suns.

People would marvel that with his countenance he could be so effective as a scout. Krause would answer them with Freddie Hasselman's wisdom: "You don't have to be a chicken to smell a rotten egg."

His first really big break seemingly came in 1976 when wily old Bulls owner Arthur Wirtz lured him back to Chicago as the team's general manager. It was quite a promotion, and it was in his hometown, which puffed Krause up with pride. Yet within weeks he got caught up in an amazingly silly turn of events. The Bulls were looking for a coach, and DePaul's Ray Meyer told reporters that Krause had offered him the job. Krause insisted he had done nothing of the sort, but somehow the incident got blown up into a local media firestorm. Abruptly, Wirtz fired Krause, turning his triumphant homecoming into public humiliation, and it forever shaped his view of the media.

His skill as a scout meant that he quickly landed on his feet. The Lakers hired him and watched in amazement as he found them a little-known guard named Norm Nixon. But White Sox owner Bill Veeck, who had known Krause for years, persuaded him to return to Chicago and baseball in 1978. Krause's toughness and acumen were already well established in 1981 when Reinsdorf put together an investment group to purchase the baseball team. The new team chairman soon grew to admire the plucky scout, and four years later, when Reinsdorf put together a group to buy the Bulls, Krause was his first choice to run the organization, despite the fact that the team's previous owners and management had loathed him.

"Jerry's been around forever," said one Bulls employee. "He knew all the coaches, the assistants, the scouts in the league. The previous Bulls administration despised Jerry. They had all these stories and tales and ripped him all the time. Lo and behold if he didn't come back here and get the job as general manager."

His resurfacing in basketball amazed many people, including Orlando Magic executive Pat Williams, who had known Krause for years and had worked with him in the early Bulls days. "Part of the saga of the Bulls is the incredible scent, the life of Jerry Krause," Williams said. "It's phenomenal. He starts out in Baltimore, then gets hired and fired in Chicago. So he's out, and he ends up going to Phoenix. He bats around and ends up with the Lakers. He ends up working for me in Philly. He's hired back by the Bulls, and Arthur Wirtz ends up firing him after a few months on the job. He's gone, just gone, and he wheels out of that, and he battles his way back and works for Reinsdorf. His life story and what happened to him is phenomenal. He's a hard worker who has really paid his dues. He may make a mistake but it won't be from a lack of effort."

"I would run into Jerry in the early '80s when he was still scouting baseball," said Bruce Levine, a radio reporter who had covered Chicago sports for many seasons. "Jerry was known in the scouting business as just a very tough cookie, very similar to what he is now. Very intense. A guy that would spend 15 hours a day going to baseball games. College games. High school games. Professional games. I've developed a large group of scouts who are friends of mine in baseball. They all admired Jerry. Some of them didn't understand him. But they all admired his work ethic."

Many of the people competing against Krause as scouts in baseball were former players and coaches, people of standing in the game. Krause, on the other hand, came from no where, so he had to outwork them, had to fight through the circumstances with a fierce, unflinching determination.

"Jerry is a great success story," Levine said. "If you can get by the little peccadilloes in his personality, the guy is just a tremendous worker who has tunnel vision on getting whatever project or thing he's doing done. That's the only thing on his mind. That and fishing and his wife. Those are the three things. He's just a totally dedicated person. I have nothing but good things to say about him, although there are days he will walk by me, just like he walks by other people. Not out of rudeness, but in the sense he has other things on his mind. I still find him to be a very amazing executive who has never gotten enough credit because everybody assumes Michael Jordan and Scottie Pippen would have won by themselves anywhere they went. That's a great argument, but I don't believe it.

"This is a guy who loves challenges, just like Michael Jordan," Levine pointed out. "Krause and Reinsdorf both do. They all love challenges, and they're all very competitive. I think Jerry in his heart would love a chance to rebuild this from the ground up and show people that it wasn't a fluke, that it wasn't just Michael Jordan."

Reinsdorf knew why he was booed at public appearances. He was also part owner of the White Sox, and back in the 1980s, when he was trying to get a new Comiskey Park built, Reinsdorf threatened to move the Sox to Florida. As it turned out, Reinsdorf said, he decided to accept about $10 million less per year to keep the Sox in Chicago, but the city's sports fans were slow to forgive or forget.

Krause's public image drew lightning for entirely different reasons, Reinsdorf said. Mainly, Krause had the drive and demeanor of a pit bull. "He has his foibles, I understand that," the owner said. "If I could make him 6-feet-2, thinner and better looking, I would do it. I think he'd be even more popular. And if he could learn to bullshit the press, I think that would make him more popular. I've told him many, many, times, 'Why can't you be more like Roland Hemond (the longtime White Sox general manager)?' Roland Hemond was the master of making the press happy without telling them anything."

Krause, however, would never consider such an approach. He once worked as a newspaper copy boy and had entertained thoughts of being a sportswriter (he worshiped legendary Chicago newspaperman Jim Enright, "The Monsignor") but Krause had a deep distrust of the media.

There was little question that his attitude toward the press had worked against him. "Jerry's never been able to project a good personal image," Jackson observed, "and that's been the thing that's destroyed his public persona as far as the audience goes here in Chicago. They see him as someone like the mayor. The mayor always gets booed in public. Jerry represents that kind of guy. He has to do a lot of the dirty jobs. The fans remember the dirty jobs, and they remember his comments. What has happened with Jerry is that he has alienated a lot of sportswriters, and the sportswriters form the public opinion.

"Jerry Krause is an enigma to the athletic world," the coach said. "So it's everybody's challenge to define him as a person. He's a Damon Runyon-type character who is undefinable. But Jerry's a watchdog. He keeps the press away, he keeps the public away, he keeps company policy always. He's ever vigilant at mind control and spin control to the point that it wears people out. He has a tendency to alienate people. I don't know if there's ever been a story done on him here in Chicago where he hasn't had a conflict with the writer.

"He's willing to call people up on the phone and challenge them. 'Why did you say this?' And, 'That's a lie!' And, 'You missed the point!' He'd done that to the point where he's sort of made himself an unlikeable character."

"It's just a shame that it's such an antagonistic relationship between the media and Jerry," Chicago radio reporter Cheryl Raye, who has covered the team for about a decade, said in 1995. "It's sad, when he gets booed at a ring ceremony. There's no reason for it. I couldn't believe it. . . . Some people just need a villain, and Jerry fits their profile."

"Jerry's style may not be liked by the media, but it's highly effective," said a Bulls employee. "He's so preoccupied with winning, he can't pull out of it sometimes. Which leaves him walking by people, as if he doesn't see them. And he probably doesn't."

Actually, Krause had maintained what appears to be a good relationship with the current group of writers covering the team, including John Jackson of the *Sun Times* and Terry Armour of the *Tribune*. "In my personal dealings with Jerry Krause, I've never had a problem," Armour offered. "He's been honest with me. I've heard people say that he's a liar, you know. I've never had him lie to me about anything. I talk to him off the record a lot. I like dealing with him. But, I've told him this in private, too, it doesn't come across to the public."

Because Krause was so set in his ways, Reinsdorf held little hope that his image would ever improve dramatically. Besides the superficial things, though, there was little that the team's chairman wanted to change about Krause, even his occasional personnel mistakes.

"All general managers make mistakes," Reinsdorf said. "Jerry's incredibly loyal, but the main thing is that he gets results. He gets results because he works very hard, and he has a good eye for talent."

He also wasn't afraid to make unpopular and seemingly unorthodox moves to make the team better. In fact, some observers have made a case that the Bulls won their championships largely because of Krause's peculiar vision. When he was named to his post in 1985, the Bulls were considered not much more than an undisciplined young superstar and a collection of questionable players.

"Like everybody else, I was in awe," Tex Winter said of seeing Jordan in practice for the first time in the fall of 1985. "He was a high wire act at that particular time. I often said back then it was more a degree of difficulty, a gymnastic feat, with Michael in those days than it was a matter of basketball."

"I had a brutal start," Krause has said of his first months running the Bulls. "I had nine players I didn't want and three I did. I wanted Dave Corzine, I wanted Rod Higgins, and I wanted Michael. The rest of them I couldn't have cared less about. And they were talented. All of them were very talented. But it wasn't a question of talent."

"Jerry took away a lot of things that this franchise didn't need," Jackson admitted. "It didn't need certain types of people on the club. He had a certain idea of what type of person he wanted. He brought in character, or what he liked to think of as character. Good solid people. People who wanted to work hard."

Krause's first draft pick was little-known Charles Oakley out of Virginia Union, a move that was roundly booed. Yet Oakley immediately showed his worth as a power forward and became immensely popular in Chicago. Still, that didn't stop Krause from trading him a few seasons later for New York Knicks center Bill Cartwright, another move that was pilloried. Although he had a dubious medical history, Cartwright showed that he was just the low-post defender the Bulls needed to become a championship team.

Perhaps Krause's two biggest moves were the hiring of veteran Winter, who designed the Bulls' famed triple-post, or triangle, offense, and the development of Jackson as a NBA head coach.

Krause fired three coaches before finding the perfect leader for the Bulls in Jackson, and each firing was accompanied by a public outcry for Krause's head.

FINDING PHIL

Jackson had had some success in the CBA, but most NBA general managers would never have considered him head coaching material. "I thought I was ready to be an NBA coach at age 35," Jackson recalled. "I had served two years as an NBA assistant in New Jersey. But I really didn't have a clue then, and I know that now. So I went to the CBA and had some success, but still nothing came in my direction. I had no mentor in the NBA. My coach when I played with the Knicks, Red Holtzman, had retired and was out of the game. Although Dave DeBusschere, my former Knicks teammate, was a general manager, he had no control over my destiny as a coach. Jerry Krause was like the only person that really stayed in touch with me from the NBA world. And he had just gotten back in it. But that was my connection. Jerry had seen me play in college, and we had a relationship that spanned 20 years."

Jackson himself was known as something of a strange duck during his playing days with the New York Knicks. In *Maverick*, his 1975 autobiography written with Charlie Rosen for Playboy Press, Jackson recalled his exploration of 1960s counterculture, including candid accounts of drug use. The book was also an excellent basketball tome as well as a personal story of spiritual growth. It was not, however, the type of book commonly associated with a head coach or authority figure.

"The only thing in that book that's an embarrassment for me today," Jackson said, "is that people have picked out one or two phrases and said, 'This is who Phil Jackson is.' Sportswriters in the past have seized on one experience with psychedelic drugs or some comments I've made about the type of lifestyle I had as a kid growing up in the '60s and '70s. I've tried to make sure people don't just grab a sentence or phrase to build a context for someone's personality."

"I've never read the book," Krause once said. "I didn't need to. I knew about Phil's character. Besides, I'd hired other colorful personalities before."

Yet perhaps no one quite so colorful as Jackson. Shortly after coming to the Bulls in 1985, Krause called Jackson to interview with new Bulls head coach Stan Albeck for the job of assistant coach.

"I was coaching in Puerto Rico," Jackson recalled, "and I flew up directly from San Juan. It was a quick trip. I had to drive into San Juan and catch a morning flight. When you live in the subtropics, you get a lifestyle. I was wearing flipflops most of the time. I wore chino slacks, because of their social standards down there, and a polo shirt. I had an Ecuadorian straw hat. Those hats are really expensive. They're not like a Panama, which costs 25 bucks. It's a $100 hat. You could crush proof it. As a little flair item, I had a parrot feather that I'd picked up at a restaurant. I had messed around with a macaw in the restaurant and pulled a tail feather out and stuck it in my hat.

"There was a certain image I presented. I had a beard, had had it for a number of years. I was a little bit of an individualist, as I still am. I have a certain carriage about myself that's going to be unique. I just came in for the interview. I don't know how it affected Stan Albeck. Stan was a good coach. He'd been around and had some success.

"Stan and I had a very short interview. It wasn't very personal, and I knew right away that Stan wasn't looking to hire me, although Jerry Krause had locked us in a room and said, 'I want you guys to sit down and talk X's and O's.' Stan found a different topic to talk about."

"Stan came back to me after the interview," Krause recalled, "and said, 'I don't want that guy under any circumstances.' When we brought Phil in again to interview for the assistant's job two years later, I told him what to wear. And to shave."

Krause fired Stan Albeck after a season, then hired Doug Collins and brought Jackson in as an assistant. In 1989, when he fired Collins, Krause promoted Jackson. "One of Jerry Krause's greatest decisions that he gets no credit for was finding Phil Jackson in the CBA," observed Reinsdorf.

Krause was likewise criticized for drafting Scottie Pippen and Horace Grant in 1987, but the two developed into tremendous talents, another major factor in the Bulls' growth into a championship team. Krause was particularly proud of the fact that he traded up picks in the draft to select Pippen that year.

Despite his immense pride in his personnel moves, Krause seemed to have no great problem acknowledging his mistakes. For example, 1986 picks Brad Sellers out of Ohio State and Stacey King out of Oklahoma never panned out, and his trade for Dennis Hopson was a bust. Then there was the decision in 1996 not to sign first round pick Travis Knight, who became an immediate contributor for the Lakers.

And even when players did work out, the general manager sometimes alienated them, as with Pippen. Although he was considered one of the five best players in the league, Pippen angered Krause and the team's coaching staff when he refused to enter a 1994 playoff game against New York with the Bulls down a point and 1.8 seconds left. Jackson had called for the last shot to go to Kukoc, the Croatian import Krause had courted into coming to Chicago over the complaints of both Jordan and Pippen.

Pippen, who had led the team to 55 wins and back into the playoffs despite Jordan's abrupt retirement that season, was angered that he wasn't given the privilege of the last shot, which he thought he had earned.

The incident left Krause eager to trade his star forward in the aftermath, but it had been extremely difficult to find a deal that would bring a player of comparable value to the Bulls. Finally Krause had put together a deal with Seattle that would have brought power forward Shawn Kemp plus a draft pick that would possibly have given the Bulls Eddie Jones out of Temple. But at the last minute, Seattle's owner backed out of the trade, and a series of news stories followed, revealing Krause's plans. Pippen, who was already unhappy over his contract, was further enraged that the team planned to trade him. The incident touched off a running feud with Krause in the press that would simmer for years.

In addition, Horace Grant, the team's talented but mercurial free-agent power forward, had rebuffed Reinsdorf's and Krause's attempts to re-sign him. He departed for the Orlando Magic after a series of acrimonious press conferences, including one in which Reinsdorf called Grant a liar.

The ensuing turmoil had left the fans eager to pump up the volume on their rejection of Krause.

"Poor Jerry's been kicked around from pillar to post by everybody, including me," observed longtime Chicago sportswriter Bob Logan in 1995. "But he got what he wanted in life. He's running the franchise. He's got three championship rings. Yet I don't think he's ever spent a day where he's completely satisfied. There's always something else he wants, or something that doesn't quite work out."

The relationship with Pippen certainly fell into that category. The star bristled at the idea that Krause "discovered" him. "How in the hell is he gonna find me in the draft if I'm the fifth player picked?" Pippen asked. "If he 'found' me in the draft, I would have been picked in the second round, not the fifth player taken in the draft and not to the point that he had to work his way up to draft me from the eighth pick.

"He's such a down guy," Pippen said. "I get drafted at fifth, then he wants to turn around and say, 'Well, we have to pay you as the eighth pick, because we had the eighth pick. He pissed me off from the very first. He's been a liar every since I've known him. But you know, when you're young like that, you try to learn, to look, listen and learn, instead of being so vocal."

"That's crazy," Krause responded. "We traded up for him and paid him commensurate with the fifth spot."

The resentment Pippen and other players expressed about Krause was that in his boasting about deals he came across as a credit-taker, as if he was taking credit for their careers. "In a heartbeat" was how Jordan described Krause's inclination to want credit for the Bulls' accomplishments.

Jordan was asked if he agreed that he and Krause would be linked in basketball history by their accomplishments together. "I disagree with that," he said. "I know you're looking at it in terms of the players who have been brought here, some of the trades. But those are not always what they seem. What we have to do — and when I say 'we' I mean the coaches and some of the players — we have to convince Jerry of certain things, to do those. It's not always his intuition or his knowledge. Sometimes it's someone else making the suggestion, but he'll take the credit in the long run."

One team advisor said the players reminded him somewhat of children reacting to a destructive parent in a dysfunctional family. Sometimes children in a troubled family attempt to exclude the problem-causing parent from the family, so they cut off emotional attachment and "divorce" themselves from the offending parent.

The players, the advisor explained, often looked at what Krause did, not what he said. For example, Krause may have said he didn't want to break up the team, but his actions, his several attempts to trade Pippen, spoke louder to the players. Because the repeated trade attempts had deeply offended both Pippen and Jordan, their response was to essentially divorce the general manager from the family, in this case the team.

"There's the old saying that there's three sides to everything," Chip Schaefer said. "There's the plaintiff and the defendant and the truth. Is Jerry the 100 percent architect of everything that happens with the Chicago Bulls? No, he's got a staff, and he's got help with his decisions. Phil coaches them, and the players ultimately have to play. There are stories of the Steve Kerrs, those guys who have called the Bulls themselves and said they'd like to come to training camp to try out. But does he deserve credit for many, many things? Certainly. I think what he is at heart, and what he always claims he is, which is really accurate, is that he's a scout. He has the heart of a scout and the mind of a scout. To watch basketball and basketball tapes all day long, which would drive me crazy, he can do. He can be in a restaurant at 2 o'clock in the morning, after a full day of basketball, having a meal and live like that. That's his lifestyle. It's not mine, because I'd rather be with my family. But I think when things require tact and diplomacy and things like that, oftentimes that's where he struggles. He's not really what I would call a people person in a lot of ways."

Krause also took pride in finding the right administrative people to work for him and often referred to them as "my puppies." It was obviously a term of affection for Krause, who had several long-term, loyal employees working for him, but it also indicated perhaps a lack of perspective.

"The modus operandi of both Jerry Reinsdorf and Jerry Krause is that they like to find and hire people, kind of discover people and give them a chance," Schaefer said. "I think you can see that with the White Sox. They could have hired Tommy Lasorda, but they went for Jerry Manuel, who nobody had ever heard of before, to be the team's manager."

Their approach bred loyalty, or should have.

"The Jerrys have this attitude that you should be loyal to us forever," Schaefer said. "It's not just enough to do your job and do it well. You've seen in print where Reinsdorf has said Jerry 'found' Phil in the CBA. Phil's attitude is that, 'Yeah, you may have found me, but then I've done my job, too.' Krause's attitude about Scottie is, 'I plucked you out of Hamburg, Arkansas, and this is how you treat me!' Well, the fact is that if he didn't pluck him, somebody else would have plucked him."

It was Krause's great misfortune to have a run-in with Jordan in his first few months on the job. One of Krause's first personnel moves was releasing Rod Higgins, Jordan's best friend on the team.

"We traded Rod Higgins," Krause said, citing the litany of moves that had angered Jordan over the years. "But we brought him back twice. Michael was upset about that. Trading Oakley. Getting Cartwright. He didn't want Bill around. I got my job to do. He's got his job to do. Walter Davis was another one. He begged me to take Walter Davis. I wouldn't do it."

The "injury debate" was by far the worst of the issues, even though Reinsdorf said that years later Jordan admitted privately that he had acted foolishly. The Bulls opened the 1985-86 season, Jordan's second year, with three straight wins, but in the third game at Golden State Jordan suffered a broken navicular tarsal bone in his left foot, an injury that had altered or ended the careers of several NBA players. He would miss the next 64 games while the team sank in misery.

But then in March, with the Bulls' record at 22-43, Jordan informed the team that his injury had healed and that he wanted to resume playing. Immediately Krause, Reinsdorf and the team's doctors questioned that decision.

"I was scared to death," Krause has said of the situation. "I didn't want to go down in history as the guy who put Michael Jordan back in too soon."

"It was like a soap opera," Reinsdorf recalled. "We were too honest with Michael. We let him hear the report from the three doctors we consulted with over when he could come back. All three said the break had not healed enough. They said if he did play there was about a 10 to 15 percent chance of ending his career. Michael was such a competitor. He just wanted to play. I thought he was entitled to hear what the doctors had to say. I never thought he'd risk his entire career. It just didn't make any sense to me. But Michael figured that the 10 to 15 percent risk meant the odds were 85 to 90 percent that he wouldn't get hurt. To me, it didn't fit any risk/reward ratio. Here the reward was to come back and play on a team that had already had a bad year. Why risk your whole career for that reward?

"But Michael insisted that he knew his own body better than I did. So we reached a compromise, that he would play gradually, just seven minutes a half at first."

"The thing that got Michael and me off on the wrong foot," Krause said, "was that he thought I said to him, 'You're our property, and you'll do what we want you to do.' I don't remember ever saying it that way. He just misinterpreted me. I was trying to keep him from playing because he had a bad foot and the doctors were saying, 'No, no, no.' And Reinsdorf was telling him about risk.

"The doctors agreed there as an 80-20, 90-10 chance of him not being injured again if he played that year," Krause said. "Jerry said to Michael, 'Let's say it's 90-10. Do you know what risk-reward is?' Michael said, 'What do you mean?' Jerry said, 'Let's take a bottle with 10 pills in it. Nine of them will cure your headache, but one of them will kill you. Would you take one of the pills? Now, is that risk worth the reward?' And Michael still wanted to play. He was a kid who wanted to play. And I couldn't blame him. But that's where it all started because we said 'We're gonna hold you back.'"

Jordan was infuriated by what he saw as a stall by Bulls management. "Here you are dealing with big businessmen who make millions, and my millions are like pennies to them," he told reporters. "All I wanted to do was play the game that I've played for a long, long time. But they didn't look at it that way. They looked at it as protecting their investment, to keep their millions and millions coming in. That's when I really felt used. That's the only time I really felt used as a professional athlete. I felt like a piece of property."

"It's against the law to own another person as property, right?" Chip Schaefer said. "I mean that was abolished. I think that Michael Jordan is a proud man, and he's a proud African-American man.

Those comments don't generally sit well with proud African-American men, to be referred to in that way. It was particularly politically incorrect to make reference to that. Michael, he doesn't forget. Look at his whole thing with *Sports Illustrated*. They wrote a cover story on his baseball experience that he didn't like one bit. Now he doesn't read the magazine, he doesn't talk to them, he doesn't even recognize them anymore. He's like part elephant. He doesn't forget. He's strong of mind and a little bit of a martyr when he wants to be. He's like that. You don't mess with him."

Jordan played that spring and went on to set his spectacular 63-point playoff scoring record against the Celtics in the first round of the playoffs, which the Bulls lost in a sweep. "Michael had a situation with Jerry that I knew nothing about," Jackson said. "I wasn't there. But it was the reason Stan Albeck was fired. It was the reason why some things happened early in his career. They told Michael he could not play. And at that time he lost respect for Jerry. He told him, 'You don't know my body.' As a consequence, Michael has always kept the fact that he will play in any game he wants to play in his own contract. And he will train any way he wants to train in his own contract. He wants control of himself. He doesn't want to lose that control in any way to this organization, basically because of that situation."

And that was the essence of the conflict between Jordan and Krause. "It's all control," Jackson said of Krause's attempts to run the organization. The real net result of the incident was that it hardened Jordan's disdain for Krause, leading the star guard to berate publicly many of the general manager's personnel moves over the years. "Jerry's gotta be his own man when it comes to picking talent," Winter pointed out. "He certainly wants everybody's input. Finally the decision has to be made, and oftentimes the decision he makes is not one that I might like or what Phil might like or what Michael might like. But we certainly are mature enough — we should be — to accept the final decision and then we're all together on the thing."

Instead of seeking Jordan's opinion on trades and other moves during his first years with the Bulls, Krause sought the opinions of Robert Parish in Boston or Brad Davis in Dallas, players he had known for years. "Michael Jordan was a very young player when he came here," Krause recalled. "The first probably four or five years of my time here, there were two players that I talked a lot to about players, One of them was Robert Parish. The other was Brad Davis. Those relationships had built up over years.

"I talked to players, but I didn't talk to Michael because he wasn't old enough to understand at that point. And they could tell me things because they had played against guys. And they could do it without hurting their own organizations. Neither one of them could hurt their own organizations."

With Jordan in obvious conflict with the GM, it wasn't long before Bulls players began calling Krause "Crumbs" behind his back, implying that Krause often left evidence of a healthy appetite on his clothes. Before long, the Chicago media were reporting that it was Jordan who had made up the nickname. Krause, however, determined it was another player, and soon that player was no longer a Chicago Bull.

The player who supposedly made up the name was Charles Oakley. "There are countless incidents related to food involving Jerry," Chip Schaefer said. "He loves Charles Oakley, or so he says."

"Krause actually got the name Crumbs years ago when he was a baseball scout," Reinsdorf said. "Other scouts gave him the name. Then Michael found out about it."

"There's no question that he's got some baggage," Schaefer said of the general manager. "He just aches to be recognized. He's an interesting guy because there are times you feel genuine . . . pity's an awful strong word, but you feel that. Then there are other times that he'll do things, and you won't feel that way. You'll feel that all the torment he gets is self-imposed. 'You didn't have to do that to yourself.' Then other times you do feel compassion for the guy and wish things wouldn't be the way they are."

By all accounts, Krause was a man of intense loyalty. Conversely, he could be unforgiving when he felt that someone had violated his trust and loyalty. The case of veteran assistant coach Johnny Bach was a classic example. "In essence, Johnny fired himself," Krause said of Bach's dismissal from the staff after the 1994 playoffs. "I told him many times that assistant coaches shouldn't be holding press conferences. Assistant coaches should have lower profiles. We cautioned him about that time and and again, yet he kept doing it."

"It was Jerry Krause's relationship with Johnny Bach that created a very uncomfortable situation," Jackson said. "It made this have to happen eventually. It had gone all wrong. It was bad for the staff to have this kind of thing because we had to work together.

"Jerry basically blamed Johnny Bach for a lot of the things in *The Jordan Rules*. And there's no doubt that Johnny did provide that information. Jerry felt that Johnny talked too much. And Johnny, in retrospect, felt that animosity that Jerry gave to back to him, the lack of respect, so Johnny refused to pay allegiance to Jerry just because he was the boss."

Krause said that in recent years he learned that Jackson actually provided far more information for the book than Bach. "Phil and the players had much more of a role than Johnny Bach," author Sam Smith acknowledged.

"Phil lied to me," Krause said. "Phil actually got Johnny Bach fired."

"It was Phil's idea to fire Bach," Reinsdorf agreed. "Phil told me that the bad relationship between Krause and Bach had made things impossible. It was Phil's idea. Nobody told him to do it."

"It had gone on for too long a period of time," Jackson said. "I could have kept them apart, at bay from one another, I suppose for a while longer. But I didn't like the fact that it wasn't good teamwork. That was my staff and my area. I agreed to do it. I felt it was a good opportunity because Johnny had an opportunity to get another job in the league quickly. It worked out fine for Johnny, although I would just as soon have not put him through the disappointment, or have to go through the situation myself."

Krause said he had an almost tearful reunion with Bach in 1998 after learning the circumstances. Regardless, the situation had made a clear impression on Bulls staff members in 1994. Don't cross Krause. And even if you haven't, make double sure not to give the impression that you have.

The Chicago media had long portrayed Krause as a non-athlete seeking to bond with the athletes he employed, yet always facing painful rejection. In 1991, when the Bulls finally defeated the Detroit Piston Bad Boys in the playoffs after years of trying and failing, Krause was deliriously happy as he got on the team plane after the game. "He comes in the front of the plane and he's celebrating," Jackson recalled. "He's dancing, and the guys are going, 'Go, Jerry! Go, Jerry, go!' He's dancing or whatever he's doing, and when he stops, they all collapse in hilarity, this laughter, and you couldn't tell whether it was with him or at him. It was one of those nebulous moments. It was wild."

You could argue that Krause had moved through a career of nebulous moments. Jackson said that in years past, Krause would approach him about making a pep talk to the team. "He'd say, 'What if I go down to the bus and say to these guys, 'We gotta get this one tomorrow.' How do you think that'll make them feel?'" Jackson said. "I'd say, 'Jerry, I don't know. I don't think that will really work.'"

Usually Krause would be good about checking with the coaching staff on player issues. But Jackson said that when Krause was at his worst he would charge right in and confront certain players. "The thing that happened with Pippen (the drawn out public infighting in 1994 and '95) was avoidable," Jackson said. "The things that have happened in the past were avoidable. Somehow or other they got pushed to greater limits. But that's part of who Jerry is. He wants to directly confront when he feels that there has been a problem. He wants to challenge and overrun people and be brusque. He's very brusque and sets people on edge just by walking into the locker room sometimes. We've had to talk to him about his manner in the locker room. On the other hand, Jerry keeps his space very well. He doesn't overrun us, the coaches. He allows a coach to do what he wants to do as far as strategy and how he wants to handle the players. Jerry has a very good attitude about protocol.

"He's just a very unusual guy."

In part, Jordan's treatment of Krause had been a response to the outbreak of hostilities between the general manager and Pippen. Although Jordan had occasionally taunted Krause in the past he took a much more aggressive approach after he returned to the game in 1995.

"He seemed to let a lot more things hang out, Michael did at that time," Jackson said. "More honest with his feelings, more outspoken. He would speak about things that he hadn't before. But there's always been that thing. Jerry will tell you, 'I'm the one person who told him he couldn't play, and Michael's gonna hold that against me for the rest of his life.'"

"I express myself more vocally now than I would have 10 years ago," Jordan agreed.

"Michael's now in a position where he can hammer him more," observed another team employee. "In the past, Michael was at a level where he couldn't quite do that. Now Michael's the most powerful person in sports, and he can do whatever the hell he wants. He feels a lot easier showing how he really feels. He felt a lot of the same things in '91 and '92 and '93, but he realizes now that he can say them. I mean, you're talking about the greatest individual, the greatest team player in the history of sports."

However, Levine, the longtime Chicago radio reporter, said he would be hard-pressed to think of any circumstances that would bring anybody to judge Jordan harshly. "To portray Michael as anything but a terrific guy for what he's been through, I think is incorrect," Levine said. "Personally, he's done me favors. He's done other media people favors over the years. I remember back in '89, '90, '91, he would come out to Children's Hospital every Christmas, without any publicity. I would ask him to come out, and he would come out and tour the hospital, just walk through the whole hospital going from room to room and child to child. It was a very touching thing.

"Would he do that now?" Levine asked. "I wouldn't ask him now because he's too big. But that's the type of guy he is. He's a giving person. There's no question he's also takes advantage of who he is. But who wouldn't? I've seen other sides of him, but for a superstar whose time is demanded and begged for by everybody, he's tremendous. He's a tremendous person, because he knows that people don't deal with him as a person but as an object. He's very much like a very beautiful woman who can't get by the fact that people focus only on her exterior. Because people are so taken by what she is on the outside and what she is physically, just the same as Michael has become the biggest superstar in sports since Muhammad Ali. He can't go anywhere without people wanting something from him.

"He's gotten a pass from a lot of media people in the sense that if we've heard bad stories we haven't always followed them because he's been so good to us personally," Levine said. "Is he a perfect person? No, he's not perfect. But he's been so giving of himself on and off the court, to charities and to people that if I heard a bad story about him, then I would go to him. And I have gone to him and told him what's out there on numerous occasions just so he knows that it might get out.

"Does Michael break the law? No, Michael doesn't break the law. Does he hurt other people? No, he doesn't other people. The only thing Michael ever does is drive 120 and gets stopped by policemen. When they see who he is, either he gives them an autograph or they let him go because they can say to their friends that night that they let Michael Jordan go."

Without question, Jordan was changed by his father's death in 1993, evidenced in part by the way he was forced to change his dealings with the media. "Up until then, he was the most unaffected superstar, because he wouldn't allow (the fame and fortune) to get to him," Levine said. "He would still sit in the locker room before the game and stretch out with us and talk for a half hour or 40 minutes about everything but basketball. He would stretch out on the floor, and we would just sit for 45 minutes and talk about everything. We'd have fun. He'd ask questions. He's a very inquisitive, a guy who wanted to learn about things. He was still learning about life and educating himself. But once the situation occurred with his father and the way the media portrayed that funeral, he never had the same feeling for media again. He distrusts most media, even people like myself who are peripherally friends with him. It just changed. He became hardened by it to a certain extent. He's still very gracious with his time, but the fun kind of went out of it for him and for us. I think we lost a lot out of it, too. We had a friend-type of relationship with him. Now, all that exists is just the interview process. There's no time for the friend part."

While Jordan may not always had the warmest regards for Krause or for a teammate who shirked his competitive responsibilities, the star displayed an uncommon drive to reach out in a special way to virtually every child or handicapped person he encountered. There were stars who when necessary forced themselves to do charity work for public relations effect, but with Jordan it was obviously a natural connection, wherever he went. "To me the test of what a person is all about is how they react around children and old people," Levine said. "And when Michael sees a child, he always gives them a big smile and shakes their hand or gives 'em a hug and takes a picture. That's the essence of Michael Jordan, he's still just this big kid."

Over the years, Jordan had made a lasting friend of Carmen Villafane, who was wheelchair bound. "They've been friends for years," said Cindy Kamradt, the United Center's guest services manager. "He buys her season tickets every year, and he never ever says anything about it. He has a number of charitable things he does on the side, away from the publicity, for which he never seeks publicity."

"We always wait for Michael to interview him when he gets out of his car at the United Center," Levine said of the outpost manned by Chicago media many game nights. "We were waiting this past Christmas. And the first thing Michael did was go into his trunk and pull out this huge gift wrapped for Carmen. He gave her a kiss and a hug and said Merry Christmas. And she gave him a gift. Those types of things are seen because we're peeking in on Michael's life. Obviously we're peeping Toms on some of his private life. That's what Michael's all about. He cares for her as a person. The human side is there. A lot of high profile people and stars who are out there all the time, they lose their humanity, and Michael has never lost it."

The difficult irony for Krause was that while Jordan had obscured, even challenged, his accomplishments as a general manager, the Bulls star had also made them possible. Not surprisingly, Krause had mixed feelings about Jordan's abrupt retirement following the shooting death of his father James in 1993. Yes, Jordan's presence was an incredible force for the Bulls. But, as Pippen alleged, Krause also relished the opportunity to build another championship team without the superstar.

"I think Jerry's stuck on the fact that no matter what he does or has done, the fact that he didn't draft Michael Jordan hangs over his head," said a Bulls staff member. "He has brought every single person into this organization, from Tex to Phil to Scottie to Toni to Ron Harper. All of them ballsy moves and trades. But he'll never get the credit he wants."

"Jerry and I have talked about it," Krause told a reporter in 1995. "Hell, yeah, we want to win after Michael because there is a certain vindication in it and there is a certain personal thing in it. Yeah, I mean, I have an ego. I don't think that it is huge, but it ain't small. And I think I'm good at what I do, and for one time I want the world to say that I won, and it wasn't because of Michael."

Reinsdorf said that he was visiting with Jordan in Las Vegas in 1997 when the star told him, "I have to reluctantly admit that Krause has done a good job."

"I said, 'Why don't you say that publicly and save him a lot of grief?'" Reinsdorf recalled. "Michael said, 'I just can't bring myself to do it.'"

In the moments after the 1997 title, one team employee watched Jordan embrace Krause. "He grabbed him and he hugged him," the employee said. "It wasn't a quick embrace because it was the right thing to do at the moment. It was a hug, a heart-felt hug. And Michael hugged Krause's wife Thelma. She was just smiling. It was almost like family."

Within weeks, though, the Bulls would be engulfed in another summer of confrontations and negotiations, and there would be no more inclination to hugs. It could be argued, in fact, that the hugs were gone forever.

"Everything is not enough."

— Townes Van Zandt

4/ Summertime Blues

It wasn't so much the grind of the seasons that had worn down the relationships among Michael Jordan's Chicago Bulls. Instead, most of their strife was acted out during the summers, in the heat of contract negotiations, when things were done and said that left all the major parties offended. They all may have been rich and famous, but that didn't mean they were immune to getting their feelings hurt. Oftentimes, just the opposite applied. The bigger the ego, the deeper the bruise.

That seemed especially true of the Bulls each offseason.

"The summertime is when all that stuff erupts with Michael," Steve Kerr observed. "We win the championship, and he goes to the podium and makes his plea for another crack at it. That infuriated management. Then it goes on all summer."

The situation hadn't been helped by the fact that Jackson, Jordan and Rodman had all been running on one-year contracts since 1996, which meant that each summer required another round of negotiations, another session of charged battles. "It's put an edge on everything, towards the end of the year for the last two years," Jackson said in 1998.

"The last two years it's been exacerbated," Krause agreed.

Reinsdorf and Jordan had enjoyed over the years what appeared to be a warm relationship. As the 1990s unfolded and it became increasingly clear that the player salaries in pro basketball were headed to almost bizarre heights, Jordan was said to be understandably bothered by the fact that he was signed to a contract that paid him in the range of $4 million annually while a dozen or more lesser players in the league were being paid twice that. At the same time, Jordan was far too proud to ask for a renegotiation. Where other athletes had routinely pouted and fretted and demanded renegotiations, he wanted no part of that. His answer was to live up to the deal he had signed in the highest fashion. Yet when he abruptly retired in the fall of 1993, there were the inevitable insinuations that he did so in part because of his contract. In 1994, a reporter asked if he could be lured back for a $100 million deal. "If I played for the money," he said testily, "it would be $300 million."

Actually, considering the billions his special performances had brought to the league coffers, the number wasn't entirely out of reason. With Jordan away from the game and television ratings falling, some NBA owners had informally approached Reinsdorf about the possibility of enticing the star back to the NBA with group funding from the league. Such a notion was unprecedented, but then again Jordan's impact on the game was also unprecedented. The idea of the league paying Jordan, though, was never pursued beyond informal discussions, Reinsdorf said.

In the summer of 1993, just after the Bulls had won their third straight championship and before his abrupt retirement that fall, there had been speculation in the Chicago press that Jordan's one-year playing contract could zoom to the $50 million range. That speculation all but disappeared with the murder of Jordan's father and the star's subsequent decision to leave basketball that October of 1993.

The Bulls continued to pay Jordan despite his retirement, which, according to one of Reinsdorf's associates, was a gesture of loyalty from Reinsdorf to Jordan. "I just wanted to give him a bonus, that's all," Reinsdorf said. "I never thought he was coming back. People doubted that he could play in the pros, but I thought he would have eventually made the White Sox as an extra outfielder."

In basketball, Reinsdorf and Jordan had been partners in the most lucrative sports/entertainment venture in history. The problem was, Jordan as a player was barred from having any real equity position in the relationship. As a result, Reinsdorf was management, and Jordan was labor. The labor costs were fixed, while the profit percentages were soaring for those with a piece of the action. Jordan, of course, was making his tens of millions off the court, using his overpowering image to hawk a range of commercial products. In a way, that position created a comfort for him. His outside income so dwarfed his player contract that he could say that he didn't play the game for money and say it with a straight face.

Still, his relatively meager player contract created an inequity with Jordan. And when he returned to the game in 1995, he returned under his old contract, which meant that the Bulls' payroll itself remained well under $30 million and that the team could continue raking in tens of millions in profit. That, of course, was in addition to the tremendous growth in equity Jordan's brilliant play had helped create for the team's owners. Reinsdorf's ownership group had purchased the club during Jordan's rookie season for about $16 million, then watched its value grow to better than 20 times that over the ensuing decade.

So there was easily the strong sense that Jordan was "owed." And that wasn't a feeling held just by Jordan and his representatives but by virtually anyone who had anything to do with the NBA.

If the notion wasn't entirely clear, Jordan emphasized it when his play and leadership drove the Bulls to their incredible 72-10 regular-season record over the 1995-96 season, culminated by a 15-3 run through the playoffs for the team's fourth championship. With the close of the campaign, Jordan's long-term contract finally expired. So then the real trouble started.

Days after the championship celebration, David Falk, the star's representative, and Reinsdorf began discussing his new contract. At first, the meetings were cordial. Reinsdorf recalled that he, Falk, Falk partner Curtis Polk and Jordan met in Falk's suite at the Ritz Carlton in Chicago, where they smoked cigars and joked "like a bunch of kids." Jordan kept ordering obscenely expensive bottles of wine and charging them to Falk, which had them all laughing. "We talked at great length how we had been together all these years, how we had struggled, how we had a great relationship. We all said we didn't want a negotiation, but just to talk it through and come up with the right number," Reinsdorf said.

At the time, there was a league moratorium on discussing figures which wouldn't be lifted for a few weeks. In the interim, they could talk but not about specific numbers. Jordan suggested that when discussions started in earnest, Reinsdorf should come up with a number. "I don't want to do that," Reinsdorf told him. "That's the ultimate negotiation."

In a private interview for this book, Jordan laid out his approach: "What I instructed my representative was, 'Don't go in and give a price. I've been with this team for a long time. Everyone knows what this market value may be, or could be. If he's true to his word and honest in terms of our relationship, listen to what he says before we offer what our opinions may be.' Falk's instruction was to go in and listen, never to negotiate. Because it shouldn't have come to a negotiation. We didn't think of it as a negotiation.

We felt it was an opportunity for the Bulls to give me what they felt my value had been to the organization."

Jordan , however, was also well aware of Reinsdorf's reluctance to turn loose money. The star believed a drawn-out negotiation would only demean what he had accomplished for the Bulls. So Jordan and his advisors entertained offers from the New York Knickerbockers.

Would Jordan have given up the Bulls for the Knicks?

"Yes," he said.

In fact, the Knicks had supposedly put together a few million in base salary for Jordan to be augmented by a mega-million personal services contract with one of the Knicks' affiliated companies. When he learned of the deal, Reinsdorf reportedly phoned the league's front office to demand an opinion on the legality of the move. The Bulls chairman was supposedly threatening a lawsuit to block the Knicks, but reportedly a high-powered source at the NBA counseled Reinsdorf against the futility of filing suit against his popular star and the Knicks.

Jordan's agent, David Falk,wanted a substantial contract to reflect Jordan's contribution to the Bulls and the game. "As I know it, no numbers were ever talked about until I was into the game," Jordan revealed. "No one wanted to put the numbers out on the table. Everyone was jockeying to see who was gonna put the first number out, which we were not gonna do. We had a number in our heads, but we really felt like it was the Bulls' place to tell us what our net worth was. And to do it from an honest state, not influenced by David, not influenced by me. Just what they felt I'd meant to the organization."

Finally exasperated at Reinsdorf's reluctance to make an offer, Jordan was pulled into a conference phone call with his agent and Reinsdorf. At the time, he was playing golf. But he told Reinsdorf that if the team wanted to re-sign him it would be a one-year deal for better than $30 million. And that Reinsdorf had one hour to agree.

"At the time they were negotiating I was in Tahoe for a celebrity golf tournament," Jordan explained. "And we had some conversations with New York (the Knickerbockers). And we were gonna meet with them right after we met with Reinsdorf, and I think that was within an hour's time. David wanted the Bulls to make their offer and discuss it before we go down and have a conversation with New York. But (Reinsdorf) knew he had a window in terms of the conversation with New York."

"That's cold," Krause would later say of the timing. "Michael's the one who made the statement." The team chairman was wounded. According to associates, he had assumed he had a personal relationship with Jordan. After all, hadn't he extended the opportunity to Michael to begin a pro baseball career with the White Sox? Hadn't he always made the effort to make clear his respect for his star player? Associates later said that Reinsdorf began to think Jordan had faked their friendship to take advantage of him, something Reinsdorf denied.

Reinsdorf said Jordan's memory was faulty on the negotiation, which came in a conference call with Falk in Washington and Jordan on the golf course in Lake Tahoe. "I proposed a two-year deal at $45 million. It had some structuring and some service clauses in it," the team chairman said. "They countered at two years for $55 million, 30 for the first year and 25 for the second. Michael was on the phone and said, 'You guys ought to be able to work it out. I'm getting off.' Falk and I had several conversations that evening and he wouldn't move from his proposal. I thought the $30 million was ridiculous, and I didn't want to commit to two years."

It was then, Reinsdorf said, that Falk mentioned that he was set to begin talks with Dave Checketts of the Knicks and that Jordan might wind up there. "I thought, 'I can't believe Michael would play in New York. I can gut this out,'" Reinsdorf recalled. Falk then suggested that if Reinsdorf didn't like the two-year deal, they could go one year for $30 million. "I didn't think it had to be done that day," the chairman said in explaining his displeasure over the threat to go to the Knicks. "It annoyed me."

But he realized he had no choice. He had to accept the terms.

"I was not happy with the $30 million deal," Reinsdorf said. "The reason I went along with it was that Falk had convinced me we needed to end the negotiations on good terms. I thought I had made a fair offer, $45 million for two years. I thought they were pushing it."

Jordan, though, could have asked for far more and enjoyed the support of public opinion that he deserved every penny. But in agreeing to the deal, Reinsdorf supposedly made a comment to Jordan that would further damage their relationship. According to Jordan, Reinsdorf said he would live to regret giving Jordan the $30 million.

"Michael is bitter at Jerry," explained one Bulls employee, "because when Jerry agreed to pay him the $30 million, Jerry told Michael that he would regret it. Michael stood in the training room one day the next fall and told all his teammates, 'You know what really pissed me off? Jerry said, 'You know what Michael? I'm gonna live to regret this.'

"Michael said, 'What the fuck? You could say, You deserve this. You're the greatest player ever, you're an asset to the city of Chicago and the organization. And I'm happy to pay you $30 million. You could say that, but even if you don't feel that way and you're going to regret it, why are you telling me that?' Luc was standing there and said, 'Really? Jerry told you he was going to regret it?' Michael said, 'He told me that. I couldn't believe my owner told me that.'"

"That creates tremendous bitterness," the team employee said.

"I said I 'might' live to regret it," Reinsdorf later admitted. "If I said anything I said I hope I don't live to regret this."

Jordan recalled: "Actually, he said, 'Somewhere down the road, I know I'm gonna regret this.' It demeaned what was happening. It took away from the meaning of things. The gratitude seemed less because of that statement. I felt it was inappropriate to say that."

The team chairman had reportedly made a similar comment to John Paxson a few seasons earlier. Paxson, who had spent several seasons working under a contract that paid him relatively little, had finally earned a substantial pay raise. Reinsdorf agreed to an increased contract but upon signing the deal told the hard-working Paxson, "I can't believe I'm paying you this kind of money."

Although Paxson, now a broadcaster with the team, declined comment, sources with the team confirmed that he was angered and insulted. Both Jordan's and Paxson's negotiations were typical of a management mentality where Reinsdorf and Krause wanted to "win" every contract negotiation with every player. That desire to get the best of the players in contract negotiations erased any good feelings between players and management, a former player said. And it usually resulted in an ill mood from Krause or Reinsdorf whenever they "lost," the player said.

"Aren't you supposed to try to win contracts?" Reinsdorf asked. The chairman said his comment to Paxson was misconstrued. The team could have signed Paxson for about $800,000 but waited until after he had turned in an excellent playoff performance, which meant they had to pay him $1.2 million. Reinsdorf said he was referring to the money he had lost by hesitating. He noted that not taking Jordan's offer for $55 million over two years was another boner. "That was a big mistake. That cost me 8 million bucks," he said, referring to the fact that he signed Jordan to another one-year deal in 1997 for $33 million.

"They really just are not very good people-people," Chip

Schaefer said of the two Jerrys. "Even Reinsdorf. I've heard him fall short there. We have our season-ending dinner and banquets and things like that. And he'll get up and talk. A favorite target for him to poke fun at is Irwin Mandel, our VP of business affairs. Irwin is a wonderful guy, a great family guy. We all love him. Reinsdorf will poke fun at him about something. It will be this inappropriate, really mean-spirited sort of thing. Jerry Krause wants to be that way, too. It's like they don't have a very good sense of humor. They'll try to poke fun at somebody or use a joke, and they'll kind of lay bombs, like they don't know what to do. They'll just make the guy feel like shit. If you actually think that about John Paxson, don't say it. I think Jerry Reinsdorf probably meant it tongue in cheek, but how is this supposedly savvy business guy capable of saying something so inappropriate or so insensitive to a guy who prides himself on being a great athlete doing the best he can for you? How could you say something like that? It's not a funny joke."

"He's loyal, he's honest," Phil Jackson said of Reinsdorf. "He's truthful. His word means something. But there's something about going in and trying to get the best every time. Winning the deal. When it comes to money, to win the deal.

"He has actually said those things, according to people I've been close to," Jackson said of Reinsdorf's comments, "and those things really hurt. Because most everybody really likes Jerry Reinsdorf.

"But," Jackson added with a laugh, "Jerry is Jerry. Jerry is . . . Jerry doesn't spend money freely, even with himself. He wants value for money. Who doesn't? The salaries that have happened in the past 10 years have been real difficult for owners to swallow. Large money. It's an amazing amount of money. I understand it. I'm not spending that money, but if I had to spend that money . . . Sometimes you're seeing a lot of money coming in, and then the ones going out are even bigger. You say, 'I wonder if the stuff coming in is going to match what's going out during this period of time.'

"It's a step of faith all the time for them to do it," Jackson said of Reinsdorf and Krause handing out large contracts. "But every time they've taken that step, there's been a reward for them. They've gotten more money to come in. And so it's kind of like this faith proposition. The more you seed, the more you're gonna reap."

In the final analysis, it comes down to faith in the NBA itself, Jackson said, "and faith in the people in this organization."

The conflict between Jackson and Krause was murkier. Reinsdorf pointed out that the two men actually had very few differences in regard to basketball philosophy. Their disagreements were more personal in nature, the team chairman said.

"It's the methods, not the philosophy," Jackson agreed. "It's how things are done.

"Jerry and I lost our cooperative nature a couple of years ago, and it was just through the hardship of negotiations," Jackson said. "I just felt that the negotiating wasn't done in a good manner. But negotiations can be difficult. Coaches and general managers, when they get caught up in it, sometimes get on the other sides of the fence from each other. That happened to us a little bit, and it's been tough to mend the bridge."

In February of 1996, word circulated through the organization that contract talks between Jackson and Krause had turned sour. Some staff members worried that Jackson would have to leave the organization. Krause and Reinsdorf were so close that Jackson would obviously lose a power struggle, one long-time Bulls employee observed.

"Two years ago, we had a couple of negotiating things that weren't good," Jackson recalled. "And Jerry (Krause) would talk to my agent and then call me up and say, 'Phil, there's no way we can do this.'"

The contract talks, sometimes emotional and acrimonious, dragged on into the playoffs, right in the midst of the NBA Finals, the league championship series between Chicago and the Seattle Super Sonics. "There was a situation in Seattle that was unfortunate," Jackson recalled. "There was all this stuff going on about coming back. I was caught in the middle of this thing. Michael was in the last year of his contract at $4.5 million or whatever he was making. We had a couple of other guys in that situation. We had a 72-10 season that year. And we were in the Finals, and there was a lot of press going on about it, and there was some bad tension about the division of the labor here."

Jackson was conducting a team practice at Key Arena in Seattle between games of the championship series, and Krause and some of his assistants had decided to come to practice and conduct a work session in the arena. During the Finals, each practice session was followed by a 30-minute session of media interviews during which reporters were allowed onto the court to question players and coaches.

About 12:30 that day, the NBA public relations staff people notified Jackson that his team's media session was over. The NBA liked to closely control the scheduling on these events, because the league didn't like to leave one team waiting for the other to leave the floor, the coach pointed out.

Upon being notified the Bulls' interview time was up, Jackson used his trademark shrill, fingers-in-the-mouth whistle to get his players' attention and announce, "OK, everybody on the bus."

"The bus was right off the court," Jackson recalled. "So we wait five minutes, and Jerry doesn't show. And I drive out. The team bus leaves, and Jerry was irate at this situation. He didn't call me, but he called my trainer and everyone else. Well, one of the things is, I always call the shots on that. I'm the guy that runs the bus and the plane and that kind of stuff. It's the team. I left him behind in that situation. Now, whether he got caught with the press or what else..."

"It was the day after Game 4," trainer Chip Schaefer recalled. "By all intents and purposes I think everyone felt that they should have been on a plane heading back to Chicago trophy in hand and hung over from a night of partying. But we weren't. There we were back at the Key Arena practicing to prepare for Game 5, and the series was not over yet. So people were in a little bit of a terse mood that day. I was actually back in the training room working on a couple of guys as practice wound down. They had their mandatory media session after that. I was the last or one of the last persons on the bus that day because I had been busy packing up my medical case.

"I sit right behind the driver when Jerry's not there," Schaefer explained. "When Jerry's there, he sits behind the driver, and Phil sits in the first seat across the aisle. I got on that day, and Phil told the driver to go ahead and leave. I knew Jerry had come over on the bus, but for all I knew he had arranged to do an interview or was going to have lunch with someone. I had no idea what he was doing. I remember turning behind me to Clarence Gaines and Jim Stack, Jerry's two assistants, and I asked them if they knew anything about him having a ride. They just shrugged their shoulders, totally noncommittal about it, and I remember turning back to those two guys and saying, 'If he doesn't have a ride back, I know who's gonna get blamed for this,' knowing full well that it would be me.

"The bus goes back to the hotel," the trainer recalled, "and I'm in my room working on Longley and Kukoc later, and my phone rings. I pick it up, and Jerry just launches into me, just launches into me. It was an expletive-laden tirade. He was on the same floor of the hotel as me, and I don't like being spoken to like that, especially on the telephone. So I hung up the phone and walked right down to his room and knocked on the door. He was still having a fit, and I looked at him and said, 'If you're gonna yell at me, yell to my face. Don't yell at me over the telephone. I don't like that.' He couldn't look at me. He just looked at the floor and said, 'I don't have time for this,' and kept yelling about how it wasn't right the bus left him. I said, 'I agree it wasn't right, Jerry. I agree.'

"He wanted to apologize the next day," Schaefer said of Krause. "He got on the bus the next morning muttering something about 'Sorry, I didn't mean to shoot the messenger.' He had called several people when he got back to the hotel to vent his frustration, and the first schmuck to pick up the phone was Chip Schaefer, so I took the brunt of it. I don't think he meant anything for me directly. He was furious at the situation. I have taken the brunt like that over the years sometimes when he gets frustrated. I have a temper I suppose if you push me hard enough, but I can work with people. We all have our point, though. I don't like being yelled at. I don't like being treated like a child or like a peon.

"That moment in Seattle in 1996 was certainly an event in my relationship with Jerry," said Schaefer, who was scheduled to leave the team after the 1998 season. "That event affected our relationship. It's like the old thing about forgiving and forgetting. People who work close with him, like Jim and Karen Stack (Krause's assistants), they're able to say, 'Oh, that's just him,' and he can behave in a certain way. And they can brush it off. But everything changes when it happens to you. I think people are accountable for their actions. I don't think you can behave in a certain way and have everyone else say, 'Oh, that's just the way he is,' and tolerate it. Why should I tolerate it?"

"I didn't appreciate what he did," Krause said of Jackson. "He never sent anybody for me. And I was standing there talking to somebody. You know what? That's all passed. That doesn't affect me. I hadn't even thought of that, OK? We're just at the point, where I think it's like divorce. Some people wake up in the morning and their children are gone. They got nothing in common. They should get divorced. We're probably at that stage."

The general manager's riding on the bus was already an issue that Jackson had raised. The coach's decision to leave his boss behind rather than keep the players waiting would quickly become a factor in both their negotiations and their relationship.

"With the negotiations that were going on at the time, that was kind of an overload situation for him," Jackson said of Krause. "And at that point, when we came back to Chicago and we won, I saw Mr. Reinsdorf heap all the praise on Jerry in the final announcement.

"They started doing a spin on the fans being so great in Chicago. The reality is that Michael had come back and proven a tremendous point. He had retired and spent a year and a half away from it. Then he'd come back and had a failure of a return in 17 games. The '95 season was not successfully finished. We had lost to Orlando, which was one of the most difficult spots for Michael to be in.

"Then for our team to win the championship on a 72-10 year was just an absolute pie a` la mode," Jackson said. "I don't care where the credit should have gone for whomever. But it was just an obvious slap in the face of the team. It was just like a pure snub."

Angered, Jackson said he considered leaving the Bulls. "The players all came to me," he recalled, "and said, 'Don't leave us. Don't go. Find a way to come back. Because we're all here. Scottie's here. Michael's gonna come back.'"

Reinsdorf would later say that Jackson turned down a five-year contract offer from the team. Jackson said if such an offer was made, it was made in passing, not as a written offer. Jackson recalled that "Mr. Reinsdorf said, 'Tell me if I'm right or wrong. From what I understand, you want to coach this team if we provide the personnel that would make it a championship team, Scottie and Michael and so forth. Because if that's the case, we'd like to offer you a five-year contract. And you'd go ahead and coach here and help us rebuild.' And I said, 'I need a break. That's really nice, but I need a break.'

"That may be what they consider a long-term offer," Jackson said. "But it wasn't clear. I said I think I've coached a couple of years too long actually for the kind of stress that this puts a person under. And (too long) for my own health, personal and mental and physical."

Jackson ultimately agreed to a one-year deal for the 1996-97 season, but his relationship with Krause suffered heavy damage. "He was offered a much longer contract," Krause recalled. "We said, 'If you're not gonna be here to rebuild, we've gotta move on.' It was very simple."

Just how badly the relationship had deteriorated became apparent with the meetings the coaching staff and general manager hold with each Bulls player shortly after the end of each season. These sessions were essential, Jackson said, because the coaching staff uses them to bring "closure" to the season, discussing with each player his accomplishments and his plans for offseason conditioning and his role on the team for the upcoming campaign. For example, it was during the 1995 meetings that guard Ron Harper and the coaches discussed his pivotal role for the 1995-96 season, a role that was a key factor in the Bulls winning their fourth title.

"We had a day off after the win," Jackson said of the 1996 end of year sessions, "and then we go into our team meetings where we debrief the players. We got into that thing. It was just a certain amount of rhythm. There's a half hour for each player. You bring them in and talk. Some players only go 15 minutes. But they have the team meeting."

The time is also used to give each player his share of playoff bonus money.

"Jerry wasn't there to start it out at 9 o'clock," Jackson recalled. "He was in his office and couldn't get there. So all of a sudden, it was 9:30, 10 o'clock, and we had three players backed up now. And I hate to have that happen to the players. They come in early to get it done. So we started doing players in a hurry, and started just cutting through what we normally would do with young players. I realized that he didn't care about this session.

"In between the sessions, Jerry was like cold," Jackson said. "We couldn't get a conversation going on. I didn't try. I mean I was just kind of feeling it out. Then suddenly he had to disappear at a certain time, and he took another 45 minutes off. We had more guys come through. I finally went to his door and said, 'Jerry, you gotta come and finish this off, or else cancel it. One way or another we cannot do this to people. You can't just not do it.'"

It was obvious that the general manager wasn't eager to work with him, and that had an effect on the quality of the sessions, Jackson said. "And all of a sudden they were like meaningless."

"Were we cold with one another?" Krause asked. "Of course we were. Because I was fed up with him."

Some employees in the organization suggested that Jackson was trying to manipulate the situation to take over as general manager. "The scariest thing would be if Krause weren't there and Phil had the power," said one employee who worked with both men. "Very scary."

Jackson's substantial ego grinds against Krause's numerous insecurities, the employee added. "Phil is a master manipulator. You're talking about the media, the players, the staff, everybody. But the one thing Phil will never be able to manipulate is the title of general manager. He'll never get that as long as he's with the Bulls."

Another employee said he thought the tension between Krause and Jackson actually was one very big factor in the Bulls' success. "Although neither one of them would admit it," the employee said. "There's that friction, but that friction makes things work. You got two polar opposites. But things are so fragile."

"There's no way that Phil could be right all the time, or Jerry could be right all the time," agreed Chip Schaefer, who was often caught between the two. "So when they have differences of opinion, it's probably healthy. Sometimes coaches and GMs have different agendas. I'm not sure how a guy can do both jobs, because you're wearing two hats. That's why leaders, whether they're presidents or kings or whatever, have staffs or people who advise them, that they can bounce ideas off of, because if one person makes all the decisions, that's too much responsibility."

Krause loyalists in the organization had suggested that Jackson had become arrogant. Asked about arrogance, Jackson said, "I've tried to be really fair and tried to stay on base and on cue and not get insulted by questions that keep coming back through the media. I've done the little things that I think have kept everything on the square with the team. But that might be their view, that I'm arrogant."

As for his ambition to be general manager, Jackson said he was the person best suited to handle relationships between management and the players. "I'm the kind of person to handle both those kinds of things and find solutions for those things," he said.

But did that translate into a hunger for power? Jackson said not. "I've never gone behind Jerry's back to the owner," the coach said. "I've never done anything to get power."

Jackson did admit that money was a big factor in his dispute with Krause. He said that was partly because the pay for coaches had inflated, exemplified by the huge contracts and power given to coaches such as John Calipari with the New Jersey Nets and Rick Pitino with the Boston Celtics. "Kind of the pay-off structure for coaches has been destroyed by John Calipari getting the kind of money he's getting in New Jersey," Jackson said. "So there's precedence. Here's guys that hadn't won at any level who are coming into the game because some team thought they were valuable at this level.

"Jerry's got a salary that hasn't done this same thing," Jackson said of Krause. "General managers' salaries didn't move up. Coaches make more than general managers. You look at it, and you say this is real tough for a guy like Jerry to negotiate. He's looking at it like, 'This guy's more valuable to the organization than I am.' I know all the personal things that must be going through his head as he's negotiating it. So it's very difficult for him to do it.

"That was my argument with Jerry Krause eight years ago," Jackson said. "I told him, 'Coaches' salaries are gonna go over a million dollars. They're gonna get paid what players are getting paid, Jerry.'

He said, 'That is never gonna happen. I tell you this: It'll never happen with this organization.' And I said, 'Well, that may be true with this organization, but you know better than anybody else, this is something you should root for, because as general manager you're gonna make money on top of it, too, because of that.'

"You could see the wave coming, that this is what was going to happen," Jackson said. "Now, guys like Jerry Krause are becoming, you know, like an oddity in a way in this league. Because teams are giving total control to coaches in places like Portland and around the country. In New Jersey and Boston, you just keep seeing these teams are now making this whole-hearted venture into a coach who's gonna be president and general manager. There must be seven or eight of them by now. Houston. And Miami."

The fact that Pat Riley, his rival in Miami, had that power, income and control was particularly galling to Jackson.

The coach pointed out that Krause and Reinsdorf didn't want to give him the money he asked for in his last contract negotiations because other coaches he compared himself with were also being paid as GMs. "That actually became kind of a marketing chip against me in the last contract negotiations," Jackson said, "which I kind of laughed about because I said, 'That's not a chip. They hired these guys to be coaches, and they can employ a personnel guy for $300,000 to do the job of general manager.' That's an argument against Jerry Krause is what that is."

The ugly process started all over again when the Bulls defeated Utah for the 1997 title and Jordan stepped to the microphone to issue a plea that he, Jackson, Pippen and Rodman be allowed to return for the 1997-98 season a shot at a sixth championship. Krause wanted to terminate Jackson's relationship with the team after the 1997 season, but Reinsdorf wouldn't let him, the coach said. Certainly Jackson was a big question, but no bigger than Pippen. An unrestricted free agent at the end of the 1998 season, Pippen would have to be traded, or the team would risk losing him without getting compensation for his immense talent.

Eventually all the details would be worked out to keep the team and Pippen intact, but not without another bloody round of negotiations.

Because the deals couldn't be worked out immediately, Jackson's status with the team was in limbo on draft day 1997. At the time, Reinsdorf and Krause were trying to decide whether to trade Pippen.

Both Jackson and Jordan had said they would not return to the Bulls if Pippen was traded.

Usually Jackson and his staff made themselves available for Krause and his assistants on draft day. But when Jackson arrived at the Berto Center that day, Krause informed him his presence wasn't required.

"He just said, 'You're not needed here,'" Jackson recalled.

Soon word leaked out on sports talk radio that Jackson had been "sent home."

"Jerry has a definite sense of respect for me," the coach explained later. "It wasn't like he sent me home. He said, 'Phil, until we make a decision on this ballclub, as long as we're seeing what the trade is for Scottie Pippen, whenever that's gonna be, and because of your desire not to come back if Scottie doesn't come back, there's no need for you to come in if we go in another direction, if we trade Scottie and you're not gonna be the coach. Today, you might as well let the coaching staff out.' That was made known to me a couple of times during the draft time. If they were going in another direction, if they were going to get a draft pick in a trade for Scottie Pippen, these were the guys who were gonna come in. And I wasn't going to be a part of the judging of the talent."

Krause's response was particularly jolting for Jackson, who realized that his dismissal on draft day might just be the last day in his long, successful relationship with the team. While it wasn't a disrespectful situation, the coach said it had the air of a brusque ending. "It was purely business," he said. "I was doing a piecemeal job. I was doing a job of handling this group of professional athletes only. That was okay with me. I understood exactly what I was asked to do. The word got out. I don't know how. I didn't try to make it public. I tried to correct it. Other people may be dismayed, annoyed, thinking that I'm not rationally handling a snubbing situation, but I'm not snubbed at all. I'm not bewildered at all. This is what my job has come down to. If I'm not on 'their team,' then I'm out. I'm basically out."

The situation resulted in the coaching staff canceling plans to hold the Bulls' annual end-of-season meetings with the players. As a result there was no sense of closure after the 1997 season, Jackson said.

Draft day 1997 passed without the trading of Pippen, and contract negotiations with Jackson became one of the team's priorities. At first, talks went surprisingly well.

"The structure that was set up for it was that Jerry is Mr.

Reinsdorf's agent, Todd Musburger is my agent," Jackson said. "And so it went pretty well for a while, and then it was just explosive. It got explosive between Mr. Reinsdorf and Todd. Jerry Krause had a license from Mr. Reinsdorf to malign Todd Musburger and as a consequence was totally disrespectful and unfair."

When the negotiations stalled, Krause released detailed information stating that the team had offered Jackson the highest-paying contract for a coach who wasn't also a general manager. The tactic infuriated Jackson.

"He aggravated the situation entirely," the coach said of Krause, "and then it became a public issue in the community. They put a spin on it that made us look really negative, that I'd been offered the highest-paid pure coaching job in the NBA. It was really distorting. It's hard to sit still when those things are done and not come back at them."

The talks had begun while Jackson was in Montana taking care of family business. "On a Sunday afternoon while I was in Montana, Todd stepped into Jerry's office," the coach said. "There was no one there but Todd and Jerry. Todd went through a half an hour, saying, 'Jerry, you know there's a lot of praise for everybody in this organization. We know that you've had a big part. The responsibility has fallen on your shoulders for five championship teams. Phil's had a big part, and Michael's had a great part. Michael's really the one.' Todd had a whole build up about it."

Then came the part where the agent informed the general manager of Jackson's asking price. "As soon as he went to the salary we were asking for, he was (thrown) out of the office," Jackson said. "Threw him out of the office. Todd had to sit out in the hallway by the aquarium. Jerry Krause said, 'You gotta get out of the office. I'm gonna make a call. I can't believe that you're actually asking for this. I can't believe what you're thinking and what you're trying to do.' So he put him out of the office, and 20 minutes later he comes out and says, 'You'll have to leave. I'll talk to you again next week, and you'll have to come back with an offer that's better.' That was it. No counter offer. We said, 'Okay, it's gonna be negotiations. They started out, and there's gonna be negotiations.' But it came down to, 'This is our offer, and this is it. This is what our offer is.' And the next thing was purely business. It was not personal. It was over the phone, and it was totally dragging him through the mud. He tried to cross Todd.

"Jerry just spent three minutes cussing Todd out on the phone," Jackson said, "just threw all the invective and spiteful things he could say. Just cussed him out. And when he was through cussing him out,

Todd said, 'Jerry, did you get it all said? Because I hope you've gotten it all said.' Todd tried to remain as calm as he could. And Jerry went through another litany of things that he said to him. The kind of things he said to him really was the final bridge for my agent. To that time, he was dealing pretty well with an uphill situation, and that just kind of put him over the edge."

It was then, Jackson said, that he realized that he was going to have to enter the fight. He told his agent, "Todd, listen. It didn't work out. I'm sorry it didn't work out. They're not gonna use you obviously. They're gonna try to disregard you. They want to negotiate with me. They want me at some level, because this is what they do. They tear it apart. They make it tough. They try to win contracts. They can't stand it. But I can deal with it. I've been able to deal with it."

"I have a good relationship with Mr. Reinsdorf," Jackson said. "In a way, I respect a lot of the things he does. That, I don't respect. That part I don't respect."

What particularly angered the coach were management's public assertions that he was trying to duck dealing with Reinsdorf during the '97 negotiations, that he was going out of his way to keep from meeting with the team chairman.

"I was traveling," Jackson said. "I was in Idaho picking up my mother, who's in a situation where she has to be in a wheelchair. She's in a walker. She's at a senior facility. So I was overnight on the road, and this kind of boiled over. And I didn't check with my agent that night. Then I came back to Montana in the late afternoon, and it's out in the media that I didn't call the owner in 24 hours. He wanted to hear from you. I didn't have any problem with getting ahold of him. I didn't dodge him or anything else. Unfortunately, when I talked about Mr. Reinsdorf having a good organizational sense, they didn't try to take it out on me. They tried to take it out on Todd.

"I don't think it needs to get like that," Jackson said.

Jackson and Reinsdorf finally began talks in mid-July. The coach said he told the team chairman that he no longer wanted to work with Krause, which Krause and Reinsdorf would later claim was not true. It was emphasized to Jackson that the contract for the 1997-98 season would be his last with the team, Krause said. "We said, 'If we do this, this is the last one.' He said, 'This is my last one.' We had agreed. Phil is Phil. All we said was, when we did the deal last summer, 'Okay, we'll do a one-year deal, and that's gonna be it, because you're not gonna stay here to rebuild this thing."

"We've got to rebuild because we got an older team," Krause

explained later in a private interview. "We got nine free agents at the end of the season. There has to be a point where you start rebuilding. You can't keep Michael Jordan at 33 years of age. You can't keep Scottie Pippen at 30 years of age. You can't keep all of these players in the years where they're best. People get old. Players get old. You cannot keep teams together. They get old. When the Yankees lost DiMaggio, they got Mantle."

On July 23, the Bulls announced that Jackson had signed a one-year contract worth nearly $6 million. "I wasn't looking to do anything that would be outrageous," Jackson said. "I wanted to be fair, and I think Jerry Reinsdorf wanted to be fair. And it got to a fair point in this thing that was good."

Yet the negotiations had left Jackson's relationship with Krause in complete shreds. That became apparent when the general manager called a news conference to announce Jackson's signing. Krause emphasized that no matter what, even if the team went "82-0," the 1997-98 season was definitely Jackson's last with the Bulls.

"The announcement that came out of my signing was negative," Jackson said. "It was very negative. Rather than saying, 'We're gonna be able to pull this year together. We started it out by signing Phil. And now Michael and Dennis are the next two to sign, and we've begun to rebuild the championship team and allow this team to go on.' Instead of something positive like that, it started out with a negative thing: 'This is going to be the last year that Phil's going to come back and coach.'"

"You could tell," Jackson said. "All you had to do was see the videotape of when I signed this year. It was pretty obvious that Jerry mismanaged that press release and kind of let his own feelings out."

"We should have just let the press release go, but Jerry met with the press," Reinsdorf said. "He said he wanted to explain it, but it came across that he was happy about it being Phil's last year. And he was happy about it, because he and Phil weren't getting along. Then we start reading things throughout the year about how we're pushing Phil out."

"I certainly didn't mean to say it with glee," Krause said. "Sometimes I don't do it right."

"We have an investment in blood. Think of it as
spiritual currency."
— *The Devil's Advocate*

5/ Open Season

Jerry Reinsdorf is a reserved man given to grand statements.
One of his statements is the new Comiskey Park where his White Sox
play. Another is the United Center. Easily the most emotional statement of Reinsdorf's career in business and sports was the Berto
Center, the Bulls' fancy practice facility in suburban Deerfield named
for Sheri Berto, Reinsdorf's longtime personal assistant and friend
who died in 1991 at age 40. The Bulls finished out the 1991-92 season
wearing a patch on their uniforms in her honor.

For the old Boston Celtics, the place that summed up their mys-
tique was Boston Garden, which was something of a basketball temple, with the ball echoing off the chipped and aged parquet floor and
the 16 championship banners hanging in the rafters.

Since Chicago Stadium was razed, the place that came closest to
that type of expression for the Bulls was not the United Center but the
Berto Center. The real fun of coaching the Bulls, said Tex Winter, was
practice "where we get to work with the greatest players in the world."

Indeed, Michael Jordan was the greatest practice player in the
history of the game, which in turn had made the Bulls the greatest
practice team. The setting for these exercises in greatness was the
Berto Center. "This is our domain, this is our sanctuary," Winter said.
"I think that this facility has been a real factor in our having the kind
of team we have."

"It's easily the greatest practice facility I've ever been in," said
Jud Buechler, pointing out that after the Bulls built the Berto Center
other NBA teams began following suit, mainly because pro basketball
clubs have become like college teams in the sense that they must
recruit free agents. The best players covet the best training facilities.
"I remember the first day I walked in that building coming from
Golden State four years ago," Buechler recalled. "It gave me a feeling

like, 'Wow!' I remember thinking, 'I got to do whatever it takes to make it here because this is as good as it gets.'"

Winter would never reveal it himself, but it was he who designed the practice gym, including the fact that the playing floor was placed over a rubber surface to provide extra protection against foot and leg injuries. "I told him I didn't care what kind of money he spent, I wanted the best practice facility in the world," Krause recalled of his instructions to Winter. Indeed, the exact cost of the facility, estimated to be between $5 and $7 million, could not be determined by the team because so much was added as the construction went along, Krause said.

In addition to Winter's work on the gym and floor, strength and conditioning consultant Al Vermeil designed the weight room, the coaches put together their ideas for their offices, and Karen Stack, Krause's longtime assistant and a star at Northwestern during her playing days, put many other touches on the building.

The Berto Center offered every imaginable aid or device for training and competition, from a state-of-the-art weight room to an indoor track, even a lap pool for rehabbing injuries. "It's an ideal facility for a basketball player to get a workout," said Bulls rookie Rusty LaRue, who spent many hours alone in the building working on defensive slide drills and other facets of his game. "To have the opportunity to have the weights, the medical equipment and the pool and the sauna and all that right there as well as the court, it's really ideal. You got it all in one place. You got your track there to do your running, whatever you want to do."

Yet the most significant of these enhancements was the atmosphere itself, a result of Karen Stack's influence. On the first level, the main hallway into the gym featured a giant mural photograph of fans faces during the 1993 league championship series in old Chicago Stadium. One fan held up a sign that read, "We Will Defend What Is Ours." Each day as they came and went, the players could feel the expectation in those faces. It was a subtle yet powerful reminder of the tremendous loyalty the Bulls enjoyed from their supporters, a loyalty they earned each day on the practice floor.

"We get along well," Steve Kerr, a gym rat who had spent many hours alone in the Berto Center grooming his free throw technique, said of the building. "I love the Berto Center. I've been on four different teams. In Phoenix, I practiced in a Jewish community center. In Orlando, I practiced in a public recreation center. And in Cleveland, I practiced in a fifth floor gym in the Richfield Coliseum that had asbestos on the walls, so believe me, I appreciate this."

In his comings and goings, Kerr often paused to study the mural of the fans. "I can tell you all those faces," he said. "I love that picture. It just captures the atmosphere of the old Stadium and the championship game. You got all the signs, people holding up NBC signs. I love that picture."

Inside the gym, toward the northeast corner of the building was a glass case, where the company hardware, the five NBA championship trophies, glistened under spotlights. With a flip of a switch, those trophies were put on display for the players as they practiced.

"You get character from those trophies and banners," said Bulls center Joe Kleine, who spent much of his career with the Celtics, "because you know that those things aren't just decoration. Those things were earned."

"It just has a championship feel," Buechler said, "because they got up the pictures of the guys who won championships, guys like Pax and Bill Cartwright. And the trophies. It's a place where you want to go. You want to go there and work."

Despite the ethic it inspired in the players, the building still served as something of a thorn in the Bulls' relationships. "There are events that happen in the course of life that are like pebbles in a pond, that sort of ripple off of it," trainer Chip Schaefer said. "As wonderful a facility as the Berto Center is, I think a lot of it started with the building of the Berto Center in 1992, when people were all forced to really be around each other a lot more. Prior to that, when we practiced at the multiplex, there were people who worked downtown, which meant there wasn't as much contact. I don't think Phil and Jerry saw each other as much. Once the Berto Center was built, we all had to be together every day, and I think that may have well been the start of it."

Before that, Krause and his staff were housed downtown on Michigan Avenue, 35 miles from Deerfield, where the team practiced and worked out.

"There was no one activating event," Schaefer said. "I think it was a series of events. If you have personalities that don't exactly mesh, then familiarity breeds contempt. If you don't care for somebody, but you're around them twice as much or three times as much as before, then you notice everything.

"The building was a wonderful thing to have for the players and stuff," Schaefer explained, "but at the same time, once you build that facility, you have people who are essentially 9 to 5 people with regular hours working with people who aren't 9 to 5, people who may have gotten in at 3 o'clock in the morning the night before who then come in at 8:30 or 9 and work till one or two. Then you want to go home and catch up on your sleep for a half hour or maybe see your family for a little bit. You'll walk out the door, and the people who are there from nine to five kind of feel like, 'He's leaving at 2 o'clock.' It creates and awkward situation."

Once asked what was the greatest misperception of a pro basketball team, Schaefer was ready with an answer: "The time. I get amused when I hear a radio update for read something in the paper about the fact that we don't play until Friday, and the report will say, 'The Bulls are off till Friday,' like we're all sitting around doing nothing or I could jet off and play golf for three days at Hilton Head. We're working all day, almost every day, and it's a grind."

And so several things factored into the Bulls' problems, the personality conflicts, the misperception about time, the lack of communication. As the trainer explained, the Bulls became something of a "house divided," and division fell along the lines of Krause's people, who came to be known by the code word "the organization," meaning the scouts and various administrative people, and "the team."

"The 'team' is the group of people you see on the bench during a game," Schaefer said. "But I never wanted it to be that. It was kind of a shame. I think people are going to look back years from now and say, 'What a shame. What a shame that we all couldn't kind of rise above it.'"

THE SCREEN

Another vital aspect of the Berto Center was the privacy. For much of the NBA's history, its teams have left their practice sessions open to the media, mainly because pro basketball always seemed to be a struggling business in need of any attention it could get. That situation began to change with the popularity that Magic Johnson and Larry Bird and Jordan brought to the game in the 1980s. Jordan's popularity, in fact, swelled so suddenly that it threatened to overrun his team. To keep a safe distance from hungry fans and to keep a circle of family and friends around him in his early years in the league, Jordan soon took to traveling with an entourage. The problem was, that also distanced him from his teammates, a situation that Phil Jackson sought to remedy when Krause named him head coach in 1989.

"I was anxious about having a good relationship with Michael," Jackson recalled. "I was anxious about selling him on the direction in which I was going. You knew what Michael was going to give you every single night as a player. He was gonna get those 30 points; he was gonna give you a chance to win. The challenge was, how to get the other guys feeling a part of it, like they had a role, a vital part. It was just his team, his way.

"He had such hero worship in the United States among basketball fans that living with him had become an impossibility," Jackson said. "Traveling in airports, he needed an entourage to get through. He had brought people along on the road with him. His father would come. His friends would come on the road. He had just a life that sometimes alienated him from his teammates. It became a challenge to make him part of the team again and still not lose his special status because he didn't have the necessary privacy.

"So I knew that we had to make exceptions to the basic rules that we had: 'OK, so your father and your brothers and your friends can't ride on the team bus. Let's keep that a team thing. Yeah, they can meet you on the road, but they can't fly on the team plane. There has to be some of the team stuff that is ours, that is the sacred part of what we try to do as a basketball club.'

A big part of Jackson's drive to create breathing space for Jordan and the team was to close off practices from the hungry Chicago media. When the team moved into the Berto Center, Jackson further enhanced the privacy by placing a large, retractable screen over the windows to the press room in the building.

"I got a curtain for our practice facility, so that practice became our time together," Jackson explained.

"Phil wanted the cover on the press room," Krause said. "That was totally his. I got blamed for it as usual." It was, to some reporters, more of Krause's personality, more of the secrecy of "the Sleuth." In reality, it showed that for all their disagreements, Krause and Jackson had a striking ability to think alike on certain issues.

"It was just the 12 of us and the coaches, not the reporters and the television cameras," Jackson offered. "It wasn't going to be a show for the public anymore. It became who are we as a group, as people. Michael had to break down some of his exterior. You know that when you become that famous person you have to develop a shell around you to hide behind. Michael had to become one of the guys in that regard. He had to involve his teammates, and he was able to do that. He was able to bring it out and let his hair down at the same time.

"We made efforts to create space for him within the team," Jackson said. "If we hadn't done that, the way he was going to treat us was that the rest of the world was going to overrun us, if we hadn't done things the right way. So we said, 'Let's not all suffer because of his fame. Let's give ourselves space and exclude the crowd.' I guess I created a safe zone, a safe space for Michael. That's what I tried to do."

The result of this effort was that the Berto Center became a shuttered enclave for the team and the organization, including Krause and his assistants. Upstairs, overlooking the floor, were the administrative offices of the coaches and general manager, which served as the inner sanctum for the team. There were the meeting rooms, the film rooms, the offices where the Bulls' plans and strategies for competition and personnel moves were concocted.

The media, of course, were kept at an arm's length with a series of electronically locked doors, but still it was a comfortable arm's length. The Berto Center press room was a cozy, well-lighted working facility, with cubicles for reporters and a bank of phones.

In this and so many other regards, the Berto Center was an extension of Reinsdorf's personality. He was intensely private, yet a person who treasured the relationships with the people who worked for him, the kind of boss who relished kicking his feet up on a desk and enjoying a cigar with one of his trusted employees (although this was not something Reinsdorf felt comfortable doing with his players). His car was a drab, late-model Cadillac, which created something of a contrast when parked in a loading dock at the United Center alongside the fancy vehicles of his highly paid athletes. His taste in dress ran to the same drab browns and muted plaids. He hardly ever inhabited a slickly tailored power suit. Instead, he maximized the casual, down to the point of spending a day in the office in his easy clothes.

"Another thing worth pointing out about Jerry Reinsdorf," said Schaefer, "is the extraordinary generosity he's shown all five of the title years for flying our entire staff to wherever the Finals are held and putting them and their families up in these absolutely luxurious accommodations, funding these extravagant dinners and recreational events. I have a friend who works for the Utah Jazz. I ran into him in summer league, later in July after the '97 Finals, and he said he just couldn't believe how Reinsdorf put us and our families up in Deer Valley in Park City for a week in this resort. He just couldn't believe that. He countered that the Jazz owner, Larry Miller, flew maybe one

25-year service veteran secretary to Chicago for a weekend where she had to pick up half of her hotel. There was no comparison at all. Those are the things that are unspoken about Jerry Reinsdorf.

"In Chicago, people compare him to Bill Veeck," Schaefer added. "Jerry Krause worked for both of these men, and Krause speaks of his great love for Bill Veeck. Yet Veeck and Reinsdorf are like night and day in their management styles. Veeck was out there with his peg leg in the middle of the bleachers, drinking a beer with fans. That was his reputation in Chicago, as a real man of the people. I think spiritually Reinsdorf shares an appreciation of the common people with Veeck. Reinsdorf just can't quite pull it off. He doesn't know how to do it, or something. It's almost weird."

Reinsdorf, rather, was still that shy Brooklyn kid, which wasn't entirely negative. After all, the troubling stereotype in sports is that of the meddling owner, who in his eagerness to be around the players, gets in the way of the organization, trying to make coaching decisions when he doesn't have the expertise to do that. In basketball, Reinsdorf had been just the opposite of that, to the degree that while he allowed people to do their jobs, he had also made himself too distant. The players rarely if ever saw him, and as a result, there were virtually no relationships there, no emotional connections that can be so important in helping to overcome the cynical atmosphere of pro sports. On the other hand, Reinsdorf's allowing the team to breathe had certainly been a big factor in the winning of five championships.

"Jerry Reinsdorf is the most loyal person that I've ever met, particularly to the employees that have done well for him," said longtime Chicago radio reporter Bruce Levine. "Sheri Berto was his confidant and one of his very best friends. What more proof do you need than naming a building after her and making sure that her family is taken care of."

Perhaps it stood to reason that a man who cherished his privacy and close relationships would have a disdain for the process of public relations. Unfortunately, that would come to be viewed as one of Reinsdorf's failings. He loved baseball and had expended much energy in the running of the White Sox, but his involvement in baseball had created one public relations disaster after another. By Reinsdorf's own admission, his early threats to move the team out of Chicago if he didn't get public cooperation in building a new Comiskey Park became the bedrock of his negative public image. In the wake of that came his role in the ugly relations between baseball's owners and its players. Added to that were the machinations over his tinkering with the White Sox roster.

For years, Reinsdorf had led the charge in fighting against the game's escalating salaries. Then, when it became clear that the fight had been lost, he turned around and gave a massive contract worth tens of millions to the snarling Albert Belle, one of the game's least popular players. The move stunned many people, including Phil Jackson, who saw giving Belle a $55 million contract as one of Reinsdorf's few mistakes. "Maybe," Jackson said, "Albert Belle for $55 million was kind of like a gut reaction, a knee-jerk reaction, a slap in the other baseball owners' faces, saying, 'OK, you guys didn't want to go my way, so I'll beat you by bidding this amount of money for this slugger, if that's what you want, bidding wars.' That might have been a knee-jerk thing."

Besides, that knee-jerk response, there had been little that Reinsdorf had done that could be classified as a true blunder, Jackson said. "He just doesn't make mistakes."

At the same time, many of the owners initiatives have been misinterpreted or misunderstood by the public, largely because Reinsdorf seemed to disdain the process of communicating with the fans of the teams he managed. Nothing illustrated this better than a 1998 letter to the *Chicago Tribune* from a disgruntled White Sox fan. Just because Reinsdorf was from Brooklyn didn't mean he knew anything about baseball, the fan wrote.

"I don't care about public relations," had been Reinsdorf's patent answer on these issues. What Reinsdorf appeared to mean was that he didn't care about popularity contests, or the process of ingratiating himself to the media. He shared with Krause a low regard for standards of journalistic integrity. But that disdain for the process had often come across as a disregard for the fans, his paying customers, and their response to Reinsdorf and Krause had been the boos ringing in the rafters of the buildings Reinsdorf worked so hard to build.

"He gets a bad rap, because he's such a tough businessman and a good businessman that people cannot separate the two," said Bruce Levine. "They can't separate the tough businessman from the good person. He's made some tough decisions. He's made some wrong decisions just like everybody does. But he's been a great Chicagoan. He's brought the two newest stadiums to Chicago, the United Center and Comiskey Park, where before that, the last stadium that was built for professional sports was 1929."

Quite clearly, to Reinsdorf, public relations was a foul, even dishonest, business. Loyalty, on the other hand, was a concept that extended beyond life itself. That, in turn, helped explain the bond he shared with Krause. For nearly two decades, Krause had been a loyal and trusted assistant. Where Reinsdorf's White Sox experience had been paved with frustrations, his and Krause's efforts with the Bulls had returned him gold. They had pushed on together, through one hostile public environment after another, always taking immense satisfaction in the aftermath that they were right, that the public perception was nonsense.

"When we win, I have a thing," Krause said. "I hug Thel, and I hug Jerry. The nicest thing that ever happened to me was when we won the first one in L.A."

It was 1991, in the cramped locker room area of the Forum, Krause said. "In that sweaty little room that we were in, we were huggin' and thinking of each other. And that's what this whole thing has been. I hugged him and said, 'This one's for you.' And he hugged Thel and said, 'This one's for Jerry.' We were just like on the same page. It made me feel so good that night that we were thinking about each other.

"It's a special relationship, because we struggled to get that damn first one," Krause said of his 13 years running the team with Reinsdorf. "Seven years it took us, and we busted our asses to get that thing. He had so much faith in me. Jerry Reinsdorf had more faith in me than anybody in my life, and it's a special relationship there."

"Krause and Reinsdorf are a management team," Bruce Levine said. "They communicate together. Jerry Krause has the basketball knowledge. Jerry Reinsdorf has the business knowledge. And together, they have not gotten enough credit for being one of the great teams themselves, handling this thing and making it into the Beatles of the 1990s."

It was through his baseball connections that Reinsdorf learned in 1984 that he might have a chance to purchase the Bulls. He had grown up in Brooklyn, where his industrious father worked alternately as a mechanic and a cabbie and ice cream truck driver before settling into a business buying and reselling used sewing machines. In Brooklyn, "being a Dodgers fan was almost a religion," Reinsdorf explained, and he worshipped just as hard as every other kid on Flatbush Avenue. He was also a Knicks fan (Carl Braun was his favorite player), and later in life, even after he had finished law school and was well on his way to amassing a fortune in real estate investment in Chicago, he would hold in awe the Knicks teams of the early 1970s coached by Red Holtzman. As Reinsdorf built the market value of Balcor, his real estate investment company, he realized that he might be able to live the ultimate businessman's fantasy: owning a major league sports team.

In 1981, Reinsdorf and partner Eddie Einhorn purchased controlling interest in the White Sox from Bill Veeck. They soon began an aggressive revamping of the team, structured around Carlton Fisk, which led to a divisional championship in 1983. A year later, Reinsdorf was in New York having dinner with New York Yankees owner George Steinbrenner, who was also a minority owner of the Bulls. Reinsdorf told Steinbrenner he would love to own and operate the NBA team in Chicago.

Lester Crown, another of the Bulls' ownership group, phoned Reinsdorf in September 1984 and told him Steinbrenner had relayed the conversation. "He asked me if I was serious," Reinsdorf recalled, "because some of the other owners in the Bulls really wanted to get out and that we should talk about it. I met with Lester, and he said that he and Lamar Hunt didn't want to sell, but that 55 to 58 percent of the team was available to purchase. I worked out a deal with Lester in October of 1984 before Michael Jordan had played a game."

But they couldn't consummate the deal because the Bulls were embroiled in a lawsuit with Marv Fishman, a Wisconsin businessman who had attempted to buy the team many years earlier and had been rebuffed. Soon, the Bulls owners settled the suit and closed their deal with Reinsdorf. Pulling together a group of 24 investors, Reinsdorf bought 63.7 percent of the team. "I will be visible, I will be seen," Reinsdorf said in announcing the sale. "I will be actively involved with this franchise. . . . I have a theory about how to run a basketball team, and I've always wanted an opportunity to run one."

Upon taking over Reinsdorf was both stunned and elated to discover that the team had never bothered to employ a season-ticket sales force. He told Krause, "Oh, boy, look what I've found!"

"The state of the franchise was terrible," Reinsdorf once recalled. "The practice facilities were terrible. The offices were terrible. They were dingy. The team charged employees for soft drinks if they wanted them. Morale was terrible. The franchise was understaffed. It wasn't that the people running the Bulls were bad, but they all had other things to do.

"I just didn't like the whole culture of the organization," Reinsdorf said, "and I didn't like the way it was being coached. I felt we had to break from the past, and I wanted someone as a general manager who believed what I believed in. I believed very strongly in two things: 1) A championship team is built around defense. You must remember this was at a time when the NBA was at a peak for points being scored, but very few teams really played any defense; 2) I wanted the offense not to be isolations and one-on-ones. I wanted all five guys participating and sharing the ball. I wanted the Bulls to duplicate what Red Holtzman had done with the Knicks."

Reinsdorf announced in late March 1985 that he was replacing Bulls GM Rod Thorn with Krause, who would become the vice president for basketball operations. "I want a team that will play Red Holtzman basketball," Reinsdorf said in announcing the changes. "An unselfish team, one that plays team defense, that knows its roles, that moves without the ball. Jerry Krause's job will be to find the DeBusschere of 1985 and the Bradley of 1985."

"I wouldn't have taken the Bulls job had it not been for Jerry," Krause once explained. "Michael or no Michael. I had worked with Jerry with the White Sox for several years. I had turned down chances to come back in the NBA during that time. I'd had a couple of strikes against me, and I didn't want to come back unless I knew I could work for an owner I felt comfortable with and that I knew would back me and do the things that needed to be done."

"Krause was atop the scouting hierarchy at the White Sox," Reinsdorf said, "and I had gotten to know him. There had to be a cultural change in the Bulls' organization, and Krause believed the same things I did."

Putting Reinsdorf's grand vision of Red Holtzman/ Knicks basketball into effect would take years and numerous personnel moves. Krause's first was to fire Kevin Loughery as coach. Then he turned his attention to cleaning up the roster. Reinsdorf made other changes beyond Krause's personnel moves. He hired a platoon of season ticket salespeople and produced a new source of revenue. He upgraded the team's broadcasting contracts and moved the team's practice facility from a dingy gym named Angel Guardian to the Deerfield Multiplex. (In 1992, the Bulls moved on to the new Berto Center.)

By 1988, the team had given up flying commercially and had begun using a charter service, mainly to avoid the hassle of taking Jordan through public airports. Combined with Jordan's brilliance and the new atmosphere in the league and the changes brought by Reinsdorf, the Bulls' fortunes began to rise, if not dramatically, at least perceptibly. "Michael's first year started slowly," explained longtime team vice president Irwin Mandel. "The first year we sort of stopped the financial skid. It took a little while to become profitable. Then the numbers started to look real good his second year. I was very excited that finally, the light at the end of the tunnel had arrived. Each week he was becoming more and more popular. There was the feeling that next year he's going to be even more popular. This is a guy who's bringing excitement here, bringing the fans back. He's going to make us successful and popular and profitable."

"It was a no brainer to make the organization better," Reinsdorf said. "It probably was one of the worst in sports. That part was easy."

MEDIA DAY

On many days, the reporters covering the Bulls would wait in the press room until the curtains covering the window to the gym were raised, signalling practice was over. Often, when they would go into the gym to attempt interviews, the reporters discovered that Jordan, Pippen and most of their teammates were gone, leaving only Jackson to answer their questions.

Yet there was always one day out of the year when reporters were granted wide access to the team. That day was appropriately titled "media day," and it came at the opening of training camp, a time when the team's players and coaches were made available for photographs, video shoots and interviews.

Anticipation usually ran high on media day, but most of the questions were mundane queries about the upcoming season or what players and coaches did for their summer vacations. Yet, with the brewing controversy, media day for the Bulls in 1997 was far from mundane. Radio, TV and print reporters from across the Chicago area were curious about the increasingly public rift between Krause and Jackson. After all, in his press conference signing Jackson, Krause had emphasized that this was definitely the coach's last year with the team.

Some team employees had hoped that Krause would see the futility of discussing these issues and that the general manager would avoid media day altogether, thus avoiding the questions and more controversy. Instead, Krause came down from his office in the Berto Center and walked out onto the floor amidst the dozens of reporters gathered there. Very quickly, the GM would find himself in a swirl of trouble by making comments that would cast him as the man who was "splitting up the Bulls."

Afterward, some team employees could only shake their heads because many of the ensuing heartaches and headaches could easily have been avoided.

What made matters worse was that Krause and Jackson were in the middle of a personal feud that had boiled over in the weeks leading up to the opening of training camp. "The way it started was his daughter got married," Jackson said. "And in a kind of unfortunate turn of events, he and his wife didn't invite us to the wedding. Which is fine. I understand that. But there are people on our staff that they invited and people in the organization that were invited."

What particularly upset Jackson was Krause's invitation to Iowa State coach Tim Floyd, long touted as Krause's favorite choice as Jackson's successor. Over the years Jackson had been known to dub his competitors with tweaking nicknames. For example, he once referred to New York Knicks coach Jeff Van Gundy as "Van Gumby." And in the spring of 1998 he made a smiling reference to Utah Jazz center Greg Ostertag as "Osterdog."

Jackson also had a nickname for Floyd — "Pinkie."

"Pinkie Floyd was there," Jackson said of the wedding. "It was an occasion that Jerry Krause used as a business opportunity to bring Floyd to meet everyone."

The Krauses further deepened the snub by explaining it to a newspaper reporter. "Thelma (Krause's wife) spoke of it this year," Jackson said. "It was in the paper. The big deal was, 'Phil's a professional. He's an office worker. We didn't invite all of our office workers.'"

Thelma Krause told the *Sun Times* the wedding was an intimate affair. "We do not have a social relationship," she said, explaining that she and her husband weren't invited to Jackson's 50th birthday party.

"The reality is that Jerry is all professional," Jackson said. "He's all business. There is no personal. He's business 24 hours a day."

The late September wedding snub soon led to a blow-up between Jackson and Krause at the Berto Center. "He kind of was hanging around the coaches' offices acting friendly," Jackson recalled. "And he walked in the office where we were just kind of joking around as an office group. So I just stood up and walked out. He was acting like nothing had happened.

"I just walked out and went down and checked on the players," Jackson said. "When I came back upstairs, his secretary came in and said, 'Jerry wants to see you in his office.' And I said, 'Tell him he can come see me in my office.' And I went in my office. Then she called back said, 'He wants you to know that you are to meet him in his office and that he's still the boss here.' So I went in his office and told him, 'Don't come around and act friendly and everything else when you know that you're not friendly.' He said, 'Well, I didn't invite Frank (Hamblen, assistant coach), and I didn't invite (Bulls VP) Steve Schanwald.'

"I said, 'Well, you crossed a bridge right there by your definition, by your snub or whatever else. Believe me, I don't care. But when you invite the next coach that's coming in and you use that as an opportunity to introduce him to the people in the community and to the owner and stuff, and then tell me it's not business, it's personal.'

"Then he came back," Jackson said, "with how Pinkie Floyd had been his friend for five or six years. I said, 'Sure, Jerry, I know he's your friend.' I've been in that same position where Floyd is. One of his puppies. He's been watching him for a while."

Very quickly, the discussion escalated into an argument, Jackson said. "It went from there to 'Well, that's why I wanted to have the owner meet you. We wanted to make sure you understand this is your last year. I don't care if you win 82 games or not. This is your last year.' That kind of shut the door for me. I said, 'OK, the big deal is that we get along.'

"We had an ensuing fight that lasted about 10 minutes, and it was pretty loud and pretty boisterous," Jackson said. "But at the end we settled down. And he said, 'This is what the owner was gonna tell you. Instead of him telling you, I will tell you what he was gonna tell you. Make sure that the drift of your thing comes out that this is the way that it has to be. And make no doubt about it that this is our intention that this is your last year.' And I said, 'Jerry, I've known that it's been my last year since Mr. Reinsdorf came to Montana and we talked about it.' And we went through a few things that had been a hardship. And we aired a lot of things that had to be aired, and we've been much better since that time. There had been animosity and we were coming apart, so we kind of cleared the air."

Later, just before media day, Krause read some comments Jackson had made to reporters in which the coach seemed to be waffling about his status with the team. "He called me up to the office that day," Jackson recalled, "and he said, 'I want you to get this straight. This is indeed your last year. We want to get that straight to the media. We don't want any of this hedging.'"

THE ORGANIZATION

At first only two or three reporters gathered about Krause on the Berto Center floor on media day. But then their number grew until nearly 20 or more encircled him. The GM began by discussing the effects of the NBA's new labor agreement, how unsettling it was, how it would take three years or more to understand how it would affect the economics of the league.

Then one reporter asked him which free agents the Bulls might be interested in signing. "We've never told anybody who we're interested in," Krause replied. "I never would tell anybody that. So it's all rumor. You guys have to write something and announce something and have something to talk about on talk radio and all that stuff. You gotta have something to do. You gotta make a living. That's part of the function of the media. And it's part of my function not to tell you who we are interested in."

Another reporter asked if the upcoming season would have a sense of finality? "All I'm concerned about, I want to win this year, and go and do what we have to do this year," Krause said. "Then myself and the scouting staff and the organization will take care of the future. We'll do our planning and do our organizing and the things we have to do regarding the future. But right now we want to concentrate on what we have to do this year to win with this team. That's why we brought everybody back. To make another run at it."

Among the players who failed to report for training camp was Rodman, who remained unsigned, although Krause said he had hopes of signing him within days. "If we sign Dennis," he said, "it will be another large donation to Dennis. There's gonna be a lot of money spent, so that's the thought in mind, that we'll go out and win this year and then plan for the future. Those things will take care of themselves as they happen."

Another reporter pointed out that the "finality of Phil rubs people the wrong way. Around town Phil leaves the door open at times in comments.

"What is the real story?" the reporter asked.

"It's both of our decisions," Krause replied. "I think you ought to ask Phil about it. But it's both of our decisions, you know. I don't see why . . ."

Seemingly exasperated, the GM paused then and started over by referring to the public reaction to his July press conference announcing Jackson's new contract. "I think when people thought that I made the statement at the press conference, it was in the press release," he said. "It was right there for everybody to see. And I think when I made a statement ... the last time I talked to you guys, some people . . . or one of the last times I talked to you as a group, some people thought I was saying something that wasn't in the press release. It was there."

His comments left the reporters around him with increasingly confused looks. "We had agreed to it," Krause said finally, "and that's the way it is. I don't know why it would rub somebody wrong. There's a time in life when people separate."

"People think you are saying it in such a way that you take joy in it," a reporter said.

"No, there's no truth to that at all," Krause said. "I don't take . . . I think people think . . . I've heard some people say that I'll take joy in the day when Michael leaves. I have no such thoughts in my mind. Hell, I'll probably cry when he leaves. But the point being that you have to go on. You know, this is an organization. We've been very successful. I'm really proud of what the organization has done.

"I look back on my early days in the league when Red Auerbach was in Boston," Krause added. "When Red lost Bill Russell he just didn't just roll up the tent and say, 'I'm done. My career's over. Russell's gone.' He went and rebuilt the team and found at that time Dave Cowens, made trades and got Paul Silas and whatever. Then that run ended after eight or nine years later after four or five championships (actually two), and then he turned around. Sure enough he didn't give up and say, 'I quit. Cowens is gone.' He went and he found Bird, Parish and all those guys. Well, we're very much in the same situation.

"I'm sure Jerry West, when he lost Kareem and Magic, didn't just roll up the tent," Krause said of the Lakers executive. "You've seen what he's done. He's done a tremendous job. He's rebuilt that franchise. Well, that's what my job is. People say I look forward to it. Well, nobody looks forward to a great player leaving. But what you do is, you say there's a challenge in front of me. And any red-blooded general manager is looking forward to a challenge. I mean, hell, that's what you live for in this business. There ain't no poor people in this business, so it isn't a matter of us being destitute or anything. We're always looking for challenges. As a result, what's the next challenge? With me, it isn't monetary or anything like that. It's building a ball club. And when you lose great players, you lose great people in your organization, you go out and you rebuild. And that's a great challenge. And that's the challenge I live for. Well, not live for, but certainly like to be a part of."

A reporter pointed out that if a lot of players left at once, a team suddenly could find itself scrambling to find the right players to replace those who left.

"A lot of them have left before," Krause replied. "We have a team that won three championships, and two years later we won a championship with 10 new players. So this isn't something we haven't done before. We've done this before."

He used that example to explain that players and coaches alone don't win championships, that sound organizations do. But as he made the remark, Jackson stepped onto the floor to begin his interview session. And as they often do, reporters hurriedly departed their current interview so as not to miss anything newsworthy Jackson might say.

Within an hour after the media session had ended, a befuddled Krause found his way down to the press room looking for reporters who might have a recording of his comments. He was sure he had been misquoted, that he had said coaches and players "alone" don't win championships. Unfortunately, few media representatives remained in the press room. Eventually, Krause would get in touch with John Jackson of the *Sun Times* who would confirm that Krause had said that "coaches and players *alone* don't win championships, organizations do."

"I was right there when it happened," Terry Armour of the *Tribune* agreed. "He was heavily misquoted. I saw everybody run from him midway through the quote and run over to Phil. They didn't even get the end of the quote."

The group of reporters went to Phil Jackson and told him that Krause had said that coaches and players don't win titles: "It's organizations that win championships."

"He would say that," the coach said. "The organization is based on loyalty. Scottie sees that and has to wonder what loyalty really does mean."

The comment would come to be a theme for the players throughout the season, galvanizing their disdain for Krause and Reinsdorf. Even team employees loyal to Krause would express dismay at the GM's choice of words, at his decision to attempt to discuss the situation with the media, because Krause's comments would set in motion a nasty public relations karma that would come back to haunt the two Jerrys again and again.

"Everything I've ever heard or seen from Jerry Reinsdorf, that's just the opposite of what he wants to do," Chip Schaefer said. "His philosophy, and Jerry Krause has spoken many times of Reinsdorf's philosophy, is, 'Don't do anything until you have to; a lot of times things will take care of themselves.' But Krause blew that. He committed to putting the cart before the horse ten months before it even needed to be done."

Even Jackson privately expressed sympathy for Krause and how the situation had blown up in the GM's face.

Later, Krause's associates would complain privately that Jackson could have spoken up and taken the pressure off of Krause's comments. The worst part about Krause's ill-timed statements was that it left both Krause and Reinsdorf in limbo. If they defended themselves against the public anger, then it seemed they were attacking Jordan and Jackson, both very popular figures, which only made the situation worse.

As for Jackson, the coach merely followed Krause's instructions on what to tell reporters. "It would take wild horses to drag me back this time," Jackson said on media day. "This is the final year. It's time to start something different. In the conversation I had with Jerry Reinsdorf in negotiations, this would be the last year. We're not having any illusions, like last year. We don't want the same situation . . . if something should happen like we accidentally win a championship. I assured (Jerry Krause) I'd walk out at the end of the season, and he assisted me in that belief."

Jordan had not made himself available to the press on media day, but the next day, after the team's first day of practice, Jordan was ready to address Krause's opening day comments. "I'm very consistent with what I've always said," Jordan told reporters. "That's what I mean. If Phil's not going to be here, I'm certainly not going to be here."

What if Jackson goes to another team next season? a reporter asked. Would Jordan follow?

"No," he said. "Totally. I would quit. I wouldn't say quit, I'd retire."

The assembled reporters went on to ask Jordan a host of questions, including the following:

• Would Krause's comments affect the team on the court?

"Not unless Jerry plays. And he doesn't play. So once we step on the basketball court we gotta do our job with whoever is out there. There are a lot of things being talked about, I'm pretty sure. But once we step on the basketball court that's where we have to live up to the expectations that we accept for ourselves. That's two championships back to back and five championships in seven years. So that's what we have to live up to."

• Would the comments hurt Jordan's relationship with Krause?

"I don't deal that much with Jerry at all. In my negotiations, I deal with Jerry Reinsdorf basically. On a day-to-day basis, it's come here and do my job, doing what I have to do with the coaches and the players. I don't have to see the general manager at all. I don't have to deal with him."

• What do you think of Krause's comment that players and coaches alone don't win championships; organizations do?

"I don't agree with him in that sense, because as a player I feel we go out and do our job. We do what we have to do each and every day when we step on the basketball court. Sure, they (the team's management) have responsibilities to do whatever, to make our jobs easier, to do what they have to do for the organization, but I mean, I didn't see any of the organization playing sick last year. In Game 5, I would have liked to see some of those organization guys step out there and play. And I didn't see that. I saw the team step out there and play. They may have paid for the plane to get us out there. But when we step out on the basketball court, the players and coaches certainly have to go out there and do the job they've practiced for for eight months. And the organization is certainly gonna provide us what we need to get to the basketball court, but once we're out there we have to do our jobs. And that's what wins championships."

• Did he think Krause's comments would have an effect on the team?

"None. None at all. Because he doesn't play the game. He does his job, whatever that job may be, but we as players, we bond together and we do what we have to do on the basketball court. We don't let that bother us at all."

• Was he offended that management seemed to be pushing Phil Jackson out the door?

"I think that's very obvious, because management has already said that this is Phil's last year. So, I don't know if that's Phil's step. I know Phil's not gonna go against a situation where he's not wanted. He's looked at it as if this is probably his last year. We just gotta go out and play the game of basketball this year and deal with what we have to deal with. Certainly we don't know what the future is going to hold. That's the organization's decision. That's not our decision. If Phil's not going to be here, then I'm not going to be here."

• Could he use his influence with Reinsdorf to bring Phil Jackson back?

"I don't know. I've never really looked at it in that sense. I don't know what my influence is. You see how Jerry Reinsdorf operates. My influence doesn't have anything to do with his decision making. I'm not gonna sit here and knock heads with Jerry. If he has his own vision for this team and what its future holds, then we take that and we deal with it. If that means Phil's not here, that means Phil's not here."

• Was there a personality conflict between Phil Jackson and Jerry Krause?

"I don't really know. It could be. I always felt Phil was for the players, no matter how you looked at it, because Phil was once a player. Now does that not calculate into what Jerry is saying, or maybe how he wants the coach to be for the organization? I can't answer that. But I've always felt that Phil was for the player. Players first. Those 15 players step on the basketball court, that's his first and foremost desire and concern. I'm pretty sure he's got to have an organizational concern, too. We all do. Because we want to live up to the high standards that this organization has been built upon."

• Did the disagreement between Jackson and Krause make for a bad way to end the Bulls' great run?

"It's a bad way to end an unbelievable run. You would want it to be better down the stretch, or when the curtain is finally closing. I think that we as players can't worry about that. We have to go out there and have our own individual, our own team, goals to live up to. The management stuff is something you'll have to worry about in the future."

• Was he upset that Bulls management seemed eager to end this magnificent run before the fact?

"That's their prerogative. I can't say that they're doing something wrong. Certainly, maybe not what I prefer. But I'm a player, and they're the organization. They make all of the decisions. Once this thing changes, once they try to make the transition from this team to possibly another team, I wish them success. But I've always believed that what we're trying to do is sustain and maintain the success."

• Was he nostalgic about this probably being his last season?

"Every year that I play, I always view it as my final season, because you never really know. But I don't think that's gonna alter the way I play basketball. If it alters it this year, then I certainly won't be the type of player I've been in the past. I won't have had the same focus. When I step on the basketball court, each and every year, each and every day could be my last. So I always take that approach. That shouldn't change if this is my last year."

Although they were measured, Jordan's comments only helped cement the impression that Krause and Reinsdorf were forcing Jackson and him from the team.

Jackson then made a point of discussing Krause's comments in a meeting with his players. "We talked about it as a team actually and said, 'We have to have good mental health as well as good physical health.'" the coach said. "This is part of the mental health."

With Scottie Pippen facing foot surgery and Rodman disgruntled, Jackson was worried that the team would open the season struggling and that the discord with management would become a major distraction.

"The challenge is if the paranoia or insecurity linger with failure," Jackson said privately. "Those things can breed the kind of dark thoughts that can sway the mental health of a coach or a team. Those are the things that we have to watch for. I feel real confident about my team, about our relationships, the team's relationships, about my staff, about our dedication towards winning this year. All those things are real strong, so I can't see anything upsetting the apple cart as far as the mental or spiritual aspect of it. We're pretty unified as a team as to what we're gonna do regardless of what happens, the innuendos that are gonna go on or the slights that are gonna happen, the backhanded comments that might be made."

Krause's comments and the responses from Jackson and Jordan brought a round of media commentary nationwide lambasting the Bulls' front office. Typical of the response was a column by Gwen Knapp of the *San Francisco Examiner* who wrote, "Krause could have let the players age gracefully into the sunset, let Jackson's natural curiosity lead him elsewhere. Instead, the general manager has sullied the whole outfit. And he hasn't even done it artfully . . . Krause's gig is charisma free, all unembroidered pettiness.

"In Krause's fantasy basketball league," she said, "Michael Jordan is just a tool, easily replaced. And the photocopier is more valuable than Phil Jackson. Last week, Krause pointed out that the team trainer has five rings."

Later, Krause and Reinsdorf would fume privately that Jackson didn't speak up more to ease the public relations nightmare that grew out of media day. But the coach wasn't about to extract the GM and team chairman from the circumstances. "They created this animal," Jackson said later, "and I'm not bailing them out. I made a decision. I'm just a person they plugged into this thing, this situation. It was the right thing they plugged in, and everything's worked graciously for us behind all that. That's great, but this isn't a real estate holding, or the stock market, where you just happened to buy a lucky piece of stock. These are people you're dealing with. And that's the thing that I think they're missing."

In reality, the Bulls' biggest concern in October had little to do with "future considerations." Rather, it was the soft tissue in Pippen's foot, injured against Miami in May in the playoffs and slow to heal. That, too, entered into the controversy when Krause faxed Pippen a letter in September threatening to take action against the star if he played in his own charity game.

It wasn't so much the content of the letter that infuriated Pippen but the harshness of its tone and the manner in which it was delivered.

The real issue, though, was corrective surgery and the timing of the operation. Decisions were difficult in the charged atmosphere of training camp. But four days after camp opened, the surgery was performed, and the Bulls announced the star forward, so critical to the team's success, would miss a minimum of two months.

"Each year we start off with some sort of challenge, and this makes it even more so," Jordan told reporters. "We know that it goes without question that if he was here we'd be that much better of a team. That's the situation and you deal with it and move on. ... First and foremost, Scottie's got to take care of himself."

The week brought more news in that Rodman agreed to a one-year contract with a $4.5 million base and performance incentives that could boost it to $10 million. But then he refused to sign it, supposedly because he feared some of the incentives would be impossible to reach.

Reinsdorf had said Rodman would be welcomed back only if he gave up the bad behavior that had stained his 1996-97 performances. At first, Rodman had offered to play for free, but later changed that to a demand for $10 million with "a money-back guarantee."

"I've learned one thing: Don't predict anything from Dennis," Jackson told reporters. "If you do, you just set yourself up."

Jordan pointed out that with Pippen's injury, the team needed Rodman to be on his best behavior. But a stalemate developed and dragged on through training camp and the start of the ambitious exhibition schedule.

After a preseason opener at home, the Bulls jetted to Lawrence, Kansas, to meet the Seattle Super Sonics in humid Allen Field House on the University of Kansas campus. Jordan had a Carolina blue affection for Kansas coach Roy Williams, an assistant during Jordan's playing days at UNC. The sold-out crowd in the grand old arena was well aware of that affection and returned it to Jordan upon his introduction. Sitting courtside, Krause's eyes tightened into a glare as the fans stood and pounded out their respect for the Chicago star. True to the pattern that would follow Jordan in every building, the arena sparkled with the pop of flash cameras. "Like a laser show," Krause observed.

The evening brought Scott Burrell's second game with the team. Krause had tried to trade forward Dickey Simpkins to Charlotte for Burrell in February 1997, but the Hornets opted instead to send Burrell to Golden State. Finally, a month before training camp opened, Krause had managed to get Burrell from the Warriors in a trade for Simpkins. "I'm nothing if not stubborn," the GM said as he watched Burrell guard Seattle's Greg Anthony. It was just this ability to defend smaller quicker guards that made Burrell a player Krause coveted.

"He'll be important later in the season," the GM said.

Afterward, Jordan offered the same appraisal, that Burrell would be important. "But it'll take time."

After Kansas, it was back to Chicago briefly for an exhibition loss followed by a transatlantic jump to Paris to play in the McDonald's Open in mid October. The city was still in shock from the death of Princess Diana in an auto wreck six weeks earlier. The Bulls landed and headed immediately to practice. "Bon jour. Bon jour," Jordan, accompanied by his son Jeffrey, told a crowd of French teen-agers after the workout.

Joining Chicago in the international exhibition tournament were Paris-St. Germain, Atenas de Cordoba of Argentina, Benetton Treviso of Italy, FC Barcelona and Olympiakos Pieaeus of Greece.

Paris used to be a place Jordan could enjoy before he was engulfed by his worldwide fame. "I used to come every other year when I first got into the league and I used to sit out at some of the restaurants outdoors and not be bothered," he told reporters. "Basketball has grown here due to the Olympics, Dream Team or whatever. It's become a major sport worldwide now. It's just hard for me to go anywhere now unnoticed — in the sense of getting out in the public and trying to enjoy myself without people bothering me. This was like my last area that I could go to where no one really knew who I was to some degree. And now it's been exposed."

Nowhere was the sense of adulation greater than on the playing floor, where opponents didn't hesitate to hit him up for autographs. "I try to oblige them," Jordan said. "I don't have a problem separating autograph seekers from the competition. But once the ball is tossed up, the only autograph you are going to get is maybe a jump shot or two in your face."

The Bulls made quick work of the tournament field, but not without a cost. Jordan developed a sore toe. "It hurts him and he can't jump," Jackson told reporters. As the team headed back across the Atlantic to Chicago, it was announced that Jordan would miss the final three exhibition games, although the injury wasn't viewed as serious.

A much bigger concern was Rodman, who still had not signed his contract by the time the team got back home. Immediately Jordan and Jackson went to work on him. "I talked to Michael a couple of days here and there," Rodman said. "He says, 'Don't leave me out here hanging to dry.' The guys gave me a lot of support. The least I can do is give something back."

With the proper prodding, the 36-year-old forward signed up for another season. "The players and the people of Chicago, they gave me a lot, so I figured I might as well come back and give them one more year," he told reporters. "The people of Chicago and the players ... other than that, I wouldn't have come back at all."

Asked why he had hesitated, he replied, "Just to make sure in my mind that my interest was still there. You've been in this league so long and you've done so much, you've got to find some motivation to keep you going. I've just got to go out there, get on the court, get around the guys, get around the atmosphere, get my feel for the game again. Once I get on the floor, I'm not going to give less than 100 percent."

NOTHING FINER

That Friday, October 24th, Rodman accompanied the team to Chapel Hill, North Carolina, for an exhibition game at the Dean Smith Center on the UNC campus. At first, it was announced that Jordan would not play, which created a swell of fan disappointment. Then came the calls from Jordan's old friends back home. With his toe feeling better, he decided he better suit up after all.

Up to that point in the young season, there had been no friction, no embarrassing moments between Krause and the players. But just before game time at the Smith Center, Jordan went to use the restroom and spied Krause's feet dangling underneath the stall. From that point, Jordan, as he had explained to Jackson, couldn't help himself. Krause was just too inviting a target. If he was going to invade Jordan's pre-game routine, he was going to pay the price.

"He was in there," Ron Harper recalled, "and Michael said, 'I'm not going in there yet, Phil. I ain't goin' in until Jerry leaves.' It was almost time to go out on the court. It was a sad scene then. He was killing him in the can. It's a thing where Jerry will embarrass himself if Jerry gets a chance. You won't have to embarrass him. He'll find a way to embarrass himself. So we tend to let Jerry embarrass himself, and guys just laugh at him. But the guys want to be a part of it."

"It's a ribbing situation," Jackson said. "Jerry ends up using the bathroom when the team's trying to get ready. You know, the players use a pecking order. It goes down to Dennis is taking a shower, Harp's in the bathroom, Michael's in the bathroom. And that's it. It usually goes in that kind of routine. Michael goes in the bathroom, and Jerry's in there in the bathroom. You know, it's like, 'What are you thinking about?' I don't go in the player's bathroom. This is a place where a guy wants to be alone and get his business done before a game. This is a team kind of thing. Those are the things that Jerry gets himself embroiled in that have just alienated himself from the team a number of times. So he goes back there and gets some kind of grief. I don't know what was said. I never know what's said in that situation. I just hear kind of a ruckus going on."

With the laughter ringing in their ears, the Bulls took the floor that Friday evening against the Philadelphia 76ers. It proved to be an evening of humorous embarrassment. In the first quarter, Jordan stole a 'Sixer pass and broke into the open court. All 21,000 fans in the Smith Center gasped in excitement. His Royal Airness was about to treat the home folks to a rim-rocking slam.

Instead, he missed, and the ball popped away from the rim. Ready to roar in delight, the crowd instead let out a giant groan.

Moments later, during a pause in the action, Harper came up to him and whispered, "Nice dunk."

"That tells you what kind of friends I've got, doesn't it?" Jordan said afterward and laughed.

In the hallway outside the locker room at halftime, he had encountered a scout from another team. "You're not gonna put my missed dunk in your scouting report, are you?" Jordan asked with a wink.

"I'm never immune to an embarrassing moment," he admitted after the game. "It's just one of those things where I misjudged my time, my jump. I missed it. If I'm gonna miss a dunk this is the proper place to do it."

With one final exhibition against the Sacramento Kings the next night in Chicago, the Bulls finished their preseason schedule and turned their thoughts to the opening of the regular season the following Friday, October 31, and how they would survive without Pippen. Jordan called the upcoming season, his thirteenth in the league, "my biggest challenge ever."

He told reporters he would play 48 minutes a night if that was necessary to deliver the sixth championship. "I'm gearing myself up for a long season — all 82 games and 15 playoff games," Jordan said. "I don't know what burnout is. I haven't burned out so far, so why worry about it?"

"We don't want to wear him out," Jackson said. "But he just wants to win, as usual. He just wants to win."

That Wednesday the players gathered with an array of fans for the team's annual preseason luncheon. "When we win the championship," Jordan told the group, "I think we'll see the road we took and look back at this sixth championship and appreciate this as being the most important championship we won ... just because of the cards we've been dealt."

The next day, Pippen predicted Jordan would produce yet another amazing answer to a challenge. "The competitiveness is going to come out. He's going to try to shoulder as much of the load as he can," the injured forward said.

Steve Kerr agreed: "Michael feels that we've got something to prove and — though I don't know what it could be — that he's got something to prove, too. So you know he's got something special in mind."

Timed to open with the start of the season was a new CBS SportsLine web page dedicated to Jordan's array of commercials for a variety of products, from sunglasses to sports drinks. Wouldn't such a site have undue sway over young minds? a reporter asked.

"Michael's commercials are pieces of art," replied CBS' Mark Mariani. "There are a lot worse things kids can get into on the Internet."

That Friday night, October 30th, they opened the season in Boston, and it became immediately apparent just how badly they would miss Pippen. The Bulls pushed to a big first-quarter lead against the Celtics, but without Pippen there to control the tempo of the game, Chicago couldn't hold the edge. And the young Celtics ran and pressed and ran and pressed some more, leaving the Bulls grabbing their shorts and sucking wind.

Chagrined, they headed home with a loss. The next night at the United Center, they held their ring ceremony and revealed the team's 1997 championship banner, to hang alongside 1991, 1992, 1993, 1995 and 1996. The rings featured a Bulls logo made up of 46 diamonds and five sculpted NBA title trophies and inscriptions "World Champions" and "Team of the Decade."

The 20-minute ceremony before Chicago's home game against Philadelphia brought another brace of boos for Krause. Reinsdorf was present, but wasn't introduced.

Pippen was obviously emotional when he stepped to the microphone and thanked the fans for 10 years of "wonderful moments."

"I've had a wonderful career here," he said. "If I never have the opportunity to say this again: 'Thank you.'"

"I said then that we'd win a championship by the time I leave," Jordan told the crowd. "Well, we're the five-time champions, going for six, and ... we're certainly going to win the sixth."

"Did you like the green? You did, didn't you? I should go back to the green."

— *The Devil's Advocate*

6/ Dennis Rodman's Illusions

Since his earliest days in the league, Dennis Rodman had been an open book, one of those people who lived his life on the edge, right there in plain view for everyone to see. As open books went, his was a fascinating mix, one part mystery thriller, one part comic book, one part experimental poetry. That's why fans in Chicago swooned over him after he joined the Bulls in October 1995.

A thousand zany incidents later, they still loved him. Sometimes maybe too much, both for their sakes and his. He stopped after practice one day to sign an autograph for a young teen-aged fan outside the Berto Center, and long after he had departed she was still trembling with excitement. Asked just what it was about Rodman she found so appealing, Jennifer Santiago replied that she, too, played basketball on her school team and she could identify with his hustle and energy. Then there was also the matter of his image. "He's not afraid to show, like, who he is," she said. "He can be famous, but he doesn't let other people decide who he is. And I think that's important."

In one brief answer, she had summed up something of immense significance to Rodman — never being something you're not. He had played for two great coaches in the NBA, Chuck Daly in Detroit and Phil Jackson. "That's one thing you really got to have on a team," Rodman observed. "You got to have a coach that makes you feel at home, that you feel comfortable with, that's there's no pressure to go out there and be someone that you're not."

Many observers figured that with the tattooed man's third season in Chicago, the thriller-mystery part of his persona would deepen, with strange plot twists and more unusual turns, including suspensions and weird acts. Reinsdorf even cautioned him about it before offering the new contract. Rodman would be welcomed back only if he gave up the bad behavior, the team chairman said. Since Rodman's earliest days with the Bulls, Phil Jackson and the other coaches and players hadn't known what to expect from him on any given night. A couple of hundred games later, they still didn't.

The scary part, said Tex Winter, was that even Dennis had no idea where his raw, exposed nerve and boundless energy would take him next. Make a wild, full-stretch dive for a loose ball? Kick a cameraman in the groin? Declare he's ready to quit the game? Produce an unexpected play of pure unbridled heart, one that turns the entire United Center on its ear? Each and every one of these items, plus countless others, was on the Rodman menu. All of them set on edge by Rodman's acknowledged fantasy to finally leave the game one night by stripping off his uniform and walking naked off the floor.

Would it happen?

No one, not even Rodman, knew for sure.

Could it happen?

You betcha.

On the other hand there was a part of Rodman that was as old-fashioned as family values. The contrast was sometimes dramatic. For example, Rodman, the supposed rebel, treated Winter with a reverential respect. When the Bulls were on a road trip, it was Rodman who would knock on Winter's door in the evening, looking for extra videotape to study. The old coach and the player with the wild hair shared a love for the technical aspects of the game. Rodman would never have wanted that information out. It was bad for his rebel image. But it was true.

Perhaps the strangest sight was the two of them sitting together on the team bus, said equipment manager John Ligmanowski. "There's Dennis with all his gold earrings and nose rings and tattoos and all his wild shit on. And there's Tex. There really isn't anybody more conservative than Tex. He went through the Depression. He was a Navy pilot. He's so tight he saves old shoeboxes."

"I enjoy Dennis," Winter said when asked about Rodman. "I enjoy coaching him. I talk to him about his life a little bit, but I'm not gonna correct him or tell him how to live his life. That would be a mistake. At my age, I think he sort of looks upon me as a grandfather figure. He's willing to listen, and he's very receptive, especially in the coaching aspect of it. And he's been fun to work with on the floor as far as that's concerned. I am concerned when we go into a ball game because he is an emotional guy. We don't want to take that energy away from him. One of the reasons that he's such a terrific player is that he's so energized. He gives this basketball team that same kind of energy. And if you squelch him, if you say, 'Dennis you can't do this and you can't do that,' well then he's probably not gonna be nearly the basketball player that he is."

Jason Caffey, Rodman's backup, even considered Rodman something akin to a mentor/coach. "Dennis is quiet," Caffey explained during the 1997 playoffs. "But he'll give me direction if I need it out there on the court. He'll guide me through. He's a great person to listen to, and he gets me through some tough times when I'm out there. He knows a lot of ball. He's very smart as far as basketball and things like that."

Even so, the Bulls had often been left to deal with whatever boiled to the top of the Worm's cauldron. The team's means of coping with that for 1997-98 was a contract that paid him a base of $4.5 million with a batch of incentives aimed at keeping him behaving and playing. If Rodman met those incentives, his pay could rise to nearly $10 million. Reluctant as they were to turn it loose, Krause and Reinsdorf knew it would be money well spent, if they could keep Rodman's open book turned to the same chapter as the rest of the team.

After the hold up on his contract during training camp, both Rodman and the Bulls had experienced a tenuous beginning to their third year together. At age 36 did he feel like going through another long, pressure-filled NBA season? The thought of that made him long for his early days in the league in Detroit as part of the Motor City Bad Boys, in the sweet old 1980s, before the league became so image conscious, before everything became so corporate.

Reinsdorf had called the Pistons "thugs" and Rodman a "lunatic" back then. But for Rodman, there was a huge thrill to being a part of that band of intimidators. "I miss the attitude," he admitted, "the attitude of how we approached the game. We knew we were gonna go out there and beat your ass. Simple as that. We knew that. We were just gonna go out there and whup your ass. That was the mentality I loved right there. And you don't have that today. You don't have that today at all."

The Bulls were a team driven by Jordan's immense will, but with the Pistons "not just one person had to do it," Rodman said. "It wasn't just one person who had the heart of a lion. I think everyone on that team had the heart of a lion and the heart of a tiger and the demeanor of an elephant. We'd just run right over you. That's what I miss about it. No one could beat us. We could barely tolerate each other some times, but in the end everyone got along."

If only the Bulls could have taken a lesson from that. Then again, the Pistons shoved their way to two championships and fell victim to the stress and pressure. The Bulls had already tallied five and had set their sights on a sixth. Each and every one of those titles had taxed them personally. The long run was a great tribute to the ability of Jordan, Pippen, Jackson, Krause, Reinsdorf and the rest of the team. Despite their differences, they all knew that winning a sixth title would put them one ahead of the Los Angeles Lakers Showtime team that won five in the 1980s. Like it or not, the Bulls' key figures were all linked for the ages by their accomplishments. Still, as the strife-filled 1998 season wore on, none of them had time to think about the ages. They were just trying to get through the moment.

From the opening night loss in Boston, the Bulls rebounded with three quick home wins, then jetted to Atlanta for a Friday night game against the red hot and undefeated Hawks in front of 45,790 fans in the Georgia Dome. For some reason, Rodman was unusually talkative in the locker room before the game. At home, he always retreated from the open pre-game locker room sessions with reporters to lift weights and snack on a meal of take-out chicken or spaghetti. Then after home games, he rarely made himself available for comment. On the road, he had no place in the visiting team locker room to retreat, so he simply stuffed his head between a set of head phones, turned up the volume and waved off reporters who stepped up with interview requests. An inveterate studier of video-tape, Rodman was one of the best-prepared athletes in the NBA in terms of scouting the opponent. He often used the pre-game hours to study his assignment for the evening.

But on this night in Atlanta, something prompted him to talk freely. "I like the way it is this year," he said. "It's more relaxed. If you lose, great. Whatever. It's a more relaxed atmosphere. We've won the two championships. We ain't going out there to kill our-selves trying to win 70 games.

"It'll be more comfortable," he predicted.

He was asked if the threat of terminating Jackson at the end of the season was management's way of keeping the pressure on the Bulls to keep winning?

"There ain't no pressure," Rodman said. "Who gives a shit really? I'd just like to say, take me, Scottie and Michael and Phil to another team. Let's just go play for the minimum (the NBA minimum wage is about $260,000 a year) and win a championship."

"Would that be fun?" an interviewer asked. "Or is that too much work?"

"Would that be crazy?" he said. "You'd take all four of us and go somewhere else next year and win a championship."

Immediately speculation centered on which team would offer the best accommodations for the four expatriate Bulls. "The Clippers, that would be close to the Los Angeles beaches that you love?" an interviewer suggested.

"Would that be crazy?" he said. "Go to the Clippers? All four of us?"

"That would be cool," a writer pointed out. "You know they'd love you in Los Angeles. You'd be right there in Newport Beach. The one negative would be Clippers owner Donald Sterling."

"He'd screw it up somehow," Rodman agreed. "He would. Easily."

"On the other hand, you could go to the Sacramento Kings," somebody pointed out.

Rodman's face immediately soured. "No," he said, "we'd have to be L.A. boys."

"The key would have to be that Scottie gets the big contract he deserves, and you, Michael and Phil would have to take big pay cuts," a writer pointed out, referring to the fact that if the Bulls' stars changed teams it would be nearly impossible under the league's salary structure for them to make as much money as they made in Chicago.

"We'll play for the minimum," Rodman said. "Why not? That would be crazy. That would be great, though. Absolutely marvelous. I would tell them, 'You guys got to sign Scottie.' They should give Scottie something like $20 million, or give him something, a bunch of land or something. Something like that."

"Buy him Pluto or the moon," suggested *Trib* writer Terry Armour, sitting nearby.

"That would be great," Rodman said. "You know Scottie's bitter about this. Been with the Bulls all these years. But there's no way they're gonna pay him with a big deal. He's gonna have to get the fuck out of Chicago."

The thought of that brought the flight of fantasy back to earth. The Bulls without Pippen weren't close to the same dominant team. That had been immediately obvious on opening night against the young Celtics when Chicago got a giant early lead only to lose the game at the end. Among his many skills, Pippen was a master at controlling the tempo of a game, keeping it running according to Chicago's game plan. Without a doubt, Pippen's absence put more pressure on all the Bulls, but especially Jordan, who would have to pick up the offensive slack, and Rodman, who was going to have to do more defensively.

Rodman was heading into the season hoping to win his seventh straight league rebounding title, something unprecedented. Then again, Rodman had turned 36 during the '97 playoffs. "I feel more fit than I did last year at this time," he said after the excitement of the Clippers fantasy had died down, his voice dropping to almost a whisper. "Bodywise. Healthwise. The older you get the wiser you get. You learn how to take care of your body."

He said there was no difference between 35 and 36, adding, "It just depends on if you maintain that level, that's all. Age 40 will be a big difference. I don't want to be playing until I'm like 40 years old. I don't want to be even be playing when I'm 37, if I don't have to. If we win the championship this year, it'll be like, 'OK, great.'"

It was pointed out to him that "no where can you earn the millions like you do playing basketball."

"It's good," he said, "but who knows if you're gonna keep making that money or not, especially with me. The only way I can make money from here on out is to stay with Chicago. I can't go to another team and say, 'OK, give me a million dollars.' I mean that's money, but it's . . . But the idea of winning another ring with another team? It's like, 'Damn, another long-ass year? Ohhhh.'

"If we don't win it this year, I can tell you right now there won't be no more Chicago Bulls. I'll tell you that right now. There won't be no more Chicago Bulls, not like they are now. That's the bottom line."

There was a time in Rodman's life when he faced giant concerns about what he would do after basketball, but no longer. His celebrity since joining the Bulls had brought an astounding flow of off-court opportunities. For the 1996-97 season, there had been Rodman's "World Tour" show on MTV. It did reasonably well in the ratings, apparently because it appealed to rebellious teens. But it was still cancelled.

"You know what that was?" Rodman said of the show. "That was almost spontaneous. It wasn't programmed to be a commercial type deal. It was, 'Just go do something, and we'll follow you with the camera.'

"What happened this year is that they got too many stupid ass shows that they brought in," he said. "Now all of a sudden they had to fire a lot of people and cut back. They cut the show. But the shows they got now are just damn stupid. So I don't even watch it."

Taking the show's place were the buckets of cash he has begun raking in on the pro wrestling tour. In one weekend alone during the summer of 1997, his take was huge from the World Championship Wrestling "Bash At The Beach" event, where he and Hollywood Hulk Hogan took on Lex Lugar and The Giant at Daytona Beach, Florida, in a pay-per-view event.

The money left him thinking of a long-term relationship. "You could easily do wrestling for the next 20 years and not do anything," Rodman said. "Ric Flair is almost in his 50s. Hulk Hogan is in his 40s. Most of those guys started out when they were 18 or 19 years old. Then, when they get to the point where they have enough juice, they look like they're 50 or 60 years old.

"The wrestling is easy. I can always make a couple of hundred thousand on that."

"Is that the easiest money available?" he was asked.

"Absolutely," he said. "The one thing about pro wrestling, everywhere they go, they're packed. They can pack any stadium. Easily. People believe in it. People think, 'Damn, this is really going on!' But that other thing they got going on, that Ultimate Wrestling shit, did you ever see that? That is some crazy shit. That's where they just go out there and beat your head in and kill. The hell with that. I'd rather go out there and make the money the easy way, bounce on your back a couple of times and try not to hurt people."

He accused the NBA of being almost as orchestrated as pro wrestling. The league, he said, had made it impossible for bad boys, like his old Detroit Pistons team, to operate. "The NBA won't allow that," Rodman said. "The NBA has gotten so soft now. It's so predictable. It's gotten to where you can't do anything. It's more of a business. It's more like an orchestra being run by the hand of a conductor who says when this side plays and then when that side plays. So it's a very good time to get out now. I'm happy that I've been in a good situation where I can make money and have a good time and the fame and fortune. I like to have that wherever I go. I'm not still here just to have that. I'd rather be a normal guy, a regular guy when I leave the game, not one of those guys who comes back to be an assistant coach. That's stupid."

Surprisingly, Rodman offered the opinion that the NBA need-

Young Jordan on the move, tongue out. *Photo by Steve Lipofsky.*

Jordan at work in the post. *Photo by Steve Lipofsky.*

Jordan matured into the world's greatest practice player. *Photo by Steve Lipofsky.*

Jordan, shown here in 1995, always worked to relate to less talented teammates.
Photo by Steve Lipofsky.

The Bulls' coaching staff in 1994. Jackson, followed by former assistants Johnny Bach and Jim Cleamons, then Tex Winter and trainer Chip Schaefer.
Photo by Steve Lipofsky.

Jackson working the officials in 1995 with Tex Winter working the clipboard in the background. *Photo by Steve Lipofsky.*

Rodman, said Jackson, "was just a very unique individual." *Photo by Steve Lipofsky.*

Fans in every city let Pippen know in December 1997 that they wanted him to return to the Bulls. *Photo by Steve Lipofsky.*

Pippen's lighter side was regularly available to his teammates. *Photo by Steve Lipofsky.*

The big facilitator on the move, looking a bit like Magic Johnson running the break.
Photo by Steve Lipofsky.

Toni Kukoc had shown flashes of offensive brilliance since coming to the NBA from Croatia in 1993. *Photo by Steve Lipofsky.*

Guard Ron Harper came into his own as a Bull in 1996. *Photo by Steve Lipofsky.*

The Bulls' bench in 1996. From left to right, trainer Chip Schaefer, Tex Winter, Jackson, assistant coach Jimmy Rodgers and assistant coach Frank Hamblen. *Photo by Steve Lipofsky.*

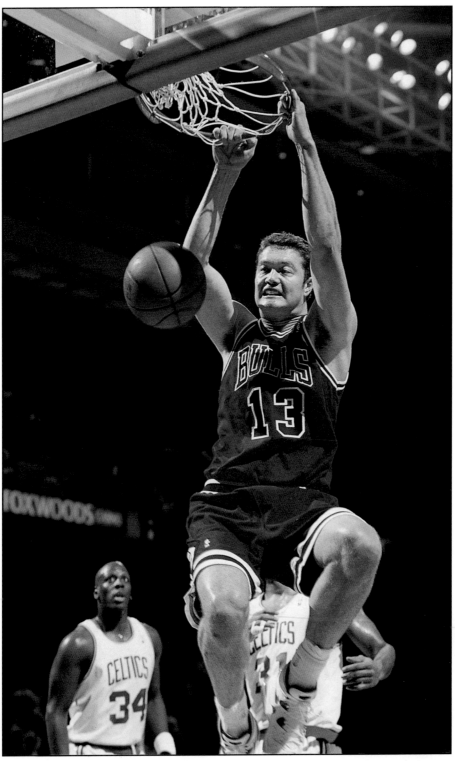

Center Luc Longley often struggled with Jordan's expectations. *Photo by Steve Lipofsky.*

Jordan in his return in 1995. *Photo by Steve Lipofsky.*

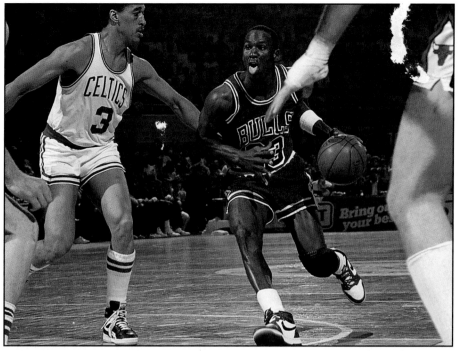

Jordan attacking the Celtics for an NBA-record 63 points during a 1986 playoff game. *Photo by Steve Lipofsky.*

The old regime. Trainer Mark Pfeil, head coach Doug Collins, and assistant coaches Johnny Bach and Jackson during the 1987-88 season. *Photo by Steve Lipofsky.*

Jerry Krause

Tex Winter

Jordan, his parents, and wife Juanita at a Michael Jordan foundation gathering in the early 1990s. *Photos by Rick Firfer*

For all of his gaudy personal style, Rodman was fundamentally sound in many phases of the game. *Photo by Steve Lipofsky.*

Jordan in 1997, at the height of his powers as a mature player. *Photo by Steve Lipofsky.*

ed to police the bad boy behavior off the court of young stars like Isaiah Rider and Allen Iverson and even old-timer Charles Barkley.

"Those guys shouldn't do what they're doing off the court," Rodman said. "You have to be a father figure in the game of basketball. Like me."

"You're saying that you can be a bad boy, but still you have obligations to the game and to the fans and to be a role model for children?" he was asked.

"You can always be a bad boy," he said. "But you know what? One thing people don't realize about me, there are all these crazy things that I do, but you never, ever hear about me off the court doing these kind of things. Because I'm always under control. And nobody ever says anything about that.

"The sad thing about it," he added, "I know how to have a good time. The atmosphere may be destructive or wild or calm. I know how to do that. I know how to control everything. The main thing many people want is for you to be out of control when you go out and party, when you're out in restaurants and bars. I like to do that on the basketball court where it's legal."

The league had ordered Barkley to hire bodyguards to keep him out of trouble in bars. Perhaps Barkley should have considered Rodman a role model in that regard. Rodman had long made use of discreet guards when he was out and about. And he paid his bodyguards well. One of Rodman's guards reportedly had purchased an $83,000 Porsche and a $23,000 Harley Davidson motorcycle. Not bad for an off-duty Chicago cop.

"Charles Barkley should think like you," a writer told Rodman. "When he goes out to bars, people lay in wait for him, hoping to anger him and make him punch them. That way they can file a lawsuit against him."

"I wouldn't try to fight in a bar," Rodman said. "I wouldn't do it no matter what. That's what a lot of guys go to bars to see. An athlete. The first thing they want to do is try to piss him off. I've been called many names from gay lover to homosexual to faggot. But it doesn't bother me. At least I must be somewhat important for people to know about me."

He was asked about the adjustment to being an actor in his first feature film, "Double Team," which was panned by many critics. "I saw a lot of people saying, 'That movie's gonna suck. He's a bad actor.' But I don 't give a damn," he admitted. "Shit, I never acted before in my life. I'm better than Shaquille O'Neal, I can tell you that.

I'm a lot better than that."

For his next film role, he said, "I'm gonna play *Bad, Bad, Leroy Brown* in Chicago next year. I'm gonna play a pimp. A big-time pimp. You know what I would be good at, though? That movie, *Boogie Nights*. I'd love to play in that move. I could easily do that."

"So, *Boogie Nights, II?*" a writer asked.

"I'd love to do that movie," he said, his voice rising. "I'd love to be in that."

"What about *The Wilt Chamberlain Story?*" *Daily Herald* reporter Kent McDill asked mischievously. "Would you do that?"

"Shit," Rodman said, struck by the thought. "Would that be great, though? He said he made love to what? Twenty thousand women in 12 or 13 years?"

"That's a lot of sex," one of the interviewers said.

"Yeah," Rodman said, shaking his head. "That's impossible. He said that to sell books."

Rodman, perhaps, qualified as something of an expert on the sexual possibilities of the NBA lifestyle. Every bar he entered, it seemed that women he had never met before were eager to walk up, lift their shirts and offer their breasts for his inspection. There was even said to be a private photo collection of these revelations. As writer and *Sun Times* columnist Rick Telander pointed out in his anecdotal book, *In The Year of the Bull*, the mercurial Rodman was a "vulva magnet."

What would Rodman be like at age 60? "A front man for the Mirage hotel and casino in Las Vegas?" he was asked.

"I don't know." Rodman said. "Hopefully I can live till I'm 80 years old. I probably can."

Public office? Politics?

"Nothing," he said. "I hope to be chillin'."

"What about coaching?" a writer asked. "Nobody watches more videotape than you."

"I don't care," he said. "I don't want to be a coach. I wouldn't even get off the fuckin' bench. I wouldn't even get off the bench, man."

"Larry Bird used to say that he wouldn't coach," the writer reminded him. "A lot of people have said that."

"Money talks sometimes to people," Dennis admitted.

As nice as the talk was beforehand, Dennis Rodman had a miserable game that night in Atlanta. The numbers? Two points and three rebounds in Chicago's 80-78 loss to Atlanta. Then in the game's final 80 seconds, he missed two key free throws and was whistled for an offensive blocking foul that negated a basket by Jordan.

Then, afterward, he said the wrong things. "I just haven't been playing," Rodman told a swarm of reporters crowded around him. "The interest level is just not there. I'm all right physically, but mentally I'm just not into it . . . I'm more going through the motions right now. If I can't get into it mentally, maybe I need to do something else.

"I shouldn't have been playing tonight," he added. "I told Phil that. It's just one of those deals, you know. I gave no effort tonight. I had no effort. It's very difficult to question my teammates. Nothing I can do about it, but I hope I can get through it."

The comments immediately drew Jordan's anger. "If that's the case, go home," Jordan said when reporters rushed across the locker room to relay the news. "If you're not into it, you don't need to be out there. Step aside and let someone else get in there and get the rhythm. Don't pacify us."

Just two hours earlier, Rodman had professed that the season was more relaxed than ever. Was he playing games? Perhaps, but those who knew him knew it was typical Dennis. He was merely expressing whatever he felt at the moment. The open book. He'd always been a conflicted sort of guy, and had done quite well by learning to have fun with those conflicts.

His teammates, however, didn't always laugh along. Jordan was simply letting it be known that the Bulls didn't have time for the crap. That was just one of the many reasons that Rodman seemed to enjoy being a Jordan teammate. He knew that when he popped up with something silly, Jordan would be there to bark him back into line. And if a quick tongue-lashing didn't do the trick, Phil Jackson hadn't hesitated to call Rodman into his office, where the coach, Jordan and Pippen could tackle him in a triple team.

"Dennis has to be disciplined," Jackson explained privately. "You gotta discipline him, and sometimes he has to be disciplined like you're a principal in a school. You bring him in and talk to him. And sometimes you have to discipline like you've got the sergeant at arms and the athletic director with you. I've brought Michael and Scottie in a couple of times to discipline Dennis. I have to bring them in because Dennis is one of the leaders of the team. And they'll be in there, and Michael will say, 'Dennis, as a leader of the team, these guys look to you for leadership.' And that's the one thing that always catches Dennis. Dennis really wants to be a leader, but it's tough for him because he leads from such a difficult spot. His leadership is really important to our team. You don't think of it as leadership. You think of it as a detraction."

Sure enough, Jordan's words did the trick in Atlanta. Rodman regained his enthusiasm a night later against the New Jersey Nets and helped lead the Bulls to a win. In the aftermath, the team and the city wrote the incident off as just another quirky episode. Besides, they had little choice. "We need Dennis' fire," Jackson explained. "We need the desire, intensity, full-out play. The big thing is that Dennis has got to want to play. He's going to have to feel that this is his business and it's what he wants to do more than anything else, for us to be successful."

Jackson acknowledged that there was some legitimacy to Rodman's feelings. Any player still able to compete at age 36 held a certain dread for the grind of the NBA regular season. Jordan himself had often called it "monotony."

Rodman had great respect for Jordan, but the two rarely talked. Rodman, though, wanted to make sure he ran out right after Jordan when the team jogged onto the United Center floor before a game. He always liked to be seen next to Jordan, to pose in photographs next to the star. Who could blame him? By just sharing Jordan's spotlight, Rodman had made more than $30 million off the court in his first two seasons with the Bulls.

Ah, the money.

"Dennis, are you amazed at the money you've made?" a writer asked in 1997, reminding him that he was nearly bankrupt when he came to the Bulls in October 1995.

"I've done it the old fashioned way," he replied. "I've earned every penny of it, so I haven't took anything for granted. I've worked my ass off for it. I wish I was like a big-time star, where it would just come to me." He snapped his fingers with an open palm as if was pulling in dollars. "Where people would just give it to me."

"But you've done well?" he was asked.

"I've done well," he said, "but well is not good enough."

It was pointed out that, with the millions flowing in, he was almost secure.

"I was secure the day I was born," he said with a smile.

THE SOFT PARADE

The latest surprise Rodman had dropped on Chicago was his new downtown bar. Dennis Rodman's Illusions opened with the idea of featuring a variety of Vegas style acts but quickly evolved into sort of a juke joint with a $10 cover. It opened in November with a private party for his friends and teammates, all of whom showed up, except for Jordan and Scottie Pippen. Even Jerry Krause and wife Thelma were there, making an appearance along with the Famous Diva Sisters, a lesbian act; Miss Nude America, who was clad in almost nothing; and eight showgirls in leopard outfits.

"It was a typical wild Dennis scene," said one laughing Bulls insider, noting that the Krauses made a quick exit.

Whatever the Worm did, it was over the top. As the 1997 playoffs were set to open, Rodman had scheduled a book signing at a Miracle Mile bookstore in Chicago. He was set to arrive on a float with two live tigers and a group of gay people dressed as animals. Apparently, the book store got queasy about the deal, and the city didn't like Rodman's request for a parade permit. The book store management asked if Rodman couldn't just slip in the back door for the signing to promote his book, *Walk On The Wild Side*.

"Dennis does not walk in the back door," Rodman's manager reportedly told the book store management. It supposedly cost Rodman $50,000 alone to cancel the parade.

Although his first book, *Bad As I Wanna Be*, was a runaway bestseller and was made into a TV movie, his *Wild Side* title made a quick turn toward miserable failure. The same fate seemed to await his ex-wife's book, *Worse Than He Says He Is, or White Girls Don't Bounce*. Rodman walked into a bookstore during the 1997 season and picked up a copy of his wife's book for purchase. At the counter, he asked the clerk how many the store had sold. The clerk said it was the first of his wife's books that someone had actually purchased. "In that case," Rodman said, "I'll put it back. I don't want to be the first."

One of the Worm's entourage later purchased it for him quietly.

Many athletes will go to great lengths to perpetuate an image, but none further than the fickle Rodman, who got a kick out of suggesting that he was super hip and even sexually conflicted, far from an "ordinary" guy.

Surprisingly, many of the staff members around the team found Rodman to be the most likable Bull. Of the Chicago superstars, Rodman was the closest thing to a regular guy. "He doesn't warm up quickly, but when he does, he's a friend for life," a Bulls insider said of the Worm.

Jordan was nice, but he could be moody. Pippen was a good guy, too. But staff members on the team noticed the way Rodman treated the people around him. Most fans didn't see this, of course, one Bulls staff member explained. "They don't get past his hair."

Back when he was a Detroit Piston Bad Boy, one of Rodman's favorite pastimes was hanging out with teenagers in mall game rooms (growing up in Dallas he had gotten the nickname "Worm" from his antsiness playing pinball.) He was also known for handing out big bills to the city's many street people, and one time he reportedly took a homeless man to his house, fed him, gave him a bath and handed the wide-eyed fellow $500.

This "giving" side was just more proof that Rodman was hardly the typical NBA player, the kind of actions that prompted former Piston teammate John Salley to say that Dennis Rodman was one of the few "real people" in the NBA. Certainly he was unlike many other NBA players in that he had not come up through the ranks of the great American basketball machine, he had not been on scholarship his entire life, wearing the best shoes and equipment and staying in fancy hotels where the meal checks were always paid. Rodman had missed all of that.

The first child of Philander and Shirley Rodman, Dennis spent the early years of his life in New Jersey where his father served in the Air Force. Philander Rodman showed a propensity for living up to his name, so much so that finally Shirley Rodman grew tired of strange women calling the house. When Dennis was three, she packed up her family and moved it back to her native Dallas. It was there that Dennis spent his formative years, a wormy little momma's boy who spent long hours pining for his father, which proved to be a debilitating factor throughout his childhood and adolescence.

His two younger sisters, Debra and Kim, would become high school basketball stars and later college basketball All-Americas, but Dennis had no such luck. If his adolescence had a context, it was a shyness framed by fear and insecurity. To make matters worse, his younger sisters both grew taller than he was, leaving Dennis behind as a frail runt, the kind of guy who had to fear for his lunch money at school each day.

In tenth grade at South Oak Cliff High School, he tried out for the football team and didn't make the cut. Although he was only 5-9, basketball was a little better. He at least made the team but quit midway through the season because he never got to play. Next he tried the bass viola for a time but gave up on that, too. Like many teen boys, his self esteem was the size of his pinkie, which meant that "hangin' out" became his activity of choice. In game and pool rooms. Fastfood parking lots. Rec centers. Anywhere a few driftless hours could be killed. It was a world that reflected his career aspirations. While his mom was an English teacher and his sisters were on the fast track, Dennis' future prospects were limited. He figured he might be able to finish high school, get a job and maybe buy a car.

He got a job as a valet at a local car dealership but was soon fired for taking a joy ride. He did manage to graduate from high school, yet his lack of success seemed all the more pronounced when compared with his sisters' accomplishments. Both were high school hoops stars on their way to celebrated college careers. At 6-2, Debra would play for Louisiana Tech, and 6-foot Kim went on to excel at Stephen F. Austin.

Dennis, meanwhile, was headed nowhere, cast into a sea of slack after high school, a series of menial day jobs and a part-time night gig mopping and sweeping up at Dallas-Fort Worth Airport. It was there, on the dare of a co-worker, that he stuck a broom handle through an airport gift shop grate and stole 15 watches, which he later passed out to friends.

Within days, he was arrested and jailed, only to confess under grilling by detectives. The charges were dropped after Rodman gave police details on how to recover the property, but not before he spent a night in jail, during which, Rodman later admitted, he was "scared shitless."

Ultimately, Rodman's life would be rescued by his pituitary. He grew almost 10 inches in one amazing year, yet even that only increased his isolation. By age 20, he was almost 6-7 and had out-grown his clothes, leaving his only attire the oversized coveralls from his job washing cars. About the only place he didn't feel like a geek was the playgrounds. Pickup basketball had become his refuge, and his height was one of his first real advantages in life.

It was one of his sisters' friends who got him a tryout at Cooke County Junior College in nearby Gainesville, Texas. He figured there was little hope, but the coaches jumped at the opportunity to sign an athletic big man and gave him a two-year ride right on the spot.

He became an immediate starter at center at Cooke and averaged double figures in rebounds despite the fact that he was playing organized ball for the first time in his life. It didn't matter. College seemed so strange. He dropped out after a few months but not before catching the eye of Lonn Reisman, an assistant coach at Southeastern Oklahoma State. The college was in the tiny farming community of Bokchito, Oklahoma, population 607, several hours north of Dallas. Rodman was very skeptical of going, but then again, he had few choices.

One of his first tasks there was serving as a counselor for the school's summer basketball camp. Within days of his arrival, Rodman befriended 13-year-old Bryne Rich, a white camper from a nearby farm. The previous Halloween, Rich had accidentally shot and killed his best friend while quail hunting. The ensuing months had left him almost paralyzed by depression, so much so that his parents feared for his future. Then one day the next summer, Bryne came home from camp all enthused about the new counselor he had met, "The Worm," Southeastern's new basketball recruit.

Bryne and Rodman formed an almost instant brotherly attachment and were well on their way to helping each other out of the shadows. Within days, Rodman was invited to dinner. Once there, he was invited to sleep over for the night, and he wound up staying three years with the Rich family, an experience detailed in the book *Rebound, The Dennis Rodman Story*, authored by Rodman, writer Alan Steinberg and Pat Rich, Bryne's mother.

On the court, Rodman became something of a force in NAIA basketball, averaging nearly 26 points and 16 rebounds over the next three seasons. He led the Southeastern Oklahoma State Savages to a district title and into contention for the NAIA national title (with young Bryne serving as an assistant manager for the team).

That performance, in turn, led to the Pistons selecting Dennis with the 27th pick in the 1986 draft, which marked the next giant step in the amazing turnaround in Rodman's life. As a rookie, Rodman found himself thrust into the titanic playoff struggle between Detroit and Larry Bird's Boston Celtics, who after winning three championships over the previous six seasons, had started their trek into decline. The Celtics, however, managed to survive one last hard-fought, emotional battle with the Pistons in the 1987 playoffs. Rodman's defense on Bird had caught the eye of keen NBA observers, and the rookie caught the rest of the basketball world's attention when he opined afterward that Bird was overrated.

Of course, the predominantly white media and pro hoops fan base treated Bird like an icon, but they were outraged at having a Pistons' rookie call their hand at it. For Rodman, this iconoclastic beginning was just the first of many notices he would send. Before long, the coaches, players, fans and media involved with the NBA would get the message: He was far from the average player. In fact, the defense and rebounding of the shy young forward were key factors in the Pistons defeating the Celtics in 1988 and rising to league championship contention. The Pistons lost to the Lakers that year in seven games, with Rodman's anguish being that he had taken an ill-advised jump shot in the closing moments of Game 6. If he had dunked, the Pistons would have been world champions. "I should have gone to the rim and torn it down," he said afterward.

The next season, the Pistons gained a rematch with the Lakers in the championship series, and Rodman's defense and rebounding were a factor in Detroit's sweep. Afterward, he stood in the din of the championship celebration in the Pistons' locker room and talked about pinball and the natural hyperactivity that fed his hoops antsiness. "My friends knew I was hyper. Real hyper," he said of his days growing up in Dallas. "They knew I wouldn't settle down, I wouldn't sleep. I'd just keep going.

"And now I just focus my energy in something I love to do. Now, I just play basketball, go out there and have a lot of fun and enjoy."

Back in the netherworld of Dallas, he had worked briefly pounding fenders in an auto body shop. You could still see some of that in his game. But like any smart player with unrefined offensive skills, Rodman made his living on the offensive boards. When the Pistons had the ball, he would often back away from the lane, his hands on his hips, his eyes always on the guards working the ball on the perimeter. He watched intently, waiting to make his move, waiting to get that special little piece of position for an offensive rebound. That was his primary study, his soul's joy of joys. Sometimes, after he had snuck in and stolen an offensive rebound, he would dribble out to the perimeter, stand there with the ball in one palm and punch the air with his other fist. He would usually do this in the Palace of Auburn Hills, the Pistons' fancy arena, where the crowds would bathe him in warm applause, and he would stand there, soaking in the ineffable glow of limelight.

After watching him in the 1989 Finals, Chick Hearn, the great Laker broadcaster, declared that Rodman was the best rebounder in the game. That night, after the championship, when he learned of

Hearn's assessment, the 27-year-old Rodman was stunned. "The best rebounder?" he asked, his eyes blinking in the first light of understanding. "In the game? You mean they put me in front of Oakley, Barkley, all those guys? I wouldn't say that. I think I'm one of the best ones, one of the top 10. But I can't be the best rebounder. I'm just in a situation where they need my rebounding here. I rebound with the best of them even though I'm not as bulky as some guys. I use my ability to jump and my quickness to get around guys."

It was Chuck Daly who had persuaded him to become a rebounding specialist and defender. Rodman bought into the plan and worked to make himself a marvelously versatile sub. Quick enough to stay with Michael Jordan or any other big guard/small forward in the league. Motivated enough to play power forward. Even tough enough to survive at center against much bigger bodies.

At Daly's suggestion, he had made this approach his mission after the 1987 Playoffs. "I just came to training camp and said, 'Hey, I want to play defense,'" Rodman recalled. "Then the 1988 playoffs really got me going. I just told myself, 'It's time to start focusing on something you really want to do.' I just feel like defense is something I really want to do."

He moved into the starting lineup for 1989-90 and helped the Pistons to yet another championship. From there, however, Detroit's guard-oriented offense declined, although Rodman's game was really just beginning to emerge. The primary ingredient was more playing time. He played 2,747 minutes in 1990-91 and responded with his first 1,000 rebound season. The next year he dominated the league in the category, pulling down 1,530 rebounds in 82 games to average a career-high 18.7 rebounds per game.

Even with his break through, the Pistons were swept by Chicago in the 1991 playoffs, and although they made a playoff run in 1992, Daly moved on to coach the New Jersey Nets, leaving Dennis without the fatherly coaching connection he badly wanted. He still averaged 18.3 rebounds in 62 games in 1992-93 for the Pistons, but those were troubled days that led to the end of his tenure in Detroit. That October of 1993, the Pistons traded Rodman to the Spurs, thus igniting the next amazing stage in his transformation, which left him searching through a series of tattoo shops, piercing pagodas, alternative bars and hair salons to find the real Dennis.. As Rodman explained it, "I woke up one day and said to myself, 'Hey, my life has been a big cycle. One month I'm bleeding to death, one month I'm in a psycho zone.' Then all of a sudden the cycles were in balance."

TUMBLING DICE

Rodman's days in San Antonio were notable for only a few reasons, one of them being his meeting Jack Haley, a deep reserve for the Spurs who was on a short-term contract. Haley watched in amazement that winter of 1994 as Rodman moved in and silently took control of the Spurs' power forward, giving David Robinson the kind of help that he'd never enjoyed before.

"I figured they were padding his stats," Haley said. "I figured no one could get 20 rebounds a night. So I started counting his rebounds. I'd come to him in a game and say, 'You got 17. You need three more.' Or, 'You need two more.' Or, 'You're having an off night. You only got five.' One game, he said to me, 'How many rebounds do I have?' From there, we developed a slow dialogue."

Perhaps it was the fact that Haley is one of the least threatening people in the NBA. Whatever it was, this casual acceptance somehow accelerated into a full-blown friendship about midway through the season.

"It really shocked me," Haley said. "We were at our team black tie dinner. Dennis and I had talked a couple of times. After the dinner was over, I'm standing there with my wife. I'm in a tuxedo. He pulls up in his Ferrari, and he says, 'Hey, would you and your wife like to go to dinner with me and my girlfriend?' We say, 'Sure.' And we went to a restaurant and had a nice dinner, and he said, 'Do you guys want to go to a bar?' I said, 'Yeah, we'll go to a bar.' He takes my wife and I to a club, and it says right on the door, 'San Antonio's number one gay and alternative nightclub.' I think he was just trying to shock me to see what kind of guy I was. So we went in, and they had a male stripper up on the stage, stripped down to a G-string. I shocked him and slipped one of the guys a buck. Ever since then, we've been good buds. I let him know, 'Hey, this is not my world, but I'm not shocked by it.'"

Indeed, Haley found he could hang rather easily on Rodman's zany planet, among his offbeat circle of friends, including a growing number of celebrities, models, hairdressers, gamblers, coin dealers and whoever else happened to nudge in beside Rodman at the craps tables of life. Almost overnight, the pair became inseparable, tooling around in Rodman's pink-and-white custom Ford monster truck, watching television at Rodman's house amid the clatter of his 15 exotic birds and two German shepherds, jetting back and forth to Vegas and L.A., carousing all night, tossing back shots of

Jaggermeister and Goldschlager, boating on south Texas' bluegreen lakes. Instead of a sullen, depressed guy, Haley discovered a Rodman who was ebullient, bubbling from a ceaseless energy further hyper-charged by nibbling chocolate-covered coffee beans. "If you're within the elite circle, he is the life of the party," Haley said in 1995. "You can't shut him up. He's hilarious. A great guy to be around."

Still, to observers, they seemed like an odd couple. Here was Jack Haley. Nice guy. Clean cut. All-American. And there was Dennis Rodman. Obviously on the highway to hell. And honking his horn to get into a passing lane.

Most relationships have a dark side, and for Rodman and Haley, it was their shared passion for gambling. For Haley, it was baccarat. For Rodman, it was rolling bones. During the season, they would catch a quick plane to Vegas whenever the opportunity arose. In the summers, they flew there nearly every weekend, making as many as 19 trips in one summer, always staying at the Mirage, where, Haley said, "they treat us like royalty." Eventually, Rodman would wear out his welcome at the Mirage but not before he had done more damage to his bank accounts.

For years, Chuck Daly had worried that Rodman was going through all of his money, that he was throwing it away on the craps tables in Vegas. Time would show that those fears were well-founded.

"Dennis is not a shy gambler," Haley said in 1995. "He plays for very big stakes. That's one of the things we have in common. I'm a big gambler myself. We spend a lot of time in Vegas. We're out there a large portion of the summer. We fly in and out. I mean Las Vegas is a big part of our lives. Dennis plays nothing but craps. I'm a baccarat player. Of course, we'll play each other's. I'll play craps with him, and he'll play baccarat with me. If we play say eight hours a day, he'll be on the crap table seven and a half hours."

On the bad nights, Rodman would lose as much as $30,000. At times, though, things got worse. Much worse.

Haley said, "The biggest night I've ever seen Dennis have, I think he won $89,000 one night. I've seen him drop $200,000 in a weekend. Part of the $200,000 he lost, though, was the $89,000 he had won the week before. He won 89 the trip before, and we went back, and instead of the average $500 bet, it was a $5,000 bet. The next thing you know you're in big trouble.

"One thing that impressed me more than anything, he was losing and he was losing huge. We pulled up at the airport to get out of the taxi, and the cab was only six bucks, and he said, 'I got it.'"

Rodman just didn't seem to know when it was time to let somebody else pick up the tab, just as he didn't know when it was time to quit.

"Later we went right back at them and recouped a portion of the losses," Haley said. "This was during the summer. During the season, you're in and out. You can't lose that much money. You set a limit for yourself every night."

Isn't the league concerned about the gambling? Haley was asked during a 1995 interview.

"What can the league say to him?" he replied. "What can they say? That's legalized gambling. They can't tell us how much money to bet. We're not Michael Jordan (referring to 1993 revelations that Jordan had lost more than $1 million while wagering on his own amateur golf rounds). We're not betting a million dollars, but we're betting more than the average player. People have to put it in perspective. If a regular person goes, and they lose a thousand dollars in Las Vegas, what's the difference if a guy making $2.5 million loses $10- or $20,000? It's the same thing."

Later, in a subsequent interview, Haley would suggest that he had overstated Rodman's losses. Perhaps. But there would soon be little question that Rodman's finances were a mess, and his gaming was part of the problem.

A MATERIAL GUY

Rodman's strange and wacky ways wouldn't have been of such tremendous public interest if he hadn't been home one night with Haley watching a Knicks game on cable.

"Dennis and I are watching a Knicks game on TV," Haley said. "Madonna is in Madison Square Garden and they interview her after the game, talking about NBA players. She makes a comment to the effect that of all the players in the league she thinks the sexiest guy is Dennis Rodman. Of course we pounce on that.

"We decided to let our PR guy contact her PR person. And her person actually said, 'Yes, Madonna is writing an article for *Vibe* magazine.' So they got back to us, and Madonna said, 'Can I interview you?' Dennis said, 'Sure.' Dennis hops on a plane after a game, flies to Miami to meet with Madonna for this supposed interview. They did a five-minute token interview, then went out on the town, danced all night and had a great time, spent the night together. From there, it was phone calls, faxes, conversations everyday."

"She had ways of making you feel like King Tut," Rodman wistfully told an interviewer. "But she also wanted to cuddle and be held."

"They got along very well," Haley said. "Madonna and Dennis saw each other several times. Then we went to Los Angeles. She has a home there, and that was the first time I actually met her and went out with her. I was very impressed with Madonna as a lady. I was kind of shocked. Her image as a hard cutthroat lady with profanity, she was nothing like that. She was polite, and in a partying sense, too. It was not just, 'Oh, hi, how ya' doin'?' She was well-spoken and outstanding. But you can feel her power and presence when you're with her. She wants it her way or no way. She's accustomed to that, and Dennis is the same way, so there was some conflict there.

"They had only been dating a month or so, and she starts talking to Dennis about having a baby. She's definitely interested in having a baby. She says to me, 'Jack, I want Dennis to have my baby.' I said, 'Why, Madonna, would you want Dennis Rodman to have your baby?' She said, 'Dennis Rodman is the perfect physical specimen to have my child.' I said, 'Well, did you ever consider the mental side?' They all laughed when I said that. That was her only response."

The Spurs were scheduled to host the Utah Jazz in a first-round, best-of-five playoff series. The Spurs won handily in the first game in San Antonio, but in the second game they went scoreless for 16 minutes and watched the Jazz control the outcome. Even worse, Rodman clobbered Utah guard John Stockton and was suspended for the critical Game 3 in Salt Lake City. Despite the suspension, Madonna showed up in Utah with Rodman.

"At this point, they were probably at their peak," Haley said. "Love is flying in the air, and everything's great. But Dennis was suspended for one game. He, of course, took off with Madonna, left Salt Lake City and went up to Park City, Utah, to one of those love resorts where they have the heart-shaped jacuzzis and the whole thing. They hid up there from the press, because there was a media frenzy. No one, management or coaching staff, knew Dennis' whereabouts but me, and I had to relay in between.

"I was eating it up, though," Haley said with a laugh. "I was on TV doing Madonna and Dennis updates for four days. It was great. And they were doing great."

The Spurs, however, were headed down in an upset with two losses in Utah. "We get knocked out of the playoffs," Haley said.

"Dennis has 22 or 23 rebounds. He plays great, but we lose the game. Dennis walks off the floor, directly into the locker room, picks up his gym bag with his clothes, walks right out of the locker room, still in his Spurs uniform, saying nothing to anyone but me, does not wait for the post game comments from (Spurs coach) John Lucas or anyone. He and Madonna get directly into a limousine, drive out of the arena while all of these people are screaming, drives straight to the airport, hops on a private plane and goes straight to Las Vegas, where they have a great time."

Meanwhile, Rodman's suspension and his apparent callousness about team issues created a storm of media criticism. Lucas and Spurs general manager Bob Bass were shown the door. Even his affair with Madonna seemed to suffer. After all, Rodman still had a live-in girlfriend in San Antonio.

"Madonna finds out," Haley said, "and a couple of weeks later Dennis is in Vegas with this other girl. Madonna comes to Vegas, checks into the suite right next to him. Rodman later told Haley that Madonna accosted him and suggested, "Let's hit a little white chapel right now and get married." Haley added, "Dennis says, 'No.' But he leaves his girlfriend in Las Vegas, doesn't tell her where he's going. He says he's going to work out. Instead, he hops on a plane and flies back to Los Angeles with Madonna and hides out."

Meanwhile, his Texas girlfriend was stuck in Vegas wondering what had happened to Rodman, Haley said. "It took her two days before she realized Dennis wasn't coming back. He's known to hang out and be flighty anyway, so the girlfriend ends up calling me in L.A. I'm there with Dennis and Madonna, and she's asking me where Dennis is. I finally have to tell her, 'You should go on home.' I sent her a plane ticket to get home."

Rodman's differences with spurs management dogged the team like a running skirmish over the winter and spring of 1995. The Spurs had their rules, and Rodman answered with an insurrection that cost him tens of thousands of dollars in fines.

"They were fining him $500 and they were fining him every single game," Haley would later confide. "I'm talking about every single day, $500 a day. Because Dennis made a concentrated effort to be late. It was his way of sticking it in their side.

"I pulled up one day to practice. He's sitting there 15 minutes early for practice. I said, 'C'mon, let's go.' He said, 'I'm listening to some Pearl Jam.' He walks into practice 25 minutes late. It was almost his way of saying, 'You're not going to control me. I'm gonna be one minute, two minutes late, every single day.'"

Perhaps the primary problem for the Spurs was Rodman's belief that David Robinson lacked commitment as an athlete. "Dennis had a real problem in his respect for David Robinson as a player," Haley explained. "He had problems with David's intensity and work ethic in practice. One thing about Dave. Dave could be the most talented player and athlete in the NBA. Dave is probably the greatest athlete in the game. Dave can go out and get 30 points and 12 rebounds without putting forth a real effort. He's that good. Therefore, he's not a big practice guy. Not a big work ethic guy. By [January], Dave would have sat out 30 practices. It's tendinitis. It's, 'I'm sore today.' Whatever it was, Dennis is a practice guy, and it didn't sit well with Dennis. That caused a lot of their problems, just work ethic.

"Dave tried everything," Haley said. "He tried everything imaginable to bond with Dennis Rodman, to get through with Dennis Rodman to form a friendship. I'm good friends with Dennis and I'm good friends with Dave. Dave would ask me, 'Why don't the three of us go to lunch? Why don't we sit down and try to talk?' He would try to talk to Dennis about basketball to form a bond. Dennis wouldn't respond. Dave is very religious. He felt that part of his quest was to get through to Dennis Rodman on a religious level, to try to turn his life around. That didn't work out at all."

Rodman's biggest problems involved his bank account. He was nearly broke despite a contract that paid him about $2.5 million annually. He owed substantial amounts of money to both teams he had played for, the Pistons and Spurs, and he hadn't paid his agent in nearly three years. Settling up those accounts after pursuing his rock'n'roll lifestyle for years meant that he had very little left heading into the 1995-96 season.

He had turned 34 on May 13, 1995, an age when most hoop stars are looking at limited futures. It was clear that the Spurs wanted to trade him, rather than deal with another year of headaches. But they were having trouble finding takers. Rodman's ideal scenario was to get with another team for the last year of his contract, perform well and sign a new two- or three-year deal in the neighborhood of $15 million.

"I'll put $5 million in the bank, live off the interest and party my ass off," Rodman told *Playboy*, just the kind of talk that made NBA general managers very nervous.

THE STRANGEST BULL

Because of NBA labor troubles, the summer of 1995 required a moratorium on all trades and contract moves, which meant that Rodman's status with San Antonio wasn't resolved until days before training camps were set to open. When a move was finally made, Rodman found sanctuary in the least expected of places, in Chicago, probably the city in the NBA where Rodman was hated most because of his brash intimidation of the Bulls during his days as a Detroit Piston.

The Bulls, though, were desperate for a quality power forward, and Rodman's rebounding and intimidation were just the elements Chicago needed to contend for a fourth league title in 1996. Even Jordan and Pippen, who had loathed Rodman as a Piston, agreed for Krause to trade backup center Will Perdue for the Worm. That news elated Rodman, who badly wanted to find a basketball home. "I had no choice," he said. "I feel like that I had a lot of negative energy going on in my life, and that was the best way to get rid of it."

Before the trade was consummated, Jackson and Krause held extensive talks with Rodman. "We had Dennis in my home," Krause recalled. "He stayed in a hotel but he came over and spent most of the days in my home. I asked him, 'Dennis, why didn't you get along with Billy McKinney (in Detroit)? Why didn't you get along with Bob Bass (in San Antonio)?' He looked at me and said, 'They all want to be my friends.' I said, 'I don't want to be your friend. I'm 56, you're 34. What the fuck do I need to be your friend for? You're sitting here with green hair and you got ear rings up your ass. We have nothing in common. I'll leave you alone.'"

The discussions convinced Jackson and Krause that the eccentric forward could be incorporated into the team. Jackson, who was himself a bit of a rebel as a member of the New York Knicks back in the '70s, grew confident that he could coach Rodman. So the move was made, and as extra insurance for communicating with Rodman, the Bulls signed Haley to a $250,000 contract. Haley would be placed on injured reserve and kept there all season, which allowed him to travel with the team and keep things running smoothly for his buddy.

"It was a tough training camp because everybody was guarded," Haley offered. "Again, you're Michael Jordan. You're Scottie Pippen. Why would you have to go over to Dennis? Michael Jordan made $50 million last year. Why would he have to go over and basically kiss up to some guy to get him to talk? They came over and shook his hand and welcomed him to the team, and this and that. But other than that, it was a slow process."

Sports Illustrated came into town the first week of the preseason and wanted to pose one of Bulls star players with Rodman for a cover shot. Jordan, who had a running feud with *SI*, refused to pose. Pippen also declined, saying privately that he didn't want to make a fool of himself. Finally, the magazine got Jackson to do the shot.

"The very first preseason game of the year," Haley said, "Dennis goes in the game, Dennis throw the ball up in the stands and gets a delay-of-game foul and yells at the official, gets a technical foul. The first thing I do is I look down the bench at Phil Jackson to watch his reaction. Phil Jackson chuckles, leans over to Jimmy Cleamons, our assistant coach, and says, 'God, he reminds me of me.' Whereas last year, any tirade Dennis threw, it was 'Get him out of the game! Sit his ass down! Teach him a lesson! We can't stand for that here!' Here in Chicago, it's more, 'Get it out of your system. Let's go win a game.'"

Asked about Phil Jackson, Rodman replied, "Well, he's laid back. He's a Deadhead, and if he wanted to smoke a joint or two, he would." Rodman laughed hard at that assessment, and when a reporter asked."Is he your kind of coach?" he replied, "Oh yeah. He's fancy free, don't give a damn. With him it's just, 'Go out there and do the job, and let's go home and have a cold one.'"

Jackson's approach with Rodman soon worked to ease any tensions on the roster. "With Jordan and Pippen, you're talking about two superstars who were not at all threatened by Dennis," Haley said. "They didn't care about his hair color. They don't care about anything. If the man gets 20 rebounds a game and they win, that's all they care about. What he does off the floor, they couldn't care less about that or anything else, as long as he comes to work. And that's what Dennis is about. 'Leave me alone. Let me have my outside life. Let me come do my job as a player. Let my actions on the floor speak for me.' The Bulls have been tremendous for Dennis. Again, everyone just gave him his space, and he just kind of slowly opened up."

Once in 1995, when Rodman's hair had been green for a while and was beginning to fade to black, Haley asked him, "Why don't you just let it go black?"

Rodman told him, "I can't let it go. My hair is part of my thing. I have to keep it colored. The fans want it. That's what they expect."

"He's very well aware of what has gotten him where he is," Haley said, "and he's very intelligent in what it takes to make himself a star.

"He has catapulted himself through outrageous hair, tattoos, body piercing and outrageous comments and hardwork basketball, he has catapulted himself to the superstardom of a Magic Johnson or a Michael Jordan," Haley said, "and to someone who's never had that, it's fun, it's exciting. He's one of the biggest names in the game, and he knows exactly why he's there."

Indeed, Rodman showed his value time and again in the 1996 playoffs, particularly when he manhandled a much larger Shaquille O'Neal and the Orlando Magic during the Eastern Conference finals. He was rewarded with a handsome boost in pay for the 1996-97 campaign but suffered through a knee injury and bouts of erratic play and misbehavior. Even so, his contributions outweighed his baggage. Thus Reinsdorf had agreed to bring him back for another run in 1997-98, but only if he behaved.

PAIR OF DICE LOST

After their win at home over New Jersey early in the 1997-98 season, the Bulls traveled to Cleveland and lost again, after which Jordan complained that they looked "like an expansion team." Then they returned home and lost in the United Center to the Washington Wizards in a game remarkable for Jordan's growing frustration. With Pippen out, teams could focus on him. Every basket became a fight. Normally a willing interview, he left after the game without speaking to the media.

Suddenly, Chicago's record was 4-4, and observers suggested that perhaps Jordan was carrying too much of the burden. He was averaging 26 points a game but, with an inflamed right wrist and sore right index finger, his usually stellar field goal shooting had drooped to the 38 percent range. "When he does try to do too much it means that he feels there's a lack of aggressiveness by his teammates," Jackson told reporters. "They don't know what to do or they're floundering. So he picks up the ball and starts carrying it on his own, and right now he's not shooting well enough to do that."

What was worse, neither were his teammates. As a team, Chicago was shooting 41.5 percent and scoring 87.5 points per game. For 1997, the Bulls had averaged 103 points per game. Without Pippen, they had failed to score 100 points in any of their eight games. "Our offense has always been able to provide Michael space to score, and the other players an opportunity to hit open shots when he's double-teamed," Jackson said. "Right now, what's really frustrating is that he's finding guys off the double-team and we're not making those shots."

"Those of us around Michael aren't contributing enough, and Michael's trying to take it upon himself to score," Steve Kerr agreed. "As a result, we're out of whack."

Kerr would finally figure that his own poor performances were a matter of worrying about the team's conflict, about the future. It was then, early in the season, that he decided just to have fun, as Jackson had been encouraging them all to do, "to live for the moment."

"We're in a shooting slump. We have been since the season started," Jackson acknowledge. "We'll break free of it, and when we do we're going to win games in bunches."

It looked like Rodman would contribute to the woes that Friday night, November 14th against the Charlotte Hornets. As game time grew nearer, he was no where to be found. The next day, headlines would report the incident as yet another sign of impending doom for the team. Yet Rodman had actually been sidetracked by nature. Driving to the United Center, he had been suddenly struck by the need to go to the bathroom. Then the urge became immediate. Unfortunately, he was in a residential area. Frantically, he got on his cell phone and dialed the United Center looking for directions to a restroom. Apparently that effort produced no results, but one of his assistants thought of a place where Rodman could stop, knock on the door to somebody's home and ask to use the facilities.

He walked into the locker room at 7:25, just minutes before the 7:30 game. "Everybody was ready to run out on the court, and Dennis comes strolling in," said one team source. "Phil looked at him and said, 'Dennis, how nice of you to join us.' You'd think he would have hurried up, but he took his time, got a shower, ate his chicken dinner and walked out on the court."

Rodman didn't appear on the bench until 7:59 remained in the first quarter. He checked into the game with 6:52 left after Jason Caffey was called for a second foul.

"Then Dennis just turned it on and got a bunch of rebounds, and we won," said a team employee. "Who else could do that?"

> "Free will, it's like butterfly wings."
>   — *The Devil's Advocate*

7/ The Wild, Wild West

For every season of their 32 years of existence, the Chicago Bulls had packed up in November and headed west for an extended road trip. In the old days, their disappearance usually cleared the Chicago Stadium schedule for a visit from the circus.

On the other hand, it could be argued that just about every year, the Bulls seemed to take the circus with them. As writer Kent McDill of the *Daily Herald* once pointed out, there was always something going on. Either one of the team's stars was making the gossip columns of the local West Coast papers after being seen in a strip bar, or something truly strange would come up. Such as the November 1996 trip, when center Luc Longley severely injured his shoulder while body surfing.

"It's always a tough haul," Jackson said of the long ride out west.

Even in the Bulls' earliest days, the excursions were marked by weirdness and bad luck. Take, for example, the sad case of Reggie Harding, who joined the Bulls in the fall of 1967 when they had lost 11 of their first 12 games. Desperate to shore up their weakness at center that season, the coaching staff had pulled in the 6-foot-11 Harding from the Detroit Pistons. One of the first players to move directly from high school to the pros, Harding had struggled with the adjustment and had even been suspended for the 1965-66 season. Sadly, time would show that Harding, who had been raised on Detroit's mean streets, could never overcome his gangster background. (He would be shot to death in 1972.) He was known for finishing practice and leaving without showering, pausing only to towel off and spin the cylinder on his revolver. Once while playing in Detroit, Harding apparently began shooting at teammate Terry Dischinger's feet to make him "dance."

Legend has it that Harding robbed the same gas station three times in his own Detroit neighborhood. According to Kareem Abdul-Jabbar, the third time Harding robbed the place, the attendant said, "I know that's you, Reggie."

"No, man, it ain't me," Reg was said to have replied. "Shut up, and give me the money!"

One night, Bulls guard Flynn Robinson awakened in the dark, cut on the light and supposedly found Harding pointing a gun at him. The Bulls, however, were almost desperate enough to overlook the strange behavior.

"I got a chance to get Reggie Harding," recalled the team's first coach, Johnny Kerr. "We needed a big center. I had heard about his pistol. Rumor had it that he carried it in his gym bag. . . . He'd play one-on-one with Flynn Robinson. Flynn would beat him, and Reggie would say, 'Get out of here Flynn before I pistol whip you.' Everybody figured he might have it with him.

"When we were in the midst of that losing streak in November '67, we played the Lakers in Los Angeles," Kerr recalled. "We needed a win in the worst way, and we had a one-point lead with just a few seconds left on the clock. The Lakers got the ball at half court, and I put Reggie in to guard Mel Counts, their big guy. I didn't want them getting an alley-oop. Counts set up out near the free throw line, but Walt Hazzard, who was taking the ball out of bounds, threw the ball over the backboard and the buzzer sounded. I was jumping around and screaming because we had finally won a game. I looked up, and Reggie had decked Mel Counts. He got up and shot two free throws and beat us."

During that same West Coast trip, Harding was called home for his mother's funeral. For the next 10 days, the Bulls didn't hear from him. Finally he returned to the team, saying that he had been appointed executor of his mother's estate and needed the extra time away. A few days later, the Bulls placed Reggie Harding on waivers.

As the Bulls struggled to prominence over the years, their West Coast trips would always seem to mix the wonderful and the terrible. For example, in November 1986 Jordan averaged better than 41 points over the team's seven-game western road swing. The Bulls lost six of those games.

By the 1990s, however, the West Coast trip had become something of a passage to greatness for the team. As Bill Wennington explained, when the team racked up six wins against a single loss in November 1995, it showed the Bulls just how dominant they could be and helped spur them to their record-setting 72-win season. Likewise, the next year they again won six games on the first western swing and knew their chemistry was still cooking. Thus, a 69-win season.

Yet the first western trip was also the time that Krause chose each year to travel with the team and evaluate the roster he had assembled. The things he saw then could help him make decisions on trades and other moves before the February trading deadline.

Krause's presence around the team also created the potential for conflict and heavy razzing on the team bus and plane. Despite the charged atmosphere between the coach and GM during the 1997 offseason, Jackson had again attempted to persuade Krause not to travel with the team.

"Basically, in my conversation with Jerry in the preseason," Jackson said, "I had asked him not to go. I said, 'You always insist on going. I don't think this is a good year to go.' He said, 'I know you could stop this stuff if you wanted to.' I said, 'Jerry, it's what they feel like. If I stood up in this situation and tried to stop this, I would alienate this team.'"

Jackson viewed the extended trips as a time for the players and coaches to bond together, to seal their unity and commitment for another championship run. Because of that, he decided to bring the injured Pippen along. The forward wouldn't be able to play, but he would undergo limited workouts and spend extra time with his teammates. "I brought Scottie along to get him back in stride with the guys, to practice with the team," Jackson explained. "There was a chance he was going to be able to come back December 10. We didn't want him to be out too long, and this was an opportunity, his first practice chance. He wouldn't have the opportunity to practice if he stayed behind."

At the time, the Bulls were not a team brimming with confidence. They had lost all three of their road games in the young season and badly needed to re-establish their prowess in the hostile environment of another team's arena. It was a dramatic turnaround. The two previous seasons they had rung up phenomenal road records of 33-8 and 30-11. "The circumstances are different," Steve Kerr, who had a bruised knee, told reporters. "I'd be surprised if we could pull off 6-1, frankly. We're not playing well enough."

"A certain understanding of going into the enemy's territory and bonding together," is how Jordan, who was averaging just under 25 points a game while shooting just under 40 percent from the floor, summed it up. "This is a great time for it, knowing we haven't had much success on the road."

This time around, the Bulls were scheduled to open with a Thursday night game at Phoenix, then visit the Los Angeles Clippers, Sacramento Kings and Seattle Super Sonics, then stop by Chicago for a two-day break at Thanksgiving before visiting Indiana, Washington and Boston. Without Pippen on the floor, the challenge against the running and gunning Suns would be controlling the game's ebb and flow, Jordan explained to the media. "If we can dictate the tempo, we're in good shape. If we let them dictate, we know we can't run up and down like they can. They're definitely looking to push the ball and outscore you. We want to keep the numbers way below 100 if we can."

Without Pippen, the Bulls were averaging only 88.4 points per game, ranking them 28th among the 29 NBA teams in scoring. Worse yet, they weren't shooting the ball well and were turning the ball over 18 or 19 times a game. Without Pippen, the game also became much harder for Jordan, because other teams found it much easier to double- and triple-team him.

"You hate to keep harping on his return, but let's be honest — the guy is one of the great players ever ... and he affects every aspect of the game," Kerr said. "Until he's back, I don't think we can consider ourselves the real Bulls."

Pippen would later admit that he wasn't exactly unhappy with the circumstances. After yet another offseason in which Krause again explored trading the star forward, the Bulls were now getting a scorching lesson in just how essential he was to their chemistry. Without him, the Bulls had no teeth. They were old, too, and like old men, they had to gum their way through games.

To ease up the offensive pressure on Jordan, Jackson figured he would try starting sixth man Kukoc, which gave Chicago something of a three-guard offense. The main problem there was that doctors had just discovered Steve Kerr would miss several games with a cracked femur, meaning that the struggling bench would get dramatically weaker.

Jackson had told his assistants of his intention to make this final season one of great fun, but just weeks into the schedule it was clearly not fun. Tex Winter watched Jackson struggle with not only his own emotions but those of his players. "We have been working on the physical, mental and spiritual sides of these players," Jackson admitted to the reporters covering the team, "to increase their appetite for the game, their hunger for playing, making basketball fun."

Winning, though, was fun, and the Bulls couldn't accomplish that against the Suns. "We lost the game in Phoenix in which Dennis had a wide-open layup down the stretch and he missed it," Jackson recalled. "We lost a game we probably should have won on the road again."

It didn't help matters that before the Phoenix game, Rodman had jetted to Oakland for a Rolling Stones/ Pearl Jam concert, then topped off the excursion afterward by stopping in Vegas to roll bones into the wee hours.

Normally, when the Bulls were dominant, the team was willing to overlook Rodman's indifference on offense. But with Pippen out, that indifference grew as yet another item in Jordan's craw.

On the team plane that night from Phoenix to Los Angeles, Krause decided to approach Jordan, Pippen, Randy Brown, Scott Burrell and Ron Harper as they were playing their usual card game at the back of the plane. The team had decided that Steve Kerr, who was injured, could go home to be with his pregnant wife. But that created a problem in that Kerr and little used rookie Keith Booth were scheduled to make a promotional appearance with Jerry Reinsdorf in Sacramento. The team chairman had not been around the team yet. What made the circumstances worse was that Krause had a speck of cream cheese on his face from a post-game snack. From several accounts of the incident, the ribbing he received was substantial. Krause spoke to the players for a few minutes without success in finding a replacement for Kerr and left.

Then, about 15 minutes later, the GM made another run back to the group to try again. According to accounts of the incident, he still had the cream cheese on his face, creating shades of his earlier days with the team, when one or more of the players concocted the "Crumbs" nickname.

Krause's second visit to the card game reportedly drew some chiding barbs from Jordan along the lines of, "What's the matter with you, Jerry? Didn't anybody ever teach you how to eat?"

"We all know that Jerry likes to eat," Harper would say later. "He don't know that he has food on his face, though. But he likes to eat, though. MJ told him. MJ said some words to him and we laughed at him. But, you know, Jerry wants to be part of the team. He'd be very successful if he stayed away."

Ultimately, Harper agreed to go on the appearance with

Reinsdorf in Sacramento, not out of any sense of allegiance to the chairman or the GM but because he didn't want the rookie Booth to be stuck alone making the appearance. As it turned out, the appearance was a nice event, Harper said, and in person Reinsdorf was great. "Jerry's a good guy," Harper said, pointing out that the team chairman made sure that the event promoter didn't try to keep the players too long.

As for Krause, Harper said, "He's brought some players to this team, but he has some players who are frustrated with the way he treats them and the things that he says. It's a cumulative thing. It's added up over the years. It's not like it's gonna go away overnight."

Jordan's answer to the losing streak was his biggest scoring outburst of the regular season, 49 points against the Clippers, the 150th time he had scored more than 40 in a game. The performance was tempered by the fact that it was the lowly Clippers, and the Bulls needed double overtime to vanquish them. Still, it was a win, and the Bulls wouldn't have gained it if Jordan hadn't come up with a Jordanesque play off his own missed free throw at the end of regulation to send the game to overtime.

The Clippers, who had only one win to go with 11 losses, held a 102-100 lead with 15.7 seconds to go in the game. Jordan was fouled, but missed his first free throw. When the second shot came off the back of the rim, Jordan got the rebound, took the ball back up top, then executed a move on the Clippers' Brent Barry for the tying layup.

In the second overtime, Jordan scored all nine of Chicago's points, giving him a run of 13 straight points, for the 111-102 win.

After the game, *Daily Herald* writer Kent McDill noticed Pippen sitting alone in the locker room. "There was a chair next to him," McDill recalled. "So I just went over to say hi and see how things were going, when he thought he was gonna come back. And I said something about what game are you aiming for. And he said, 'Well, I'm not gonna play for the Bulls anymore.' Ron Harper was standing next to him, and Ron looked down at him and made some sort of snide remark. Scottie was laughing, and then he went on: 'I'm tired of the way I've been treated, and I don't want to play for any team that Jerry Krause is on or represents. I don't want to represent Jerry Krause.' He said a bunch of that stuff. Then he and Harper started laughing about where they were going to end up, what team they were gonna play for and this other stuff. Then Scottie finally looked at me and said, 'I want to be traded.'

"It was all too jocular for me to actually write it," McDill said. "It all seemed kind of silly. I knew that the Bulls probably wouldn't trade him even if he wanted to be traded."

Later Jackson would note that Pippen's agent had come to Los Angeles. "I just heard his agent had been in L.A.," the coach said, implying that agent Jimmy Sexton's presence might have had something to do with Pippen's statements.

McDill didn't write the story after the Friday night game in Los Angeles. But on Sunday in Sacramento he saw Pippen again. "Before the game he was standing there before introductions," the reporter recalled. "And I just said to him, 'When are you going to have your press conference to announce that you want to be traded?' He said, 'As soon as you write the story.' So I asked a couple more questions. Then I went into the press room and started writing down the stuff that had happened Friday night as well. At halftime, I saw him again, and he said, 'Are you gonna write it?' I said, 'To be honest with you, I already did.' I told him what the story was gonna say, and he said, 'That's exactly how I feel. I want to be traded. I don't want to play with the Bulls anymore.'

"It obviously wasn't a well thought-out decision," McDill said, "because the Bulls aren't going to trade a player just because he wants to be traded. It's not like they were gonna get what they wanted for him in value, when a player announces he wants to be traded. At the time he was angry and had things he wanted to say, and I'm sure he wanted to stir the pot a little bit. Which he did."

Indeed, Pippen's comments made headlines across the country. "I ain't coming back," he had told McDill. "I want to be traded. I want to go to Phoenix or L.A." Even worse, he had insinuated he was malingering, saying, "Maybe I'm healthy" now.

"He hasn't said anything to me," Krause said when asked about the comments. "We spent a lot of money to bring everybody back and try to win a championship. I don't know anything about it."

Pippen told McDill his anger had boiled over a September letter Krause faxed him warning him not to play in his own charity game in the United Center. "He said he would fine me. Can you believe it?" Pippen said.

"It was a league mandate that I send that letter," Krause said.

The good news for the Bulls was that they got a second straight road victory, 103-88, that Sunday against the Kings, and their defense showed some real teeth. Randy Brown, a former King, had a strong game, and Kukoc scored 18 to help Jordan with the scoring burden.

But the team training room was the scene of another ugly exchange between Krause and Pippen and Jordan before the game. "Something happened in Sacramento in the training room," Schaefer recalled. "Jerry walked in the training room, and they said something. Michael and Scottie were in there, and he came in and they started going at each other. They get into these sparring things over drafts. Michael likes to poke fun at Jerry over his claims of drafting and finding Earl Monroe and different people like that. Michael gave a little jab that day at Krause for claiming that he discovered Scottie. Something was said that kind of set Scottie off."

Jordan had always found it amusing that Krause claimed to have discovered Monroe, a Hall of Famer, when the Bullets took him with the overall number two pick in the 1967 draft. Krause, though, took immense pride in being what he figured was one of the first scouts to spot Monroe playing for Winston-Salem State. Krause said coach Gene Shue and other members of the Bullets front office weren't as enamored of Monroe, but Krause said he persuaded them to take the high-scoring guard by offering to give up his salary for months until Monroe showed that he was indeed a worthy draft pick.

"I think that whole thing with Michael stems from Earl Monroe," Krause said. "I used to needle him. I used to say, 'Someday you might be as good as Earl Monroe. You remind me of Earl and Elgin. You're a combination of Earl Monroe and Elgin Baylor, and you might be as good as both of them someday. Earl did it on the ground. You're doing it in the air. Elgin was the first one to do it in the air. You remind me of him.' And then every time after that, 'He'd say, 'That fuckin' Monroe.' Then, he'd say, 'Where'd you take, Monroe? Second in the draft? Big fuckin' deal?'

"Well, he has no comprehension of what it took to get Earl Monroe," Krause said.

Again, these spats might seem almost foolish to outside observers, but when their egos and personalities collided, Krause and Jordan and Pippen were a volatile mix.

With an 8-5 record, the Bulls set out for Seattle, the scene of their strangest hour. On the flight up, they partied to celebrate another win. Although the news of Pippen's comments had yet to hit the streets, he partied a bit too much, perhaps over his recent freedom of expression.

"It was a trigger to a very big event this year that was rather embarrassing," Jackson said. "Unfortunately for the players, it was an opportunity for them to unload against Jerry. It set about a mechanism between the two of us. It was embarrassing. I had to discipline the players about it, or else. And risk losing by standing in between (them and management) on what they considered an affront to their world. Or I could sit there and incur the embarrassment that followed. For the most part, I pulled them aside and talked to them personally about it. Not to do this because it's embarrassing to the whole bus basically."

When the team landed in Seattle, there were two buses waiting to carry them to their hotel, one for the players and coaches and one for the broadcasters and staff people. Krause chose to ride the team bus.

"Scottie began his tirade right after that," Jackson said. "That was the thing that sprung it all open."

Obviously intoxicated, Pippen began yelling at Krause about signing him to a new contract or trading him. The harangue went on and on and turned increasingly uglier.

"Why don't you trade me?" Pippen screamed.

"I finally turned around," Jackson said, "and grabbed a bottle of beer and held it up to Pippen and pointed to it like, 'Beers. You've had too many beers to drink.' Joe Kleine thought I was toasting him. He said, 'Were you toasting Scottie? I've never seen anything like that.' I said, 'No, I was holding up a beer and pointing at it, saying, You've had too many. You better quiet down. I didn't want to have to get up.

"This is beyond what normally goes," Jackson said. "I didn't like it at all. Jerry said, 'Don't worry about it. I can take it. Don't worry about it at all.'"

"With Scottie, that meant nothing to me," Krause said later. "He was drunk, and he thought the best way to get out of here was to piss me off more."

"These days and age, if you stare at a guy something can be said," Ron Harper said of the incident. "I think that Scottie was just letting some of his frustrations out. So he said some things."

"It was the venting of his frustrations," Jordan agreed. "I think it's devastating the relationship between the two of them. I don't think Scottie can ever overcome that."

Asked later about his conflicts with Krause, Pippen replied, "I can't say exactly where they come from. We don't have any type of relationship. There are a lot of little things that have gotten to the point where they've turned into things that are big."

"I'm not quite sure what cracked in Seattle," Chip Schaefer said. "I'm not sure it was alcohol. I don't know if it was a combination of things. Something snapped hard. We all know it was an accumulation of the trade stuff."

"That's something that we will never understand," Jordan said later when asked about Pippen's relationship with Krause. "How that relationship formed and bridges were burned. The situation deteriorated even more when I was gone from the game and then even more when I came back. That's one thing I can't comment on. But we all have differences with management and certainly with Jerry Krause. Some of us can deal with it in different ways. Believe me, when I step on the basketball court, the last person I think about that I'm playing for is Jerry Krause."

Certainly part of the situation was Pippen's anger and bitterness over the contract he had signed in 1991. Considered one of the NBA's 50 greatest players ever, Pippen was ranked 122nd on the league's 1998 salary list. He had put the financial issues aside and focused all his energy on making the team a winner. He had done this thinking the team would eventually reward him. But instead the signals he received every summer from Krause's actions was that the team continually shopped him around in trades. The one thing that Pippen really wanted, beyond pay commensurate with his ability, was the respect and honor of staying with one team his whole career.

"Scottie has always held a real good idea about his place in basketball history," said McDill, who has covered the team for more than a decade. "And he thinks a player who stays with one organization his entire career has a better reputation after they're done than a player who gets traded. He's always wanted to be one of those guys who gets to play his entire career with one team. But in this situation he's being pushed out in a lot of ways."

"From my standpoint, I would love to have finished my career in Chicago," Pippen said. "It's a great tribute. And to go out on your own and not be forced out of the game."

That, in part, was his motivation for putting aside his feelings about his contract. But he felt Reinsdorf and Krause had responded to his show of good will and effort by again trying to trade him. "I had accepted the fact that I was fairly underpaid and that with the way the new collective bargaining agreement was done, it was something I was gonna have to deal with," Pippen said. "It was a process, something I was gonna have to deal with. So, you know, just go ahead and play the game."

"He definitely wants the respect, and he deserves it," Jordan said of Pippen. "I think the thing that pisses him off more is that at no time did they ever put me on the trading block. And the things that he's done, they put him on the trading block."

"Babe Ruth was traded twice," Krause responded. "Wilt Chamberlain was traded. There have been very few guys through the years who haven't been traded."

(Krause didn't note that their teams suffered terribly after Ruth and Chamberlain were traded.)

"Scottie Pippen was a great player," Krause said. "He was one of the few players who truly excited me. He's still a fine player. But, as far as trading anybody goes, I have learned that the organization has to come first. Now, Michael can never be traded. But I would have to add that any deal we'd ever talked about was somebody who would have to be a knockout for us."

As for Krause, his biggest irritation was what he saw as Pippen's whining over the 1991 contract. At the time, Pippen was coming off a serious back injury and wanted a long-term contract to protect his future. Sitting in his office during an interview, Krause recalled, "I sat right here with Scottie Pippen and said, 'Don't sign this seven-year contract. Don't sign it. It's stupid.' He said, 'No, I want the security.' So I said, 'Then don't come back to me.'

"The players can tell you this," Krause said. "When they're ready to sign a contract, I take the pen out of their hands and say, 'Look, we fairly negotiated this. Your agent did a fine job. We did a fine job. But if you don't like this, don't sign the damn thing. Give me the pen back. Because what I don't want you doing is coming to me next year or the year after, because we ain't going to renegotiate. You sign it, you live with it. You have two bad years, three bad years, we live with it. You have three great years, we live with it the same way. Don't come back to me.'

"I've never had a player give me the pen back," the GM said.

Pippen's 1991 deal also included a large portion of the money deferred. Krause said that by 1994, when it became apparent that Pippen had agreed to an inferior deal, the player asked to move the deferred sum into current dollars. "Scottie came to us," Krause said. "They had a lot of money deferred in that contract. They came to us and wanted the deferred money brought up to current, and it was quite a bit of money. And we said, 'All right, this is the end of the talk till the end of the contract. I'll never talk about this again. It's over. I'm done.' We brought the deferred money current, and three weeks later he was talking like a magpie.

"So you can understand," the GM said, "why I have hard feelings at times. And the money we brought up to current was in seven figures."

He also pointed out that the Bulls had given "Rabbi trusts" to both Pippen and Horace Grant early in their careers. Those trusts or deferred annuities didn't count against the salary cap at the time and were later ruled illegal by the league. But Pippen's and Grant's remain in effect because they were grandfathered in before the league's ruling, Krause said. "Twenty to 30 years down the road, they got annuities coming in. They're like tax free annuitities, because they're not taxing. The organization loses money on the deal, because the organization pays the taxes on it. Other general managers for other teams say they won't do it anymore because it now counts against their salary caps. But we did it for Scottie and Horace. We were so good to players that the league outlawed it."

Pippen said that in place of the money, he would have been pleased with a simple "thank you" from Krause or Reinsdorf. But neither man ever expressed their appreciation for Pippen's leadership role with the team while Jordan was gone from the game or for Pippen's unselfish approach once the superstar returned in 1995.

"Not to this day," Pippen would say later. "I would think you would do that. That's good manners. But this team has gotten so much success. It's like Krause said, 'It's this organization that's been able to win, not just the players.'"

In fact, he had not spoken to Reinsdorf in several years, since a chance encounter at a White Sox game three or four summers before the incident in Seattle.

So the anger had built in Pippen until the alcohol emboldened him to unleash it on Krause in Seattle. As it was, Pippen might have been able to undo some of the damage the next morning when he again encountered Krause on the team bus headed to practice.

"Good morning, Scottie," Krause said.

"Go to hell, Jerry," Pippen replied.

Upon hearing that Pippen had made trade demands to the media, Jackson tried to make light of it, knowing that the emotional Pippen was capable of misspeaking, particularly if reporters were gouging his sensitivity with questions. "I think he's just joking the press, personally, and throwing a barb out there," the coach told reporters that Tuesday in practice.

"We know that he's not happy with his contract," Jordan said. "He didn't have to go public, but he did. I'm not shellshocked by anything that happens. This organization is at a crossroads. The future is in front of them. Sometimes, decisions get made for business or personal reasons and not basketball."

Then Seattle forward Vin Baker weighed in on the issue. "He is one of the top three or four players in basketball," he said of Pippen. "The Bulls couldn't have won all those championships without him."

"I'm not surprised he wants to be traded," Harper told reporters. "He feels they are not loyal to him and he has been loyal to them. He has played hurt; he has won five championships. He feels they should come out and do something for him."

Pippen responded to Jackson's comments by saying he was not just trying to make things interesting. "I think I've been treated very unfairly by this organization and . . . it's gotten to the point now I don't see myself carrying on with it," Pippen told reporters. "I would rather leave things as I can remember them as a player and go on. It's very difficult. I have a lot of respect for teammates and fans in Chicago. I've enjoyed my 10 years playing (there). I never saw the day when I would have to turn the other cheek, it just sort of came to that."

He was asked what he would do if Krause didn't trade him before the league's February trading deadline. "I don't know," he said. "I'll come to that bridge when I cross it."

"You never close doors," Krause told reporters that same day in response to questions about his plans. "However, we spent a tremendous amount of money to bring this team back intact. It would take a knockout deal for us to trade any key guy on our team. If somebody doesn't knock us out, I'm not going to trade Scottie."

"For Scottie's situation," Jackson said later, "everything kind of broke. The venom kind of broke, and he said, 'I can't play for this team anymore.' He had crossed a bridge with the organization. It was very disappointing. And it took him a while. We had to come back here and really work with Scottie."

"That doesn't mean you have to leave the team," Jackson told him.

"Scottie thought he had shown himself the door, because he had had too much to drink," the coach explained. "It was over the edge."

The team returned to Chicago just before Thanksgiving, and Jackson arranged for the team's therapist to spend some time with Pippen counseling him on his anger. Over the break, Pippen phoned Jackson late one night for a long discussion during which the coach realized that Pippen seemed fairly set in his position not to play for the Bulls again. The coach knew that the team couldn't be successful without Pippen, that changing his mind would take the best efforts of a variety of people, including Jordan, Harper, Jackson himself and several teammates.

"Unfortunately, it took him a while," Jackson said. "He wasn't ready to play for another two months. And so it was a situation where he had time to cool out, to look at it and say, 'Well, my options aren't very good. I really don't have another place to go, and this is the right thing to do.'"

"We let Scottie be Scottie," Harper later said, "and let him grow into what he will put himself into. We all are by his side."

Part of the strategy, though, included Jackson and Jordan openly expressing their displeasure with Pippen's position. That Monday, December 1st, the coach and star player both suggested that they felt betrayed by Pippen's demands. "It's all right to hold it against Scottie," Jackson told reporters. "We care about Scottie, but we're going to hold this against Scottie because he's walking out on us, there's no doubt about that. Some things are personal and some things are public. Publicly, we like Scottie, but personally there's always going to be a . . . residual effect of having gone to bat for Scottie."

Jordan had already told reporters the previous Saturday that he was "disappointed, very disappointed, that (Pippen) hasn't been able to put aside his dealings with management."

Jackson and Jordan said they wouldn't have returned to the team if they had known Pippen was going to leave. "There is that kind of feeling: 'Hey, we came back to do this job together and Scottie ducked out the door,'" Jackson said.

"It would have made a big difference in terms of me and Phil and a lot of other players," Jordan said.

Jackson recalled for reporters that Jordan had come out of retirement in 1995 due in part to Pippen's great urging. "I don't think Michael forgets the fact that when Scottie was here alone in '94 and '95, that he was . . . saying, 'Come on back, come on back, Michael, and help me out with this load,'" Jackson said. "So I'm sure Michael's going to get back at Scottie, hold his feet to the fire."

Resolving the issue could take six weeks or more, the coach pointed out, and the team could become greatly affected by the distraction.

A little more than a week after Pippen's explosive verbal attack against Krause, Latrell Sprewell of the Golden State Warriors ignited a media firestorm by attacking coach P.J. Carlesimo and choking him at practice, then leaving the building only to return later and throw punches at the coach. The entire incident, Sprewell said later, was aimed at forcing the team to trade him.

The Pippen incident was far too private for any of his teammates to discuss publicly. Still it seemed obvious that Jordan was speaking subtly to his teammate when reporters asked him to comment on the Sprewell incident.

"I've been angry at coaches," Jordan said. "I've been angry at people. I've been able from the teachings and learnings of my background to control myself. Each and every person is different. I'm not saying I haven't been angry enough to think about doing certain things. But also I've been smart enough to think about the alternatives that action would cause. Some people do lose their cool. Some people don't think about those alternatives, the repercussions of their actions."

The hopeful sign, for Dennis Rodman at least, came that Wednesday when the Bulls traveled to Boston to play the Celtics and Pippen went along for the ride. "He's here tonight because he still wants to be part of the team," Rodman told reporters.

Asked if the situation was a distraction, Rodman replied, "It can't be. We're grown men playing a game, and we're getting paid lots of money. We have to be able to put the distraction aside and go out and work. If Scottie doesn't come back, that's his choice. You have to live with your own choices. For me, my choices paid off. Some people might not like the choices I've made, but they've definitely paid off. It's a different situation with Scottie."

One of Pippen's ways of dealing with the anger was to pick up the phone and call Reinsdorf for their first chat in a couple of years. "He just wanted to be traded," Reinsdorf said. "He said he hated Krause. He couldn't even refer to him by name. He kept calling him 'your general manager.'"

Reinsdorf said he told Pippen that Krause hadn't been shopping him around in trades but merely listening to other teams' offers.

"I talked to him for about 20 minutes, and he was supposed to call me back but he never did," Pippen revealed later. "He just sort of talked his way around some things. I'm still waiting on that call."

"It's a test, right?" "Isn't everything?"
— *The Devil's Advocate*

8/ December's Children

Over the years, Michael Jordan had entertained a succession of young players touted as the next apparition of his greatness. The media heralded the coming of one after another until the role itself took on a name — "Heir Jordan." As the original rebuffed each and every one of the imitators and successors year after year, the process took on a strange feel, sort of like a convention of Elvis impersonators in Vegas.

Still, the NBA from its earliest days had been a business that survived on star power. Even before the Jordan era there had been a mentality of "who's next?" As Jordan neared the end of his career, that question only intensified.

In the early 1990s, Southern Cal's Harold Miner had the sad misfortune of being labeled "Baby Jordan" and believing it. Grant Hill, too, labored under the hype as a Detroit Piston rookie in 1994, although time revealed he was a player more along the lines of Scottie Pippen. Jerry Stackhouse followed Hill into this mire of embarrassment in 1996, and in December 1997, it was Kobe Bryant's turn.

This time around, though, Jordan himself did a doubletake at the similarities. Chicago reporters noted that the 19-year-old Bryant even had the demeanor of a young Jordan in his interview mannerism. But the real comparisons came from Bryant's game itself. Not the defense, and certainly not the competitive maturity. Bryant was, after all, only 19.

But the offensive moves were another story.

"He's got a lot of 'em," Jordan himself admitted.

Los Angeles Lakers guard Nick Van Exel liked to joke that it could all be attributed to the Jordan highlight videotape that he loaned to Bryant in the fall of 1996, just days after Bryant joined the team as an 18-year-old rookie out of Lower Merion High School in Pennsylvania. "I gave him a highlight tape of Mike, and I ain't seen it yet. That was last year," Van Exel said, laughing.

Over the first few months of the 1997-98 season it became clear that Bryant had spent quite a bit of time studying the tape, because he had just about all of Jordan's moves down pat, even the famous post-up gyrations where Jordan would twitch and fake his opponents into madness.

In fact, the young Bryant was doing such a fine job in only his second season in the league that, heading into the matchup with the Bulls, many observers were touting him for the Sixth Man Award. Through the first two months of the season, when the Lakers were hampered by injuries to center Shaquille O'Neal, Bryant had scored at a clip of better than 19 points per game, the top average of the NBA's non-starters.

As a result, his flashy play generated a substantial amount of hype for the Lakers' mid-December visit to the United Center. How would Bryant do matched up against Jordan? That question offered a bit of comic relief to a Bulls team still laboring under the anxiety of the Pippen question.

In truth, the real issue for the Bulls was their difficulty scoring. The Lakers were a young, athletic team that flaunted a wicked running attack. The Bulls, meanwhile, still lacked the transition game that Pippen's defense brought them. As a result, they got no easy baskets and few easy wins.

Fortunately, just before the Lakers arrived Chicago got a preliminary test against another running team, the Phoenix Suns, and promptly whipped them in the United Center, one of the first signs the Bulls had begun to find a way to adjust to life without Pippen. It was obvious they would never get near a championship level without the star forward, but they could still compete.

The Lakers made that discovery just moments into their meeting with Chicago. Van Exel admitted there was a certain look in Jordan's eyes that told them the contest would be decided early. Indeed, the Bulls controlled the tempo, established a limited transition game and iced the Lakers by the end of the first quarter, which was fine with the United Center fans because it meant they could sit back and watch the individual duel between Jordan and Bryant.

"Michael loves this stuff," Ron Harper said of the meeting between the two. It was a scenario that Harper knew well. As a young, high-flying star for the Cleveland Cavaliers in the late 1980s, Harper was considered an early Jordan heir, until a knee injury forced Harper to remake his game. "(Bryant) is a very young player who someday may take his throne," Harper said, "but I don't think Michael's ready to give up his throne yet. He came out to show everybody that he's Air Jordan still."

While the outcome was a 20-point win for the Bulls, the contest between master and student generated a few sparks. Jordan scored 36, and Bryant produced a career-high 33. It was a night for highlight clips with both players dancing in the post, draining jumpers from the perimeter and weaving their way to handsome dunks. "I had that same type of vibrancy when I was young," Jordan told reporters afterward. "It's exciting to match wits against physical skills, knowing that I've been around the game long enough that if I have to guard a Kobe Bryant . . . I can still hold my own."

Jordan had attempted to show restraint. "It was a challenge because of the hype," he said, "but it's also a challenge not to get caught up in the hype, not to make it a one-on-one competition between me and Kobe. I felt a couple of times that it felt like that, but I had to refrain from that, especially when he scored on me. I felt a natural tendency to want to go back down to the other end and score on him. . . . But you can't. It takes a lot of discipline not to get caught up in that individuality of our games. You stick close to the system and you think team first and try to do your job."

It was especially fun for Jordan because the Lakers showed a disinclination to double-team him. "The urges were there tonight," he admitted. "Mentally, I think I'm tough enough to take on those challenges because I know so much about the game and I can make the adjustments. I feel if they're not going to double team me then I have the advantage. Defensively, I just have to get used to playing against a player who has skills similar to mine. I try to pick a weakness and exploit it."

Bryant's specific weakness was his defense, no surprise considering his age and experience, Jordan said.

If nothing else, the circumstances revealed that Bryant possessed certain Jordanlike qualities. "This kid is really, really driven. I haven't seen it in a player in a long time, not to that extent," said Laker assistant coach Larry Drew.

"Kobe's one of the most competitive guys that we've ever had on our team," said longtime Laker trainer Gary Vitti, "to the point where when we practice and we scrimmage and his team loses, he's uncomfortable to be around. In simple practice pickup games he gets mad, you can't talk to him. He goes over and sits on the sideline, and he's mad. Really mad. That's his competitive nature. He just wants to win all the time. You need somebody like that to elevate your practices."

"It's always been there since I was four or five years old," Bryant said of his competitive nature. "I can't explain it. You just don't feel right if you lose."

The observations sounded hauntingly like Bulls coaches talking about Jordan in 1985-86. Jordan, though, came to the NBA after three years of undergraduate study under Dean Smith at North Carolina. Bryant, instead, took the surprising shortcut of the '90s, going directly from high school into the pro game. Just months after taking his last high school exam and taking diva-in-waiting Brandy to his senior prom, Bryant joined the Lakers as a first-round draft pick (13th overall) to become one of the youngest players in NBA history.

As early as his ninth grade year, Bryant had begun thinking about turning pro after reading about the prodigy young Magic Johnson was, going into the pros as a 19-year-old. Throughout the 6-6 Bryant's career at Lower Merion High in the Philadelphia suburbs, there was simply no opposition that could contain him.

With excellent grades and college board scores, he could have gone to any college he wanted, including LaSalle, where his father, Joe "Jelly Bean" Bryant, who had played professional ball eight years in the NBA and eight more in Europe, was an assistant coach.

The young Bryant's polished offensive skills meant that he could hold his own in those high-test Philly pickup games that featured big-name college talent and occasional 76ers. All of which meant that he came into the NBA with a certain confidence, almost an air of assumption.

It wasn't an entirely smooth ride, though. First came the injuries that got his season off to a late start. Then, even when he did return to active duty, he found Laker coach Del Harris using him sparingly, partly because the pro game's busy schedule allows so little time for practice and developing young players. Bryant went on to average 7.1 points while getting to play about 15 minutes a night his first season.

The primary reason for his dramatic improvement his second season was the work Bryant put in over the summer. He took a quick promotional trip to Europe and completed a summer school course in Italian at UCLA, but beyond that he spent his days and nights developing his game.

"It's non paralleled," Del Harris said of Bryant's work ethic, another reason people compare him to Jordan. "He doesn't waste a minute. Before practice, after practice, during the summer, whenever. Kobe doesn't waste any motion."

"I drive myself," Bryant explained, saying that work was more important than play. "I like to go out and have fun and have a good time. But I just don't feel right. While I'm out having a good time, I could be playing basketball or something, could be lifting weights. I could be working on something."

His coaches saw this intensity as his response to the challenge of the NBA. "As a rookie he had the chance to kind of grow up a little bit,"

Larry Drew said. "It was a tough year for him last year, but he handled it well. He's got that one year under his belt. There was a little bit of maturity that goes along with that. He got to see what the whole NBA life was about. He made a good adjustment. He's not surprised by many things any more. And I try to stay in his ear as much as I can about things that happen out on the floor. He absorbs it, and he very much wants to learn."

Indeed, in the fourth quarter of his game against Jordan, Bryant stopped the Chicago star to ask a question about posting up. "He ask me about my post-up move, in terms of, 'Do you keep your legs wide? Or do you keep your legs tight?' Jordan said. "It was kind of shocking. I felt like an old guy when he asked me that.

"I told him on the offensive end you always try to feel and see where the defensive player is. In the post-up on my turnaround jump shot, I always use my legs to feel where the defense is playing so I can react to the defense."

Jordan added that Bryant's biggest challenge would be "harnessing what he knows and utilizing what he's got and implementing it on the floor. That's tough. That's experience. That's things that Larry Bird and Magic Johnson all taught me. There's no doubt that he has the skills to take over a basketball game."

Bryant said his answer to Jordan was to "try to play my heart out. Michael loves challenges. He loves to answer the bell. But at the same time, my father always taught me growing up that you never back down to no man, no matter how great of a basketball player he is. If he's fired up, you get fired up. You go out there, and you go skill for skill and you go blow for blow."

Jordan himself admitted to being a bit awed by the aerial talent on display. His Airness confided, "I asked Scottie Pippen, 'Did we used to jump like that? I don't remember that.' He said, 'I think we did, but it's so long ago I can't remember it.'"

The situation left Jordan feeling a little like he had been forced to play defense against himself. "I felt like I was in the same shoes of some of the other players I've faced," Jordan explained. "He certainly showed signs that he can be a force whenever he's in the game. He has a lot of different looks. As an offensive player, you want to give a lot of different looks, so that the defense is always guessing."

Given Bryant's abilities, Jordan quipped that the next time instructional questions came up in the middle of a game he would charge Bryant for the lessons.

"That just comes from competitiveness," Bryant explained about asking Jordan for the tips. "You want to learn as much as you can. He told me a lot of things. I'll use them."

What else did he learn from his first major encounter with Michael?

"He does a great job of initiating the offense, making the proper cuts, getting his teammates open, whether it was with back picks or moving without the ball," Bryant said of Jordan. "Even when he doesn't have the ball, he makes himself visible, makes himself a threat, allowing guys like Luc Longley and Steve Kerr to get open. Those are the things that I learned from him, how to be a threat without the basketball."

Especially impressive was Bryant's ability to post up effectively, a feature that most guards don't share with Jordan. "He's a very good low-post ball player, because he has good foot work," Larry Drew said of Bryant. "He's good on both blocks, and he really, really uses both hands well. His left hand is solid. He has so much confidence in taking that little lefthand jump shot that it's just unbelievable."

Perhaps the main lesson for Bryant was that the little things add up. In the second period, Jordan caught the young Laker off balance, went up for a jumper and drew the foul. It was a classic case of the veteran schooling the understudy. But Bryant went right back at him.

"That's the whole purpose of the game," the 19-year-old said. "If somebody scores on you, you go right back at 'em and try to make 'em work back down on the other end.

"He's a very smart competitor," Bryant said of Jordan. "I could tell that he thinks the game, whether it's the tactical things or little strategies he employs on the court. I'm checking him out and analyzing him, so that I can do the same thing. But he's just better at it, because he's been doing it awhile. He's very smart, very technical. You just don't naturally acquire that. You can go into the NBA and be in the league a while and play games, but if you try to learn, and really push yourself to learn the game, not just from a physical standpoint but from a mental standpoint, you can get better."

Beyond the Bryant interlude, December for the Bulls was a month marked by a quiet nervousness. Would Pippen return to the team, or was the championship run about to come to a premature end? Unable to answer that question, Jackson and his players had to turn their attention to a host of milestones:

• On December 5th, the team played its first home game in three weeks and celebrated by holding Milwaukee to 62 points, setting a Bulls team record for the lowest output allowed an opponent. Surprisingly, despite Pippen's absence, Chicago continued to lead the league in fewest points allowed. "They're playing better," Pippen said. "The stuff surrounding me sort of put them back on their heels. It took their mind off what they wanted to do. I think they're going to be fine."

• In a December 9th win over New York, Jordan passed Moses Malone (27,409 points) to take over third place on the NBA's list of all-time scorers. Just two weeks earlier Jordan had passed Elvin Hayes (27,313) to take over fourth place. (Wilt Chamberlain is number two on the list with 31,419 points, and Kareem Abdul-Jabbar is first with 38,387).

• The game against Phoenix on December 15th marked the 500th consecutive sellout for the Bulls, the longest such streak in the league.

It was no coincidence that the next game, the Lakers contest, brought Jackson's 500th regular season victory as the Bulls coach. He had reached the milestone sooner than any coach in league history, a fact that didn't help the public understand Krause's apparent desire to see the coach leave. "To get the guys, when they have one ring or two rings, to go out and play hard, there's the challenge," Clippers coach Bill Fitch, who had coached Jackson in college at the University of North Dakota, told reporters. "He ought to be able to coach here as long as he wants to coach."

JACKSON

After opening the season with eight wins and seven losses, the Bulls found some balance under Jackson and won nine of their next 11 games. "People think this team is easy to coach because of MJ, but Phil's had to hold us together this year," Ron Harper told reporters. "Even when Pip is healthy, this team isn't as easy to coach as every-body thinks. We have a lot of egos to manage."

Jackson had accomplished that with an open management/ open communication style that left his players singing his praises. He was also secure enough to give his assistant coaches wide latitude in their involvement, exemplified by Winter's free hand in running the offense.

The son of a Pentecostal preacher, Jackson had been raised in Montana in a strict, reclusive world that left him longing for escape by the end of high school. He found it in the athletic scholarship offered by Bill Fitch at the University of North Dakota. The 6-foot-8 Jackson developed into a two-time NCAA Division II All-American, a legiti-mate pro prospect, the only problem being that few pro scouts found their way out to North Dakota. One who did was an enterprising young Baltimore Bullets representative named Jerry Krause, who was entertained by Fitch's trick of having Jackson sit in the back seat of a

Chevrolet and use his long arms to grab the steering wheel or unlock the front doors on either side. "I had quite a wingspan," Jackson recalled with a chuckle.

After his 13-year playing career, Jackson had worked as an assistant coach and broadcaster for the New Jersey Nets before moving on to become head coach of the Albany Patroons in the Continental Basketball Association for five seasons. In 1984, Jackson's Patroons won the CBA title, and the next season he was named CBA Coach of the Year. He was doing a brief stint coaching in Puerto Rico when Jerry Krause contacted him about an assistant coaching job with the Bulls in 1985.

"I had wanted to draft Phil for Baltimore in the second round in 1967," Krause once recalled. "We took a gamble on another player, and New York got Phil. I kept up with Phil as a player through the years. We'd talk from time to time, and I followed his coaching career in the CBA. When I got the job in Chicago in 1985, I talked to him again. I told him I needed scouting reports on the CBA. Within a week, I had typewritten reports on the whole league, detail on every player. What I saw in Phil was an innate brightness. I thought that eventually he'd become the governor of North Dakota. I saw a lot of Tony LaRussa in him. A feel for people. A brightness. A probing mind."

When Krause fired Doug Collins in 1989, he knew that the 43-year-old Jackson was the perfect coach for the Bulls. He had been a member of Reinsdorf's beloved Knicks when they won the NBA title in 1973. Yet Jackson actually cited the Knicks' 1970 season, when he was on the injured list after undergoing major back surgery, as the breakthrough season in his pro basketball career. That year he sat in the stands at Madison Square Garden watching Knicks' coach Red Holtzman's every move. It was then, Jackson wrote in *Maverick*, his autobiography, that he came to understand the game. That season also laid the foundation for the philosophy he sought to instill when he became head coach of the Bulls in 1989.

"The Knicks in the late sixties and early seventies were one of the dominant teams in the NBA," Jackson explained, "yet they were a collection of very good individual players but without a dominant star that could change the context of the game. The whole of idea of the Knicks playing together was how well the ball moved, how well they played together defensively, the fact that any of the five players could take a key shot down the stretch. It was a difficult team in that regard to defend against. They were unselfish, and Red Holtzman, the mentor, was really the guy who taught us that. Surprisingly enough, he taught us teamwork through defense.

"That was the concept when I came to the Bulls," Jackson said, "that the ball had to move. They all had to touch the ball regardless of who was gonna score. Everybody had to become interdependent upon each other and trusting on the offensive end. Defensively, we were gonna play full-court pressure. We were gonna make defense where we started our teamwork."

"I think Phil came in," Tex Winter recalled, "with the basis of some very sound philosophy. I mean the philosophy of life. He recognizes that there are a whole lot of things more important than basketball. He doesn't take himself too seriously. We all take basketball pretty seriously at times. Even then, he's inclined to relax. I'm amazed at times in the course of the game how he sits back and lets things happen. He likes people to be able to solve their own problems, and so he gives his players the reins. On the other hand, when he sees they're out of control, then he starts to pull them in a little bit. I think this is his strength, the way he handles the players and his motivation, his personal relationship with the players. That's borne out by the fact that they'll accept his coaching, they'll accept the criticism, even though sometimes it's pretty severe with certain players. They accept that because it's who he is, because he's Phil."

"I've always been impressed by Phil," former Bull John Paxson said. "He's an intellectual guy, and I think that's the first thing that stood out to me. You don't run into too many intellectual guys in the NBA. The thing that impressed me is that he hasn't allowed this game to consume him. It can be so consuming for a coach. But Phil has other interests. His family has always been important to him. And he has never let the game take a toll on him mentally."

That mental strength, which stemmed from Jackson's strong affinity for Zen philosophy, would play a huge role keeping the Bulls together amidst the charged atmosphere surrounding the team. "We've been together a long time, especially Phil and me," Tex Winter said of the circumstances in 1997. "Nine years. I think we understand each other pretty well. Phil is the kind of guy who has the ability to not let things distract him. My Lord, I couldn't do it. If I were the head coach, I'd be a maniac by now. And my whole team would be out of whack. That's Phil's strength. This Rodman thing, all the things that come down along these lines, Phil kinda just handles it in a very natural, easy way.

"He's very good at handling distractions," Winter added. "As far as next season is concerned, he's said very little about it. It doesn't seem to bother him one bit about what is coming down. I've told him at times that maybe he might not be concerned but some of his staff members might be. On the other hand he sets the tone. He says, 'We're just playing this thing out. Let's worry about today. Let's don't worry about tomorrow.'"

Despite the potential conflicts of their success, the Bulls got along far better than the average NBA team. But winning championships had required more than a "better-than-average" approach. It had required a supreme chemistry. Jackson, of course, was a master at pulling all the disparate elements together. Perhaps there was no better example of this than the team's late-season signee during the 1997 playoff drive, Brian Williams. He, too, was a free agent, but salary cap restrictions and league compensation rules virtually assured that he would have to move on to another team at the end of the season. Never one to show a fondness for coaches (he had played for four different teams in his six-year career), he had nonetheless taken an immediate shining to Jackson.

"He's an excellent coach," Williams said. "In my time in the league, he's the most thorough, the most understanding coach I've been around."

Matt Steigenga, another late-season signee, expressed a similar appreciation for Jackson, especially his knack for using a player's mistakes for teaching instead of humiliation. "He doesn't berate guys, doesn't get on them," Steigenga said. "But guys still know when they mess up. I had a college coach, if he wasn't yelling there was something wrong. When he stopped yelling at a player, he didn't care about that player any more. Phil's the other way. He rarely will scream or yell or belittle a player. But he really gets a guy to see his mistake and learn from it. His mental approach and mental prowess comes through. He has that grip on players, that feeling of force. You know this man is able to lead."

Jackson liked to call his approach "Zen Christian," a mingling of his fundamentalist upbringing with his love of Buddhist and Native American culture. His strategies for success included preaching to his players about the great white buffalo or giving them obscure books to read or having them pause amid the looniness of the NBA for a meditation session. On more than one occasion, Jackson's approach has left his players shaking their heads in amusement. "He's our guru," Michael Jordan quipped when asked about Jackson's quirkiness in early 1996. "He's got that yen, that Zen stuff, working in our favor."

But make no mistake, Jackson was so compelling a figure that, while his players may not have accepted each and every of his unconventional remedies, they showed an utter and complete faith in him. And they understood when Jackson talked of the spiritual connection to the game. Jordan credited just that connection with showing him how to relate with less-talented teammates. "I think Phil really has given me a chance to be patient and taught me how to understand the supporting cast of teammates and give them a chance to improve," Jordan said.

"He's an interesting guy," Steve Kerr said of Jackson. "He keeps things very refreshing for us all season. He keeps things fun. He never loses sight of the fact that basketball is a game. It's supposed to be fun. He doesn't let us forget about that. But at the same time, this is our job, too, and he doesn't let us forget about that either. The amount of work involved and what it takes to win, and finally the feeling of success when you do win. He's constantly reminding us of all that."

That's not to say that Jackson would hesitate to get in a player's face, Kerr added. "But when he does it you know it's not personal. That's his strength. He always maintains authority without being a dictator. And he always maintains his friendship without kissing up. He just finds that perfect balance, and because of that he always has everybody's respect. And ultimately that's the hardest part of being a coach in the NBA, I think, is having every player's respect."

"Phil understands the game better than most people," observed John Salley, who had played for a variety of coaches. "And he expects certain things that he knows his guys can give him. He gets the utmost respect from his players. A lot of people say Michael really runs the Bulls. But Phil runs this team. He runs the squad. He runs practice. He runs the film sessions. He splices the film. He organizes practice. He dissects the other team we're playing against. He knows his stuff.

"He understands the players' bodies. He understands when not to overuse them. He understands when he can rest you. He knows when to watch enough film. He knows when to push his players, when not to push 'em. He knows who to yell at, who not to yell at. He knows who can take it. And he treats you like a man, as opposed to downplaying you, or talking to you like you're less than him because of his position. He's a great coach. He laughs and smiles at life."

Former Bulls assistant Johnny Bach said one of Jackson's special gifts was the ability to establish a clear team structure. "We have in the league a lot of people who think they're a lot better than they are," Bach said. "And that's what coaches have to deal with. Can you get five people to play a team game when all the rewards seem to be for individual achievement? You're talking about fragile egos. Big egos. People who had status and can lose it in this game so quickly. Phil is great at defining roles and having people face up to what the hierarchy is. Here's Michael. Here's Scottie. And he does it in a very intelligent way. He doesn't do it to put you down. But he clearly addresses the problem."

Jackson knew the faith his players had in him was no small thing. "I believe that there is a tenuous trial sometimes between coaches and players," he said. "I've found that I have the confidence of my group, so that they feel comfortable. And it's not anything where if I try experimental things that they feel threatened or can't deal with it. It's sort of something where I've had an open working forum to try a variety of styles and approaches, all of which seem to be enjoyable to them. The only thing they don't like is monotony and constancy. But we still make one thing constant, and that's fundamentals. The one thing that we always strive for is to make fundamentals and execution a part of our game."

His players used the occasion of his 500th victory to marvel at the circumstances of his impending dismissal. "It baffles me to understand that he's not welcome," Jordan said. "He certainly still knows how to coach the game."

In fact, the Bulls star rated Jackson an equal to the much revered Dean Smith, Jordan's college coach. "I think they're very similar in the fundamental aspects with which they coach the game," Jordan said. "With their caring about the players. Players first, management, everything else is second. I think their dedication to spreading the wealth is very evident. Their overall love for the game. I think you can see it in the way they coach. They're very poised in pressure situations. They don't let the game or the situation speed up their thought process. As a player, if you see that, then you tend to maintain a certain poise in pressure situations. So I think those are key components to winning."

Jackson used the occasion of his 500th win to do something he had said he wouldn't do — take the pressure off of Krause and Reinsdorf. Their selecting him as Bulls coach in 1989 "was a miracle for me," Jackson said. "It's a great success story. A lot happened in this organization that just all clicked: the players, ownership, general manager. Motivation isn't something you teach players. They have to bring that themselves. This organization, Jerry Krause and his staff, have found players who have that kind of motivation."

Asked if he was being "squeezed out," Jackson replied, "I don't think there's any squeezing going on. This is a mutual agreement that we've made, Jerry Reinsdorf and I. We look at it as an opportunity — not as a farewell, see ya' later. This is not a last gasp."

Jordan, though, refused to accept that. "It's too obvious to see the guy's success in such a short amount of time to say, 'Now, we need a change.' It's something deeper than what you see on the basketball court," he told reporters.

The star pointed out that Jackson had guided the Bulls through difficult circumstances after taking over in 1989. "We had coaches coming in and out of here," Jordan said. "We found a good one and we stuck with him and ... he gave stability to my career. We all have so much respect for him."

That respect once again proved to be the bedrock of the Bulls' superior chemistry as they worked their way through yet another challenging season. It could be seen in the excellent year Dennis Rodman was having. "He treats you like a man," the mercurial rebounder said of Jackson. "He lets you be yourself." Rodman's December hair decoration was yellow, with a smiley face in the crown.

"Dennis is staying out of trouble," Jordan pointed out. "We probably expected him to be a pain in the butt this year but he hasn't been. He's just gone out and rebounded and done his job. You have to respect that."

"Dennis has had problems with other coaches, but he knows Phil is on his side," Ron Harper observed.

Jackson, though, pointed out that one of the major differences with Rodman was the behavior clauses in his contract. "The Bulls put (behavior clauses) in the contract," Jackson said. "Rather than being a rebel, he's chosen to do the things that are appropriate. He's having a lot more fun. And he's right back at the top of the league in rebounding."

And wearing a smiley face in his hair. "I love having the most famous hair in the world," Rodman conceded to reporters. "People wonder what's going to happen next. It was Chip Schaefer's doing. Chip told me, 'Be a happy face, shock everybody.' Well, here it is."

Yet all the players knew that Jackson's respect faced a bigger challenge than Rodman's behavior. Much good will would be needed to lure the angry and frustrated Pippen back to the team. Fortunately, Jackson had the substance in abundance and was using it discreetly to pull Pippen back into the team circle. As December passed, there were clear signs that his efforts were working.

In the middle of the month, the forward appeared at the team's annual holiday party, where an 8-year-old boy asked Pippen, "Are you going to get back on the team?"

"Yeah," Pippen replied with a shy, soft smile.

A week and a half later, he began practicing with the Bulls. "I'm just trying to get myself healthy," he said. "If I have to come back and play here then, you know, that may be the way it has to be."

"It's money, blood money."

— *The Devil's Advocate*

9/ The Big Facilitator

It was supposed to be Magic vs. Michael.

At least that was the hype for the 1991 NBA championship series between the Bulls and Los Angeles Lakers. But the outcome of the title bout hinged on a development no one foresaw, least of all the Bulls' coaches, who began the series with the 6-6 Jordan defending the 6-9 Johnson. There were other disparities. Johnson and his Lakers had won five league titles in the 1980s and had appeared in the championship series three other times. Jordan and his Bulls were making their first appearance.

Many observers, such as former Lakers coach Pat Riley, who was broadcasting the series for NBC, figured the Lakers' experience made them a cinch to douse the upstart Bulls despite the fact that Chicago had homecourt advantage. That thinking looked good when Johnson and the Lakers used their experience to steal Game 1 in Chicago Stadium.

Suddenly, the pressure was on the Bulls for Game 2, and they struggled with it. Then, a huge basketball accident occurred. Michael Jordan got into early foul trouble, and forced to make a decision, the Bulls coaches switched the 6-7 Pippen to cover Magic Johnson. In retrospect that would seem logical, but at the time there was an assumption that the 25-year-old Pippen would struggle to handle the wily Johnson, the master point guard of his time.

Just the opposite happened. The long-armed Pippen was on Johnson like a Hydra, and like that, the momentum in the championship series shifted. Pippen harassed Magic into four-of-13 shooting from the floor while Pippen himself scored 20 points with 10 assists and five rebounds as the Bulls won Game 2 in a swarm.

Forget the stats, though. The tale of terror was written on Johnson's face. "I can't believe this is happening," he told reporters as the Bulls swept four straight games from Los Angeles.

"It's true," Phil Jackson said in 1998 when asked if the switch of Pippen covering Johnson was entirely accidental.

"We started to see that we were wearing him down from a physical standpoint," Pippen happily recalled, "especially myself being able to go up and harass him and trying to get him out of their offense. He wasn't as effective as he had been in the past against some teams, being able to post up and take advantage of situations. I saw the frustration there."

Pippen added that as an old man years from now, he'd probably look back on the switch as one of the defining moments in his career and in the history of the team. "It was the first year of being into the Finals and playing against one of the greatest teams with a lot of great players, future Hall of Famers," Pippen said, "and I would have to say that Finals is definitely at the top. Being able to win my first title and playing against guys who I'd always looked up to and idolized. My being switched to cover Magic was important in the series as a whole. We found another guy who could match up with their big guard and kind of wear him down throughout the game.

"It was very important to me personally to have the opportunity to defend someone I'd idolized and watched for so long," he added, "to have that opportunity to step up in such a big game and such an important time of the series, to be able to defend him and to play him as well as I did."

Pippen went on from that series to serve as the point guard leading Chicago to five championships, and in the process, he set himself up for comparisons to Johnson. Both were distinctively tall point guards, what Tex Winter liked to call "big facilitators." Both played essentially point guard on offense and forward on defense. Both led their teams to at least five titles. Both were selected as among the NBA's top 50 players in the league's first 50 seasons. Both were responsible for getting the ball to the premier offensive post weapons of their time. Johnson delivered to Kareem Abdul-Jabbar, and Pippen's target was Jordan, much smaller than Abdul-Jabbar but every bit as dangerous in the post.

"I've always had a lot of respect for Magic," Pippen said. "He always had an all-around game, could handle the ball for his size. I had a lot of respect for that."

The glaring difference between the two was Johnson's flashy passing brilliance, an extension of his sunny personality. Pippen, on the other hand, displayed a passing game as plainly fundamental and efficient as his taciturn interview demeanor.

"Scottie is no where near the passer that Earvin Johnson was," said Ron Harper, Pippen's good friend. "But on the other hand, Earvin Johnson was no where near the athlete that Scottie is."

That athleticism had evidenced itself over the years in his extraordinary defensive ability. Arguably, Pippen had established that he was the game's all-time greatest defensive forward, a force so unique as to be impossible to duplicate.

"In a lot of ways, it's difficult to compare the two," Tex Winter said. Then he proceeded to do it. "Both of them make their teammates better," the 76-year-old assistant observed. "Magic, when he was out there playing with the Lakers, certainly made his teammates much better. And Scottie has that same kind of ability, I think more so than Michael. It's my opinion that there are times — not always certainly — but there's times when Michael detracts from his teammates. You're not gonna find that much in Pippen. He's totally unselfish. Michael should be selfish because he's such a great scorer. Michael is uninhibited, and Michael is gonna look to score most of the time when he's in a position where he thinks he can, whereas Scottie on many occasions will pass up that opportunity just to get his teammates involved.

"And that's what I call a facilitator."

After he had pondered the comparison for a while, Winter concluded, "There certainly is a likeness in many ways. Magic could probably push the ball and key the fast break, for a man his size particularly, better than anybody has in the game of basketball. Tremendous vision, tremendous passing. Scottie really doesn't have that kind of ability, even though Scottie does gravitate to being a guard and does like to handle the ball and push it up the floor. He can't deliver the ball the way Magic did, but on the other hand Scottie is apt to make up for that. For one thing, he may hit a shot for you, a long three-pointer off the break, or he may get the team into the offense."

On the defensive end, Pippen is clearly exceptional, Winter said. "From that standpoint, Scottie has it all over Magic, in my opinion. As a matter of fact, we felt Magic was someone we could take advantage of defensively in that series, because Magic, he's a great team defensive player in that he wants to help and help to the extent that often you can take advantage of him. But Pippen can not only help, he can recover. He can do a job individually on a man, or lay off his man and help with the team defense. Scottie is able to do both, where I don't think Magic really had that kind of ability."

Pippen's overall versatility had been a giant factor in the success of the Bulls, Winter observed. "Phil has been able to utilize his talent to the utmost in that respect. There will be times when Jordan will cover the best player on the floor in crucial situations, but only in crucial situations. There'll be other times when Pippen in placed on someone who is hurting us. Because they're such great players, such great athletes, we've been able to get away with that type of thing."

Growing up in rural Arkansas, Pippen found himself, as did millions of other youths, identifying with Magic Johnson's brilliance. "I think I've definitely taken a lot from his game, learning how to handle the ball," he said. "I'm not the passer. Magic was a definite flashy player. His passes were so creative. Just as a great player like Michael could be creative in doing things from an offensive standpoint, Magic can make a pass just as spectacular as an offensive move."

Perhaps no one appreciated Pippen's greatness more than Jackson. While the coach obviously relished Pippen's role in the 1991 championship series, he also pointed to Pippen's coming of age against the Pistons in the Eastern Conference playoffs that same season.

"The real build up was in that Detroit series when Rodman headbutted him," Jackson recalled. "He got beat up, he got thrown to the floor. He had to guard Laimbeer. He played through a physical, combative series, in which the stories were, 'They'll beat him up, and he'll pussy out in the end and he'll get a migraine headache or something will happen.' They tried to make it a negative thing about Scottie, but the truth was that Scottie was extremely tough and resilient. He has magical games, really big games."

A perfect example was the 1997 championship series, Jackson added. "If anybody looks at Michael's game against Utah last year in Game 5, and sees how Scottie Pippen played in conjunction with Michael Jordan, with Michael just playing offense and Scottie telling him, 'Look, I'll take care of the defense.' He just ran the defense and ran the floor game brilliantly. He played an absolutely terrific ballgame. The combination of the two of them was devastating."

THE PATH TO POWER

Like Rodman, Pippen's journey to the NBA followed an unlikely route. After playing all of his young life in relative basketball obscurity, he quite suddenly and dramatically sprang to the NBA's attention in the spring of 1987. He came from the hamlet of Hamburg, Arkansas, (population 3,394), the baby in Preston and Ethel Pippen's family of a dozen children. "It was fun," Pippen said . "With all those brothers and sisters I always had a friend around."

He attended Hamburg High, where as a junior he hardly got off the bench for the basketball team. As a 6-1, 150-pound senior, he became the school's starting point guard. That failed to bring notice from college recruiters, however. The fall of his junior year, he had agreed to become manager of the football team, and if his prospects for higher education seemed bright, it was there.

Don Dyer, the basketball coach at Central Arkansas, arranged for Pippen to attend school there on a federal grant while serving as manager of the basketball team. "I was responsible for taking care of the equipment, jerseys, stuff like that," Pippen once recalled. "I always enjoyed doing that, just being a regular manager."

"He wasn't recruited by anyone," Dyer once explained. "He was a walk-on, a 6-1 1/2, 150-pound walk-on. His high school coach, Donald Wayne, played for me in college, and I took Pippen as a favor to him. I was prepared to help him through college. I was going to make him manager of the team and help him make it financially through college. When Scottie showed up for college, he had grown to 6-3. I had had a couple of players leave school. I could see a little potential; he was like a young colt."

"I really wasn't that interested in playing," Pippen recalled. "I had gone through some hard times not playing in high school, but my coach had it in his mind that basketball was the way I would get an education."

"By the end of his first season, he had grown to 6-5, and he was one of our best players," Dyer said. "He had a point guard mentality, and we used him to bring the ball up the floor against the press. But I also played him at forward, center, all over the floor."

"I felt myself developing late," Pippen explained. "I kept seeing myself getting better and better. It was a great feeling, like I could be as good as I wanted to be. I developed confidence in my abilities."

For Central Arkansas, Pippen became a two-time NAIA All-American. As a senior he averaged 23.6 points, 10 rebounds and 4.3 assists while shooting 59 percent from the floor and 58 percent from three-point range. NBA scouting guru Marty Blake had gotten a tip about Pippen, which he passed on to the Bulls and other teams. Pippen was invited to the NBA's tryout camps, and the rest of the story became the Bulls' sweet fortune. They selected him fifth overall in the 1987 draft, a story that Jerry Krause relished often with a retelling. NBA scout Marty Blake first alerted Krause about the unknown Pippen, who would later appear in the league's pre-draft camp in Portsmouth, Virginia. Krause made the journey to see Pippen.

"We watched him," Krause later recalled, "and I just got excited. I just got really shook up bad."

Krause left Virginia and informed Doug Collins, who was then coaching the Bulls, that there was a special player available and that Collins should see videotape of Pippen in the NBA's next draft camp, in Hawaii. "When we told Doug Collins about Scottie, he was skeptical," Krause said. "So I put together a video of all the players in the Hawaii tournament and gave it to the coaches. I gave them names and rosters but no real information on the players. We let them see for themselves. After they came out of the video session, I asked if they had any questions, and the first thing out of their mouths was, 'Who the hell is Scottie Pippen?'"

"I'd never heard of him," Jordan said. "He was from an NAIA school."

Krause made numerous moves to get Pippen and later Clemson's Horace Grant in the first round of the draft. "That night," Reinsdorf once recalled, "when the draft was over, we were in the conference room in the old Bulls office with the coaching staff. There were a lot of high fives going around that night because we really felt that we had pulled a coup."

"His is one of those stories that you read about happening somewhere else," said Dyer. "It's rags to riches, a guy coming from nowhere. One of those fantastic stories. Just amazing."

"Honestly, I didn't expect to be drafted that high," Pippen once acknowledged. "I figured after I went through the camps that I'd have the opportunity to be drafted. I didn't know how high."

As a player from a small town and a small school who was suddenly thrust into the spotlight in Chicago, Pippen was understandably lost. But he quickly developed a friendship with the Bulls' other first round pick that year, Horace Grant. They did everything together. Shopped. Dated girls. Partied. They both drove $74,000 Mercedes 560 SELs. They moved within a mile of each other in suburban Northbrook. And eventually, they both got married within a week of each other, serving as each other's best man.

In the Bulls' 1988 yearbook, Pippen's profile contained a question: If you were going to the moon who would you take along? Pippen's answer was, "Horace Grant."

"Scottie is like my twin brother," Grant told reporters.

"We talk about every two hours," Pippen said at the time.

"Just to see what's going on. Horace is my best friend, the closest anyone's ever been to me."

"Scottie called in one day and skipped practice because his cat died," recalled former Bulls trainer Mark Pfeil. "Horace called about 15 minutes later and said he was with Scottie because of the grieving. Johnny Bach, our assistant coach, was absolutely furious. He got Horace on the phone and said, 'You get here. You oughta throw the cat in the garbage can.' Horace, when the team got together, wanted to have a moment of silence for Scottie's cat.

"My first year here you could read their facial expressions like a book," said former Bulls assistant Jim Cleamons. "They were easily frustrated when things did not go right. But over their first three years, they learned how to play, and they learned to keep their composure on the court. They matured and grew more confident."

"I think the physical demands on Scottie were what got to him the most," said longtime Chicago radio reporter Cheryl Raye. "When he got here, he was very fragile mentally. I tie that to his being from a very small school, being from a different background, a different setting. Scottie never had any of the grooming that guys like Michael who went to big programs had. At the big schools, they groom those guys with the media. Usually they have some sort of maturity about them when they get to the NBA. Scottie did a couple of things on his own. He hired a speech coach from Chicago, a radio person, and worked on how he handled questions, what to say."

"My first year or two, I admit that I messed around a lot," Pippen once admitted. "I partied, enjoyed my wealth and didn't take basketball as seriously as I should have. I'm sure a lot of rookies did the same thing I did. You're not used to the limelight or being put in a great situation financially."

"Starting out, you could see Scottie's possibilities," Phil Jackson said. "He could rebound yet still dribble. He could post up, but he also had those slashing moves. You knew he could be very good, but you didn't know how good. He played a few times at guard in his first few seasons, bringing the ball up against teams with pressing guards, but mostly we used him at small forward. As more and more teams pressed, however, we decided we had to become more creative. More and more we had to go to Michael to bring the ball up. We didn't want to do that. We came up with the thought of Scottie as a third ball advancer, of an offense that attacked at multiple points. From that position Scottie started to take control, to make decisions. He became a bit of everything."

Key to the Bulls' growth was the maturing of both Pippen and Grant, the two young players with enough athleticism to give the Chicago defense its bite. "He's on the cusp of greatness," assistant coach Johnny Bach said of Pippen. "He's starting to do the kinds of things only Michael does."

"It's just a matter of working hard," Pippen said at the time. "I've worked to improve my defense and shooting off the dribble. I know I'm a better spot-up shooter, but I'm trying to pull up off the dribble when the lane is blocked."

Almost every night over the course of the 1989-90 season, Jordan led the Bulls in scoring, but it was Pippen who gave opposing coaches nightmares. Few teams had a means of matching up with him, particularly when they also had to worry about Jordan. A series of win streaks propelled them to a 55-27 finish, good for second place in the Central behind the 60-win Pistons, the defending World Champions.

The Bulls sailed into the playoffs with new confidence and Pippen playing like a veteran. First they dismissed the Milwaukee Bucks and followed that by humbling Charles Barkley and the Philadelphia 76ers. But Pippen's 70-year-old father, Lewis, died during the series, and the young forward rushed home to Arkansas for the funeral. He returned in time to help finish off Philly. Next up were the Pistons and the Eastern Finals. The year before in the playoffs, Bill Laimbeer had knocked Pippen out of Game 6 with an elbow to the head. The Detroit center claimed the shot was inadvertent, but that wasn't the way the Bulls saw it. To win a championship, they knew they had to stand up to the Bad Boys.

"There were times, a few years before the flagrant foul rules," Pippen recalled, "when guys would have a breakaway and [the Pistons] would cut their legs out from under them. Anything to win a game. That's not the way the game is supposed to be played. I remember once when Michael had a breakaway, and Laimbeer took him out. There was no way he could have blocked the shot. When you were out there playing them, that was always in the back of your mind, to kind of watch yourself."

The series developed as a classic, with each team winning tight battles at home to tie it at 3-3 heading into Game 7 at the Palace of Auburn Hills. The Pistons had homecourt advantage, and the Bulls could only watch as things went dreadfully wrong, beginning with John Paxson's badly sprained ankle and Pippen's migraine headache just before tipoff.

"Scottie had had migraines before," recalled former Bulls trainer

Mark Pfeil. "He actually came to me before the game and said he couldn't see. I said, 'Can you play?' He started to tell me no, and Michael jumped in and said, 'Hell, yes, he can play. Start him. Let him play blind.' Horace kind of backed up a little bit that game, too. It was more a matter of maturity than wimping out. It took a certain period of time before they would stand up and say, 'Damn it, I've been pushed to the wall enough.' Scottie played with the headache, and as the game went on he got better."

"It grabbed me and wouldn't let go," Pippen later explained. "It's something the fans will never let die. Then again, it's something I look over. I really don't think much about it."

Pippen played, but the entire roster seemed lost. They fell into a deep hole in the second quarter and never climbed out. "My worst moment as a Bull was trying to finish out the seventh game that we lost to the Pistons in the Palace," Jackson recalled. "There was Scottie Pippen with a migraine on the bench, and John Paxson had sprained his ankle in the game before. I just had to sit there and grit my teeth and go through a half in which we were struggling to get in the ball game. We had just gone through a second period that was an embarrassment to the organization."

The burden of the loss fell on Pippen. Everyone, from the media to his own teammates, had interpreted the headache as a sign of faintheartedness. Lost in the perspective was the fact that the third-year forward had recently buried his father.

Determined to prove his detractors wrong, Pippen answered with his play over the 1990-91 season. A gifted swing player, Pippen performed with determination, playing 3,014 minutes, averaging nearly 18 points, seven rebounds and six assists.

"I thought about it all summer," he said of the migraine. "I failed to produce last season."

"For Pippen, it was ultimately taking him from being a wing into a point guard role," Jackson said. "He became a guy who now had the ball as much as Michael. He became a dominant force."

Finally mature, the Bulls swept Detroit in the conference finals. Then Pippen discovered in the league championship series that he was up to the task of guarding Magic Johnson. The Bulls claimed their first championship with a 108-101 in Game 5 in Los Angeles. Pippen led the scoring with 32 points. "I thought that Scottie Pippen would be, at best, a very good journeyman player in this league," Utah executive Frank Layden told Lacy Banks of the *Sun Times* in the aftermath. "But to tell you the truth now, I'd have to think real hard not to place him as the second best player in this league. I think he's that good. I get the feeling that his development has been enhanced by playing alongside Jordan. He's picked up some good habits from him."

"It was just a matter of him believing in himself," Jordan said of Pippen. "When he got here, just playing with him, you could see he had all the right tools. It took some time for him to get his confidence on this level because he was competing against some of the best."

HARP

Ron Harper knew that as a friend of Scottie Pippen's there were just some things that you didn't ask him. For example, you didn't ask him about Jerry Krause. Pippen was an emotional guy, and you just didn't go digging into his emotions like that. "I stay away from that subject," Harper said.

It was important to the Bulls that Harper was a big, athletic, veteran guard with the ability to defend smaller, quicker players. The fact that Harper was also a sensitive, understanding person with a huge heart would make his contributions immeasurable.

"Our relationship has been as close as any player on this ball club in the short time that we've played together," Pippen said of Harper. "Our relationship started before we became teammates. From what I know of people around the league, Ron has the greatest heart of anybody that plays the game. Everybody loves him for being himself. He's always a respectful guy, he never has a change or a mood swing or anything like that. I mean he's just always the same guy, always the same even keel."

Above everything else, it was Harper's friendship and good nature that would eventually bring Pippen back to the Bulls. But it was a slow process. "That wasn't corrected in a day," trainer Chip Schaefer said of the emotional damage done by Pippen's outburst on the team bus in Seattle. "That thing happened in November, and he didn't come back till January. It took weeks and weeks and weeks of his teammates saying please come back and play. It was a big deal. It took a long time."

Of all the Bulls coaches and players, the 34-year-old Harper was perhaps the most patient with Pippen. Then again, Harper was quite familiar with the healing process, having been through a devastating knee injury that cost him a chunk of two seasons while playing for the Los Angeles Clippers. A slashing scorer, Harper had always relied on his athleticism until the 1990 injury. But major reconstructive surgery had robbed him of that, or at least he thought it had. Only with the help of then Clippers coach Larry Brown had he been able to overcome the mental barriers to regaining his aggressiveness. Harper quickly understood that at heart Brown was a teacher and a patient one. "He was the kind of coach who loved teaching young guys, who loved to work with you on your game," Harper recalled. "That's why Larry Brown has been a great college coach, because he's a great teacher and knows how to teach this game."

If there was anything that Harper admired, it was a teacher, someone full of soul and love and understanding. At Miami of Ohio Harper had majored in physical education with an emphasis in learning disabilities, and during his five years in Los Angeles had become actively involved with Widney High, a school for disabled young people. Harper himself had overcome a halting speech pattern. He knew every inch of the depths of frustration, and he knew that patience was critical to finding your way out. The process that he had been through made Harper aware of the patience that would be necessary for Pippen to heal mentally and physically. He also knew that when the time was right, the patience would have to end. Then it would be time to push.

And by January that time had come. Pippen had made public statements suggesting that he might have come back sooner, suggesting that he was ready physically before he was mentally. But that really wasn't the case, said Schaefer. The big problem was that Pippen had gone months without activity. Sure, he could dunk as he showed the media briefly. But in reality he didn't have the conditioning or health to leap and run and move constantly in an NBA game.

Ideally, he would have had surgery immediately after the 1997 season, but circumstances conspired to prevent that.

"The thinking would have been to get something done as soon as possible after the season in order to have ample rehab time," Schaefer said. "For some reason he wanted to delay it, and somehow we lost touch with him. Actually what wound up happening is that June became July, and summer league and things went on."

During the first week of August, Pippen made a public appearance in the Chicago area for a book signing and told the *Sun Times'* John Jackson that his foot was still troubling him. Schaefer read that and was immediately alarmed.

"Lo and behold Scottie reveals to everybody involved that his foot's still killing him and not any better than it was in June," said the trainer.

Schaefer hadn't seen or heard from Pippen in the two months since the '97 championship series and had presumed no news was good news. But upon reading Jackson's story, the trainer phoned the star and asked if foot still hurt. Pippen said yes, it did and that he probably should have something done.

Part of the problem, Schaefer said, was that Pippen was angry with the team and Krause over the trade talks and subsequent rumors throughout July. Once it became known that he might need additional treatment, a round of medical opinions became necessary. The situation was further clouded by the fact that Pippen played in Vin Baker's benefit game and seemed healthy, but his play there in part apparently prompted Krause to fax the letter to Pippen cautioning him not to play in Pippen's own charity game. That letter only sparked Pippen's anger.

The issue was further inflamed when the player's representative wanted another medical opinion from a New York foot guru. The team mentioned Pippen taking a commercial flight to see the specialist. "His agent wound up handing the Bulls a couple thousand dollar bill for a private plane," Schaefer said. "They wanted to know why he couldn't fly commercial."

The result of all the miscommunication and disagreement was that Pippen didn't undergo surgery until October, after training camp had started. "In theory, if all things were as they should have been, the surgery should have happened in June," Schaefer said.

As it was, the rehab took weeks, which only left Pippen to suffer atrophy. Team officials were astounded in December to discover that Pippen's vertical leap had fallen off by nearly two feet, down to a little more than a foot, due to the previous months of inactivity.

"The reality was he hadn't done anything, so it was a four or five month rehab," Schaefer said. "He had lost his explosive power. It was poor. It was much poorer."

As a result, it took him weeks of physical work, not to mention mental healing, to be ready to play. "The timing was right," Schaefer said of Pippen's return in mid January. "We probably needed a good eight weeks to get his body right, and we needed just as long to get his head right. He came back as soon as he could come back. The deficits in his strength and his power and stuff were genuine."

Even as he healed physically, it wasn't clear that he would rejoin the Bulls. Finally even Harper ran out of patience. "Finally I just told him he had to come back," Harper said with a smile, "that I wasn't going to let him leave me there by myself."

"Having a friend makes things much smoother for you," Pippen said. "You don't want to be in a situation where you don't have a close friend, because it makes you feel worse than what the situation really is."

The bonds of that friendship were strong enough to make Pippen go back in the face of his public declarations. He had said he would never again play for the Bulls.

But he did.

"I love Pip," Harper said with a sly smile. "That's my man there. Every now and then he gets on my nerves. But Pip is a great character, even though some of the fans probably don't think that. They may see all the things that he has done off the floor."

Without question, Pippen had made his share of public missteps during his career, from being arrested on a weapons charge to once accusing Chicago's white fans of favoring white players. But Harper and his teammates saw an entirely different person from the image projected to the public. Pippen's unselfishness had prompted Kerr to describe him as one of the best teammates he'd ever had. Not every Bull had those feelings about Jordan, but they did about Pippen.

Harper had even seen his goodness from afar, dating to their earliest days in the league. In the late 1980s, Harper was the star offensive weapon for the Cleveland Cavaliers and Pippen was a budding star. They got to know each other through Charles Oakley, who was then Pippen's Chicago teammate. In the offseason, Pippen and Harper began hanging out together. "To party, have fun," Harper explained.

"Since then, we've just kind of allowed things to evolve," Pippen agreed.

The Bulls got better and better in those years and played later and later into the season, meaning that Harper, who played first for the Cavs and then the Clippers, began hitting up Pippen for playoff tickets. "My season would end and their season would still be going on," Harper said, "so every time I came to town I would call up Pip and say, 'Pip, I need some seats to a game.' And he would say, 'OK, park back in the back. Tell Sam back in the back that you're coming, and I'll take care of you.' So he always gave me seats."

Then timing enhanced their good fortune. Jordan had left the game abruptly in the fall of 1993, and that next spring Harper became a free agent. The Bulls needed a big guard, a big scorer, someone to help them battle Orlando and the Magic's big guards in the Eastern Conference. Harper, at 6-6, had just played 75 games and averaged 20.1 points per game for the Clippers.

"We knew then that we needed bigger guards," Pippen recalled.

"We had B.J. (Armstrong) at that time, and had had Pax. We needed some more size to be able to match up with Orlando better, and I felt Ron was gonna be a fit for us, that he could give us that missing link, that missing component we needed to get to the next level to be able to compete with Orlando."

So Pippen went to Jackson with his idea about Harper. "Phil's always been one to listen to my opinions," Pippen explained. "Even during games he's allowed me the opportunity to orchestrate the offense or run whatever I feel like we need to get the right motion out on the court. He was just willing to listen, to see how I felt about Ron. He knew that I had a relationship with him. They tried to sort of use that to our advantage to get him. After Michael retired, Ron was a big guard, someone that we needed whether Michael came back or not."

Harper said that he and Pippen had talked about his becoming a Bull. "Once I got a chance to become free, Pip went and told Phil and them, 'Sign Ron.' That's how I became a Chicago Bull."

"When we brought Harper in, we felt that if he could regain some of his old skills, his old abilities after the knee injuries he'd had, he could be an ideal player for us because of his size," Tex Winter said.

Harper signed a six-year deal with Chicago for plump millions, then promptly found himself facing one of the toughest tests of his career — the triangle offense. Like most players, he found the adjustment frustrating, agonizing. His scoring average plummeted to under seven points a game. Then, just when he had begun to spark a connection with the offense, Michael Jordan returned to the game, and Harper's playing time shifted dramatically.

Soon the whisper circuit around the NBA had Harper pegged as finished, his legs gone, his game headed for moth balls. The circumstances left Harper understandably despondent, struggling through the lowest point in his 9-year career. "Suicide was an option," he would say later, only half jokingly. "It was something I learned from. It was frustrating, but my friend had a frustrating year, too," he said, referring to Pippen, who had spent much of the '95 season fighting with management, "and we both grew."

Out of that growth came Harper's motivation to show everybody just how wrong they were about the status of his career.

In the wake of the Bulls' 1995 playoff loss to Orlando, Jackson realized that Harper could be part of the answer and told him so in their season-ending conference — if Harper would dedicate himself to offseason conditioning. "Phil let Ron know that we very definitely were counting on him to be a big part of the team," Winter said. "I think that helped Ron no end. Phil put it to him in no uncertain terms: 'You gotta go out and get yourself ready to play.' And Ron did that, he really prepared himself."

"Phil asked me what my role was going to be on this team," Harper recalled, "and I told him, 'When Michael returns, I'll be a player who plays defense and fills the spot. If there's a chance to score, I'll score.' I think that we felt as a team that we had something to prove. And on my own I had something to prove. I figured this was going to be a very good ball club . . . I trained hard. I felt that last year I definitely didn't have the legs to play the style here. I had to learn that, too."

The situation was further clouded by the fact that the NBA endured a lockout during a collective bargaining standoff that summer of 1995, and Harper was forbidden from having contact with the team. Not to be deterred, he conducted all of his conditioning on his own, with a trainer.

And when he returned that fall, he had remade his game into that of a defensive specialist, much as Michael Cooper of the Los Angeles Lakers remade himself from a high-flying scorer into a great specialist. It soon became clear that for major stretches of games Harper could take on the toughest defensive assignment, leaving Jordan and Pippen to patrol the passing lanes for steals and transition baskets, what would become the teeth of Chicago's attack.

How valuable was Harper? That became apparent when his knee problems flared up during the 1996 league championship series against Seattle. With Harper out of two games, it became obvious that the pressure dropped in Chicago's defense. Pippen or Jordan had to take the primary assignment and were no longer free to terrorize the passing lanes as effectively as they had before.

It was no coincidence that when Harper returned for Game 6 and gave the Bulls big minutes despite his knee problems, the pressure returned to Chicago's defense, and the Bulls rode that to their fourth championship.

"It's very rare that you find guards of that size who have the ability to defend," Pippen said, "and Ron is a guy that I think is a very, very underrated defensive player. I think he could get a lot of credit for his defensive ability, and he's never been rewarded for it."

The 1996 offseason brought surgery for Harper and a slow 1996-97 campaign, but once the playoffs returned, he was again a huge factor in Chicago claiming a fifth title. Once again, he had quietly sacrificed his scoring for the team.

There were many things that Pippen prized about his friend. But

Harper's selflessness was tops among them. And, make no mistake, everyone agreed, from Krause to Jackson, that he was a huge chunk of the Chicago Bulls' substantial heart.

In the business of pro basketball, many teams make the mistake of evaluating players on their statistics. People can easily measure rebounds and points and assists, but Red Auerbach used to pay his Boston Celtics players merely on their contributions to winning. That was a point emphasized to the Bulls by stress counselor George Mumford: What are your contributions to winning?

That was why Pippen valued Harper so highly. "That's what it's all about, as far as winning," Pippen said. "You can't get anything accomplished until you get people to accept that goal. You can't go out and play selfish and be considered one of the greatest teams. You don't accomplish anything by trying to achieve a lot of individual things. You have to go out and do it as a team, and when it's all said and done, the whole team is rewarded for it in some way or another. That's what the regular season's about, to sort of get all that out of your system and realize that it's a team game. If you want to accomplish things as a team, you shouldn't have any selfishness."

To gain that, you have to have people willing to live by the quality of things, not the quantity, to live by their contributions rather than their stats. "Ron is a prime example," Pippen said, pointing to the fact that Harper often would play the first half then see his minutes reduced in the second while Jackson let others see some action. "At times, you know, he's forgotten over there on the bench in the second half. But he never complains about it, or anything of that nature."

Because Harper made that sacrifice, it meant that others on the team felt more induced to make it. "Ron is a guy who shows leadership just by him sitting over there on the bench in the second half," Pippen explained. "He's not trying to be selfish. He don't feel that this should be his time. He's just sort of sitting back and soaking things in and letting the younger guys see that you don't have to be on the court to be involved in the game at all times. I think a lot of it is just the leadership he has provided on the court. It's how he is around his teammates, his personality. He's a guy everybody has a lot of love for."

Just how badly the Bulls needed Pippen was emphasized January 8th with a smashing road loss in Miami. The Bulls took a 28-20 first-quarter lead over the Heat but scored only 44 points the rest of the way and lost, 99-72.

"There's no explanation for it," Jordan told reporters. "You just have to grin and bear it."

Jackson, of course, hated to lose to any Riley team and showed his disdain by getting ejected just before half time for arguing with the officiating crew, which included one of the league's first two females refs, Violet Palmer. "The only thing I'll say is I'm disappointed with the league for sending a crew like that out to referee a game like this," Jackson said. "From the very first play, there was a problem."

Two nights later they journeyed to New York for their first game of the season in the Garden where Jordan tantalized the Big Apple media by saying that he would "love" to play for the Knicks, "but that would be a selfish act not conferring with my family and knowing that my kids are in school, and I can't take them out. That's not great parenting."

Jordan's words combined with Jackson's comment before the game that he planned to take a year off before coaching again ignited wildfire speculation that a move was afoot.

Was Jordan reminding Reinsdorf of his close encounter with the Knicks in '96? "It would be great to play here in New York if that situation (arose)," Jordan told the media. "(Or) if I was single and didn't have to worry about uprooting my family from where they are. That would be a selfish approach. I have to think about my family when I think about moving from Chicago and going to other places."

Could it happen? reporters wanted to know. "Let me resolve my parenting issues, then I can make that decision," Jordan replied. "Right now I can't."

The next night, January 11, the Bulls returned home, and Pippen appeared in uniform for the first time since the '97 championship series. The United Center crowd greeted him with joyous applause. He played 31 minutes and scored 14 points in an 87-72 win over hapless Golden State. The timing for his return was right. The Bulls had won 13 of their last 15 games and boosted their record to 25-11.

"I just didn't have any rhythm," Pippen told reporters. "Being away from the game, my teammates didn't know when I was taking shots or what passes I was going to make. Those are things that will come in time."

He was asked if his relationships with the team's front office had been repaired. "I don't think they've been repaired at all," he said. "We haven't tried to repair them. I don't think they can be repaired. I'm just going to do my job and just allow them to do theirs."

Asked about his mental state, he replied, "This is the frustration

I've been going through for the last couple of years and over the summer, having to deal with all the trade talk and things of that nature. I think a player of my caliber deserves better, so I had to stand up and speak out for myself."

There remained the possibility that he still might be traded before the late February 19th trading deadline, although Krause had told reporters that any deal for Pippen would have to be highly favorable to the Bulls. When asked by reporters if he was convinced Pippen wouldn't be traded, Jackson said, "I remain unconvinced about anything."

"I would like to finish the season here," Pippen admitted. "I think the team is looking forward to us going for a sixth title. If something happens, that's always been out of my control."

Just as they got Pippen back, the Bulls lost Kerr for 6-8 weeks with a broken left collarbone suffered in a loss at Philadelphia when the Sixers' Derrick Coleman went up to block his shot and landed on him. "It was a strange play," Kerr said later. "It felt like he could have gotten out of the way. He landed right on top of me."

A week later, just days after Jordan had praised his good behavior, Rodman stirred the pot by missing a pre-game practice after a night of carousing at a strip club in New York.

Jackson's response was to fine him, suspend him a game and send him home from New Jersey.

"I thought it was fair, and I thought Phil sending me home was the right thing," Rodman told reporters later. "When I came back from flying home by myself, I went straight to the practice facility and started to work out. I messed up, and that is it. It's as simple as that. I didn't feel good physically, and I stayed out a little too late."

The Bulls returned home from New Jersey and found the Utah Jazz waiting. Karl Malone scored 35 and powered the Jazz to a 101-94 win that ended Chicago's 17-game home winning streak.

Immediately afterward, the Bulls departed on their second West Coast road trip of the season, with games against Vancouver, Portland, Golden State, the Lakers, Denver and Utah that would lead right up to the All-Star break in New York.

At 30-13, the Bulls were showing definite signs of life. "It's a bonding trip," Jordan said of the western swing. The last time he had made such a statement, the journey had turned ugly and sour, producing anything but bonding. This time, Krause would remain home, busying himself with scouting college talent. But the general manager would still find a way to extend his reach to the team, setting up the next round of controversy, yet another exercise in wasted effort.

"Won't be long `til I'm puttin' on my flying shoes."
— Townes Van Zandt

10/ For the Moment

It all made perfect sense in a Zen sort of way. For the third straight season, the Chicago Bulls had faced an uncertain future. They were a great team, yet the slightest disruption to their modus operandi would likely have been taken as an excuse for the team's chairman and general manager to break them apart. That meant that a major injury, internal squabbling, or just plain old everyday fear run amok could have spelled their doom. Yet that hadn't happened. One of the reasons was the Zen concept of "living in the moment," not losing concentration, not giving in to their concerns about the future.

"It doesn't affect him at all," Steve Kerr said of Jackson. "And that's to his credit. He always preaches being in the moment and living for the moment and enjoying each day for what it is. He's got a lot of little pet quotes and sayings that allude to that, and he practices that. It could be the last run for all of us, and he's gonna have fun."

Jordan agreed, saying that Jackson's dealing so smartly with the adversity of the season had been good for him "because he finally gets some notoriety as a coach. He's a wise, smart coach, not just the guy who coached Michael Jordan, Scottie Pippen, Dennis Rodman. He uses his talent to blend everybody together to have one focus. And he's doing a heck of a job of that."

By all rights, the separation anxiety alone should have been enough to splinter the Bulls into factions. But they all believed in Jordan, Pippen and Jackson, and that bound them even tighter. Jackson loved the unity of it. Zen warriors. In the moment. Doing battle.

As the season unfolded into February, it became clear that there was plenty of battle to do, on and off the court. They opened their western trip with wins in Vancouver, Portland, and Golden State, then they got waxed by the quick young Lakers in Los Angeles, and one night later righted themselves against lowly Denver.

It was in Utah, on the eve of their rematch with the Jazz, that word came that Krause had decided to unburden his mind to *Tribune* columnist Fred Mitchell.

Jackson would definitely not be back, Krause emphasized.

"If Michael chooses to leave because there is another coach here, then it is his choice, not ours," Krause told Mitchell. "We want him back. We are not driving anybody out. We are not driving Michael out of here. That's bull.

"The decision on Michael will just have to take a proper time when we will sit down and talk," he said. "We will talk about what he wants to do and what the situation is with the franchise and who is going to be here, and what our (salary) cap situation is. We would like to have Michael back. But Michael is going to have to play for someone else. It isn't going to be Phil."

Krause also said that Jackson wasn't "being run out of here. Phil agreed that this would be his last year. He did not want to go through a possible rebuilding situation. Nobody is running Phil out of town. It was a well thought-out decision."

Krause also offered up an opinion on the difficulty of rebuilding with Jordan still on the roster. "Obviously, with Michael and the salary he is making now, it would be very tough to improve our team. Our cap money would be gone. It is a highly complicated thing. I would say that no NBA team has faced this type of situation before, cap-wise."

Krause should have known Jordan would take the statement as a challenge. After all, the GM had worked with the star for 13 seasons. Krause also should have known that Reinsdorf would be angered by the statement. After all, the chairman's philosophy was to make no decision, to take no heat, until necessary. Krause had done just the opposite. He had spoken prematurely. No matter what he said later, his words only cemented the impression that he was eager to pack up the current championship team, to clear the salary cap, so that he could begin rebuilding.

Krause's comments created a bit of a media frenzy that morning at the Bulls' shoot-around before the Utah game. Jordan again emphasized that if Jackson weren't retained, he would move on, too. "It still stands true," Jordan said. "That's been my thought process for the year, pretty much. I felt that management has to make a decision in terms of what they want to do with this team, the direction they choose to go in. They have to make their choice."

The Bulls lost that night in Utah despite the fact that they had run up a 24-point lead early in the game. The outcome allowed the Jazz a season sweep of the two-game series and home-court advantage if the two met in the 1998 Finals. While the rest of the team returned home to rest during the All-Star break, Jordan journeyed on to New York to take part in the All Star events. He was sick from a cold and almost ducked out to be home and rest with his family. But a gathering of global media awaited, more than 1,000 journalists, and Jordan was ready to fire back at the two Jerrys.

He missed Friday's opening media sessions but weighed in Sunday afternoon in the locker room before the game, a crowd of reporters pressed in around him. Asked first about the situation with his team, Jordan said, "I haven't seen any light on the other side of the tunnel at all. I think management has stated their position. I don't see how it's going to work in my favor."

Did the fact that the Bulls' run seemed to be headed toward an end leave him sad?

"There is a sadness," he said. "But any time it comes to an end, there's a certain sadness."

From there, he fielded a variety of questions from reporters.

• Does this come down to a fundamental personality conflict between Phil and Jerry Krause and Jerry Reinsdorf?

"That has a lot to do with it. It certainly can't be because of his job and what he's done with the players and the respect he's won from the players. His success as a coach is certainly impeccable. I don't think that can be questioned. I think it's more personal than anything."

• You are an astute businessman. The story of you leaving the Bulls is a business story in addition to a sports story. Are you surprised that Jerry Reinsdorf would allow a personality conflict to interrupt logical business decisions?

"It doesn't surprise me. Especially when you pretty much want to control everything. And it's more control than anything. It's not quite the way they want it to be. From an economic standpoint, I'm pretty sure they're not making as much money, but they're making money."

• But they're losing value in the franchise if you leave?

"Yeah. That's the challenge they're willing to take."

• A short-term gain? When you and Phil and Scottie and Dennis leave, maybe they add $50 million to their balance sheet for next year? But the value of their franchise decreasing would seem to offset anything they gain?

"You and I understand that."

• They're so angry over the personalities that they would make that bad business decision?

"I think it's more personal than anything. They're willing to take the risk at this stage."

• Do you have any thoughts of communicating with Jerry Reinsdorf on this issue of the team's future?

"None. Jerry Krause would not speak without Jerry Reinsdorf knowing."

• So this is Jerry Reinsdorf?

"Believe me."

• Why are you taking the stand you're taking?

"You could pose the same question to them. Why would you change a coach who has won five championships when he has the respect of his players and certainly the understanding of his players to where they go out and play hard each and every day. Why?"

• The quiet argument from management is that Phil Jackson has become arrogant and that they can't stomach that anymore. Have you seen arrogance on Phil's part?

"I'm pretty sure that he's probably getting tired of Krause. And I've been there, a long time ago. I understand (Phil's) frustrations. Maybe they view that as arrogance. But what I see in Phil is an attitude to work with the players to achieve the best as a team. That means a lot to us. Now in terms of management agreeing with the relationship we have with the coach, that may be a problem with management. Phil, I think, has an attitude of pro-player to some extent, as opposed to pro organization. He played the game of basketball, so he has an understanding for a lot of things we deal with. Some of the decisions he makes veer more towards the players than the organization. I think that's a part of the problem as well.

• Have you absolutely ruled out playing elsewhere?

"It's Chicago or nowhere."

• What about Kobe Bryant and Kevin Garnett and young kids being ambassadors for the game?

"It's not about being an ambassador. That's a heck of a responsibility. What they should try to understand is the position they have and a understanding for the business. They should educate themselves about it, so they're not fooled by the business somewhere down the road. That's important. Still enjoy the game. Never get to the point where you don't enjoy the game. The game is still the game. If you didn't get paid a dime, you'd still play the game somewhere."

• The other owners of the Bulls, have any of them expressed their concern about the situation?

"No. I haven't talked to any of the owners, none of that. I was shocked by Krause's comments in Utah. I didn't know it was coming. But it didn't really surprise me. I've felt that the rift between him and Phil, or between management and Phil was pretty strong. But I thought those types of things would be decided at the end of the season, not in the middle of the season. That was kind of surprising."

• You have no personal relationship with Jerry Reinsdorf? Wasn't there a time that you had affection and respect for each other? I mean you even played for his baseball team.

"I still respect him as a business (man). I still have some personal relationships with him. But it's very evident that doesn't come into play here. If it came into play, we wouldn't have this discussion. But it doesn't come into play. I'm not surprised, because he's a shrewd businessman. He makes business decisions a lot of times. He's not afraid to go against the grain."

• Isn't there a time when personal loyalty comes into play?

"I believe in that. But everybody doesn't have the same beliefs about that."

• If Phil were back, and the core of the Bulls were back, how badly would you want to play another season? Would it be something you'd really cherish?

"If they'd keep everybody intact? I'd love to do that. I would love to come back again."

• Is this a challenge they're throwing at you, to see if you mean it?

"No, I think they've pretty much made up their minds. I'd like to think that they've left the door open, so that there can be change down the road. But it doesn't appear to be that way."

• How many more years can you play at this level?

"That's the beauty of it all, I don't know. And neither do you. I don't think anyone can know."

• You walked away once before and came back loving it. Why would somebody great still walk away, knowing that at 45 you can't come back?

"Why would a guy at this age walk into an unknown situation, when everything right now is pleasant for him with the coach. Next year whoever they bring in may not have the same philosophy, may not have the same system, may not have the same rapport with the players. It's like starting over, it's like getting divorced and then getting married too quickly. If I have a choice not to . . ."

• But no coach is going to come in and say, "Number 23, you're the eighth man."

"But see I've never had a guy come in and pacify me. I like Phil. I think Phil comes in with a certain motion, a certain thought process, a team concept, that everybody fits within that. We grew to where we respected each other, and he knew certain things to apply to me and to apply to other players. I don't want a coach to come in and say, 'Well, what do you want to do? Do you want to do this? Do you want to do that?' That doesn't motivate me. That doesn't challenge me. And now you're asking me to go into that situation unknowingly? At this stage of my career? If the system doesn't suit me, and I don't feel comfortable, or my game starts to suffer, or certain things start to change, then you leave yourself open for all kinds of speculation, which I'm not afraid of. But why would I take the risk of changing it?"

• It almost sounds like a superstition.

"It's a comfort. It's a respect. It's knowing what I'm getting instead of not knowing what I'm getting."

• Do you think there's any pressure on Jerry Reinsdorf from the secondary owners to cut costs and increase profitability?

"It could be. These are things that he wouldn't tell me. My best guess is that he's making the calls, and he's making whatever call he has to make."

• What's your role gonna be in the league when you retire?

"I'm gonna be a fan, from afar. I'm pretty sure I'll still have some contacts, because of my business, the shoe industry. It won't be every game, but I'll still come down to visit. I'm a basketball fan, so I'll still be around the game."

After answering those questions, Jordan went out and scored 23 points to lead the East to victory in the All Star Game. The performance netted the third All-Star MVP award of his career. Better yet, it again emphasized Jordan's dominance over the game, something he would demonstrate again and again over the spring. In the process he would hammer Krause's statements about the need to rebuild the team into a thin argument.

In the wake of Jordan's comments, Reinsdorf issued a statement calling for an end to premature comments about the team's future. Word spread around the Bulls' offices that Reinsdorf was angry with Krause, that the GM had lost face because of his comments.

"That's one thing that Jerry Reinsdorf does very well," Steve Kerr observed. "He stays away and doesn't get involved in all of it. He lets Jerry Krause and Phil and everybody else go about their business. Obviously, he's ended up sort of in the middle of this. But usually Krause is the front man."

Practice resumed at the Berto Center on Monday after the All-Star break, and afterward, Jackson spoke with reporters, emphasizing that he was leaving. "There is no other option," the coach said. "We've made an agreement that that's what is going on and that is the direction we are going as a basketball team. It's going to be hard to say goodbye. It's going to be really tough."

Then he quibbled, leaving the door ajar that indeed he might find a way to return, which left Krause furious but muzzled.

"I'm not saying our beds are made," Jackson said, "but they are laid out and ready to go. Early in training camp I sat down with Jerry Krause and Jerry Reinsdorf and we expressly went over this again and said this is our swan song as a team."

Then he said, "Michael has a tremendous sway in this game, as we all see from the effect he had in the All-Star game. Michael is the only one who could change it."

About Jordan's threatened retirement, Jackson said, "It makes me feel like I am standing in the way of him continuing his career. Some of it does. The other thing is that the organization is a bit to fault in it, too."

Jackson then predicted that Krause wouldn't change his mind. "That's not going to happen," he said. "I think the amount of intensity we've had over the last two seasons, the directions we've changed and the divergent paths that both Jerry and I have gone on just spelled the fact that the relationship had reached its course. It's time for him to do what he wants to do in his management of this organization, and it's time for me to move on wherever I have to go. Michael can throw a monkey wrench into things, but that's their decision and that's the way we have to look at it."

In his *New York Post* column during the All-Star break, NBC analyst Peter Vecsey had suggested that the Bulls were paying Jackson $500,000 in hush money not to speak out about the situation.

"I didn't get back from the All-Star game until Monday afternoon," Jackson later recalled. "We had practice and I didn't see his column. I had questions from reporters about this, and I didn't understand it. It was totally misrepresented. There is not anything like that in my contract. Last year at some point during contract negotiations, we said at some point that if we don't come to an agreement and we have to step away what's going to happen? There was some talk about a severance. Because we actually began thinking, 'We may not reach a common ground on this and this may become difficult for the franchise.' So we talked about it in that context. But I had no intention of taking hush money, or whatever to be quiet, or whatever it was meant as. But, you know, severance money is severance money."

In the wake of the All-Star Weekend, the atmosphere around the Bulls tightened as the trading deadline neared. Would Krause dare trade Pippen? It seemed unlikely. Not with the uproar that his comments earlier in the month had caused.

But the team did send young forward Jason Caffey to Golden State for David Vaughn, an unproven player, and two second round draft picks. The move set off immediate speculation that Krause was intentionally weakening the team.

"This is a horrible thing to say," said one longtime team employee. "I wonder if Jerry and Jerry almost want us not to win this year, so they can have the excuse to rebuild. It's an unbelievably dangerous thing to say, especially with a tape recorder on. I'm just wondering about their emotional state. You don't want to think that, but you have to wonder."

Jordan, meanwhile, was angry, pointing out to reporters that losing Caffey, an athletic rebounder, was like losing family. One reporter asked Kerr if it seemed like management was putting another obstacle in front of the team to prevent the Bulls from winning the title.

Kerr laughed. "That's a good way to put it," he said. "We were all a little dismayed. We feel like it hurt our depth. He's big and strong and athletic, and I think that really hurt our depth. They've got their reasons for doing things. There's not very good communication between players and management, so there's not a whole lot of that that goes on."

Asked if he meant that he thought management had put up an intentional obstacle, Kerr paused a moment, then replied, "No. If you look at it, both Jerrys . . . to win another championship, ultimately, is two more big feathers in their caps. I can't imagine that they would want to sabotage anything. That would be counterproductive to their own desires. That doesn't really make sense."

"You don't think it makes it easier to break up the team to say 'See, we told you?'" the reporter asked.

"You know, maybe we should call Oliver Stone and he could make a movie out of it," Kerr said. "He would have a field day with all of this."

Terry Armour of the *Tribune* figured Krause had scored one against Jackson and Jordan with the trade, a perception that also registered with many fans. "The Caffey move," Armour said, "to me is strictly — and I could be wrong here. I've been wrong before — 'see if you can win with a David Vaughn.' To me, it just looks like, 'OK, let's make some minor moves that will make it hard for us to get there.' But you know, who would want to want to do that? Realistically, who would want to weaken their case? You can accuse somebody of that, but realistically, it doesn't make sense that somebody would want to do that."

Behind the scenes, the Bulls' assistant coaches had lobbied hard for Krause to keep Caffey, but Jackson quietly agreed with the deal. He knew that Krause had no plans to re-sign Caffey, who would be a free agent at the end of the season. Plus, Jackson was hoping that the Bulls would be able to find a player like Brian Williams, who was able to guard smaller, quick centers. Williams had been a godsend during the 1997 playoffs. Obviously, no player of Williams' quality was available in 1998, so Jackson figured that a "Dickey Simpkins type" player, someone about 6-9 or 6-10 might be available to help out defensively.

"I actually wanted to bid out Caffey (for a trade)," Jackson explained. "Jason wasn't going to get a chance in this organization. He'd go through his free agency and he wouldn't be re-signed by this organization. For a kid that I liked, it was a good opportunity for him to go. But I didn't want to hurt the team. I wanted a bigger kind of a player like a Dickey Simpkins who could play centers that are small like Mourning. And Jason was a little too small to play the Shawn Kemps. He's a 6-8 guy as opposed to a 6-10, 265 pound guy. So that's the difference.

"I told them that's what I wanted," Jackson admitted privately. "We wanted a Brian Williams type player. I've always had that type of center. Stacey King and Scott Williams."

As it turned out, Simpkins was soon put on waivers by Golden State, allowing the Bulls to waive Vaughn after a few days and sign Simpkins.

"Dickey's that kind of guy," Jackson said. "The job is his to do. It's not a heavy minute role. We don't see that guy coming in there and playing 30 to 40 minutes. But he can play 16 minutes a game for us and help us out if possible."

Simpkins, whom the Bulls had traded in the fall of 1997 to Golden State for Scott Burrell, was truly elated to be back in Chicago. "It's like going off to war, then coming back," he said.

Or maybe vice versa.

Behind the scenes, Krause was furious with Jackson. The general manager alleged that the coach was supposed to explain the trade to the players but that Jackson had failed to do so, opening the door to speculation that Krause was sabotaging the team. "Phil was supposed to take care of the team, and he didn't do it," Krause said. "He was supposed to explain it to the players. But once again he left me looking like the bad guy."

With the tension, people in the organization increasingly complained to reporters that Jackson had grown arrogant. "I've heard from different circles," Terry Armour said, "that one thing that Phil may have done to rub the organization the wrong way is that he came in on a winning situation and took it to the next level.

"The belief is that, whatever reasons Doug Collins was let go for, Doug would have done it," Armour said. "Doug would have been right there to do it. Phil got arrogant. You know winning changes people, and that Phil went from being a team player as far as the organization is concerned, to saying. 'Hey, maybe I'm the guy who did this.'

"He may come across as arrogant to some people because of the way he talks," Armour added. "Some people take that as being a snob, or that he's trying to show us how smart he is. But I don't think it's that way with him. I would not consider him arrogant in his dealings with the media. He knows how to play the game, too, as far as the PR thing. You can tell when people are arrogant with the media. They embarrass you when you question them. Phil is not like that. I think, if anything, Phil might be too honest with us. Maybe it's a PR move, but Phil will answer our questions, good or bad, and he doesn't really think about repercussions."

The sensation was unique in sports. With their "divided house" in full conflict, the Bulls entered the spring playing both for and against the organization. That seemed to work well enough. Jordan and company ran off eight straight wins, dumping Toronto, Charlotte, Atlanta, Detroit, Indiana, Toronto again, Washington and Cleveland before finally losing again on February 25th when the young Portland Trail Blazers gave the Bulls only their third defeat of the season in the United Center. As they had done in the past, the Bulls answered defeat with another torrid burn of winning and would roll through March at 13-1, emphasizing to opponents and fans alike at every stop that these Bulls were indeed back to their old dominant selves, or something close.

The head of steam was aided by nearly a week's rest in the schedule after wins over Sacramento and Denver. The Bulls sat at home, healed their injuries and stoked their fires. Jordan even had time to rummage through his closets to find a vintage pair of Air Jordans to wear for what was billed as his last visit to Madison Square Garden, the game against New York March 9th when the Bulls resumed play. Never mind that the shoes were gaudy and flimsy, they were the perfect touch to send a public message, creating further anxiety about Krause and Reinsdorf shutting down the Bulls early.

It also sent a little private message to Reinsdorf, reminding the chairman of just how much they loved Jordan in New York. Boy, did they love him. The Sunday afternoon game was televised on NBC, and Jordan in his red shoes was like Dorothy standing at center court, clicking her heels three times and saying, 'There's no place like the Garden.'

One by one the Bulls' staff members and players noticed Jordan had unpacked the shoes and set them by his locker. Team photographer Bill Smith took it as a sure sign that this was indeed Jordan's last season. The rest of the public soon got the message.

"It was a big topic of conversation," Steve Kerr said of the locker room buzz before the game. "I couldn't believe it. My first reaction was, 'What is he nuts?' I was thinking this could be plantar fascitis big time. Did you see those things? They looked like cardboard put together. It's amazing how far the shoe industry has come in the last 14 years. It was kind cool, kinda neat to see. He was obviously kind of projecting an image of coming full circle. I assume he kind of broke those shoes out in the Garden. I don't know. He obviously had it on his mind that this might be his last shot here.

"I was betting guys that at some point he'd take them off and go back to the new ones," Kerr said. "But then when he hit his first four shots I changed my mind and said, 'No, he's gonna wear 'em the whole game.'"

"I overheard him telling some guys that he's got a few at home," Pippen said, "and he felt like this was probably his last game in the Garden."

"I went kind of retroactive today with the shoes," Jordan admitted. "I was joking with my wife about it. I was actually doing some cleaning up at home and kind of ran into them."

His feet covered in red, Jordan treated the adoring Garden crowd and the television audience to an old-style performance, filled with whirling, impossible drives to the baskets and reverses and dunks and whatever else popped to the surface of his creativity, all of it good for 42 precious points.

"I played up in the air a lot today," he admitted afterward. "I'm not afraid to play that way. There was a need there, and if there's a need there, I have to address it. I'm not really thinking about the moves and how excited the fans are. The oooohs and aaaahs tell you that. Some of the moves seemed to be coming from 1984."

Once he switched hands on the ball in trademark fashion for a layup. Another time he absorbed a blow from the Knicks' Terry Cummings, turned in midair and still flipped the shot in over his shoulder.

"That's a heck of a shot," Knicks coach Jeff Van Gundy said, shaking his head.

"It's just so much fun to be a part of this team," Steve Kerr said of Jordan's acrobatics, "because you see that routinely, and yet you can't ever take it for granted. You can take the total performance for granted. Forty two points, we see that all the time, but those moves that he does are just so amazing that I find myself cheering just like everybody else in the stands.

"It's one of my favorite atmospheres in the NBA," Kerr said of the Garden. "It's electric in here. The fans are very sophisticated. They understand the game. They love Michael, and yet they hate him. It's a neat feeling to be a part of it."

With Jordan's outburst and Pippen's defense in full force, the Bulls drove to a 102-89 win. The game also marked Kerr's return to duty after missing six weeks with the fractured left clavicle. Kerr entered the game with two minutes left in the first quarter and promptly threw up and hit his first shot. On the day, he would finish with eight points.

Afterward, reporters ribbed Kerr about shooting so quickly. "I don't think I've ever actually seen you shoot on your first touch," the Daily Herald's Kent McDill told him.

"I felt like Bill Wennington," Kerr replied, the joke being that Wennington was known for being so eager to get his shots in that Jordan called him "trampoline hands."

"Vinnie Johnson is gone," another reporter told Kerr, "but you might be Microwave II. You didn't waste any time getting that shot."

Kerr laughed and said he wasn't a threat to the former Pistons' sixth man who was known for heating up off the bench in a hurry. "He's got nothing to worry about," Kerr said. "They might call me like the Toaster Oven or something. But it probably wouldn't work very well."

Kerr, the league's all-time leader in three-point field goal percentage, was viewed as a critical element for the Bulls' bench. His injury, plus the recurring knee troubles of center Luc Longley had left the Bulls searching for rotations even while they won. The time off, though, worked in his favor, Kerr said. "This last two months has been great for me because, while I was healing I was really kind of getting refreshed and mentally prepared. I stayed in shape physically, and I'm just so excited to be back playing. Sometimes in the long course of a season, you can get kind of worn down and you lose a little of your spirit. I'm just so fired up to be back.

"That's one of the things about injuries, you have a lot of time to think," he explained. "I really thought about my situation here and my future, and I realized that early in the season I was probably pressing a little bit because of the uncertainty over next year, me being a free agent and nobody knowing what was happening with the team. I realized that I was gonna have probably 20 games left and then the playoffs. And then, who knows? That might be it. So I better enjoy it and be aggressive and try to have as much as fun as I can when I do come back."

His explanation was a window to how many of the Bulls felt. Scott Burrell, for example, had battled his insecurities about the triangle offense, which was predicated on the Bulls' players reading the defense and reacting, much like a quarterback in football reads defenses and reacts. That was one reason it was difficult to learn.

"Each pass is a different option, and no plays are really called," Burrell explained. "When a pass was thrown in, I had to think about it first, instead of just reacting. And you can't play while you're thinking. You gotta keep a clear mind. When I got the ball, I didn't know what to do about passing. I didn't know about shooting or doing anything else with it. The way they teach you makes it a lot easier. It takes them a long time to teach you, but after that, it's so much easier."

It was pointed out that Jordan had developed a trust in former Bulls guard John Paxson, and eventually trust in Kerr. Jordan knew that when he passed to them, odds were they would knock down the open shot. Burrell had begun to find his open shots in the offense. Had Jordan come to him and expressed a confidence?

"Nah. He's not gonna come and talk to me," Burrell said and laughed. "I'll find out for myself. If I'm open and he throws me the pass, then we'll know."

Without question, Burrell's growing comfort in the offense was adding to Chicago's depth. But the injuries and Caffey's trade had left the players questioning their ability to dominate a playoff series the way they had in recent seasons. "I don't know if we'll ever be able to get to that point from a personnel standpoint," Kerr admitted. "We're just not as deep as we have been. But I think we can still win the championship. It's going to be more difficult."

At first it was reported that Knick and Jordan friend Charles Oakley had gotten Jordan's red shoes in the wake of the Garden game. But Bulls equipment man John Ligmanowski had secured them for his private collection. Jordan admitted as much the next week. "My right foot has always been 13 1/2. My left foot has always been 13. And everybody said I tried to squeeze my foot into a 12. That was not true," Jordan said, though he admitted the shoes had given him blisters.

Regardless, the touch had been well worth it from an entertainment standpoint. Beyond that, it had allowed him to score big points in his public relations battle with the two Jerrys. "That move was a brilliant public relations move," said John Jackson of the *Sun Times*, "because it brings attention to the fact that he's serious about retiring because in his own mind he considers this his last game in Madison Square Garden, so he's looking to make it special. Obviously, this isn't an idle threat. Doing it this way, by using the red shoes, he doesn't have to come out and say it. He doesn't have to say, 'I'm retiring.' He doesn't put himself in a position to look like a spoiled athlete."

It was obvious that Jordan was campaigning against management, but he appeared to be rethinking his position, observed Bruce Levine, the reporter for WMVP radio. "I've never seen anything like it. He has been an open book to talk about the contract, where the team should go, about Phil and his destiny with Phil. But he's kind of changed his opinion over the last six or seven weeks, but it's more of a wait and see policy now. If Michael Jordan does change his mind and play for another coach, who's gonna say anything?"

Kerr agreed that Jordan was campaigning, but seemed to be doing so with a sense of frustration. "He speaks up," Kerr said, "but there's not a whole lot he can do. Everyone kind of assumes that if he wants he can just step in and just kind of take over the whole organization. But it doesn't work that way. He's wants people's respect, but he's still going to respect management. But he doesn't go overboard, like Scottie or someone like that."

Pippen was asked if he was amazed that Krause and Reinsdorf would let Jordan and the rest of the team just walk away from the game. "I'm looking toward that," he said, "so it doesn't amaze me at all. I think change is good for you at some time. Maybe it's just that time for me."

Kerr, though, had a definite opinion. "It's unfortunate," he said. "I think Scottie deserves to be a Bull for his entire career. But if it doesn't happen, it doesn't happen."

Keeping Krause from breaking up the team was obviously Jordan's goal, John Jackson said. "The reason Jordan's saying his leaving is not a hundred percent a done deal is that in his own way he's putting enough public pressure on them to put them in the position where they can't really do that. If they break this team up and try to start rebuilding next year, the team's not gonna be that great. They're talking about building another championship club, but that's gonna take another five or six years down the road minimum. They're gonna have to get through a tough period. They're gonna have to have the support of the public and the fans before they can do that. What Jordan's campaign does now is basically back them in a corner, where public sentiment is so much against them that they're gonna have no choice but to back down."

Kent McDill of the *Daily Herald* said, "Krause doesn't want to be the man who chases Michael out of the game. He just wants to get rid of Phil. He wants a coach who respects him. He likes to be a kingmaker, and he feels that Phil doesn't give him the respect he deserves for putting him in a position to be considered one of the top ten coaches in NBA history."

"To be honest," said the *Sun Times'* Jackson, "if I was Krause and I was in his position, I think I would want to change coaches right now, too. I think it's time. I think Phil's a little burned out in this job. He has changed a lot, and he has gotten a bit arrogant. The decision to change coaches is a valid one, and I think Krause is right on about that. But the problem with it is, Jordan has aligned himself so heavily with Phil. Sometimes perception is more important than reality. And the perception is that if Krause makes a coaching change now, he and Reinsdorf are showing no loyalty to Phil, they're just kicking him in the ass."

"I don't see any reason," said Kent McDill, "why this whole thing just couldn't keep on going."

PLAYBACK

If the springtime meant that Jordan had to campaign to keep his once-in-a-lifetime team together, it also afforded him rare occasions to sit back and reflect on just what his career had meant to him. Sometimes these moments would come in the hours before a road game, sitting around with a few reporters. These sessions disappeared as the season tightened. But when the mood and circumstances allowed, he would sip his pre-game coffee with cream and sugar and visit the past and sometimes the future.

If he wanted, he could have simply ducked into a private screening room at home and opened up his library of videotape, for just about any selection from any point in his career. "I got it all on tape," he explained . "Everything that was on TV, I got it."

Regardless, he had not viewed any of it. "I don't watch it because I'm still building it up, building up that library," he said. "I think a library is something where if I want to refresh my memory, I can. But right now my memory is still good. I don't want to feel like I'm losing my memory, like I have to go back and refresh it. It's special for my kids. I know where I've been, and I know pretty much a lot of the games that I've had, against who, and what my thoughts were at the time. I'm a library in terms of the game, in terms of my participation. So whenever I start losing that, then maybe that's a good place to go back and replace those memories."

How good was his memory? Asked about a 1983 game against the

University of Virginia, he knew it immediately. In the closing minutes he had stunned the crowd at University Hall in Charlottesville by soaring across the lane to block the shot of 7-foot-4 center Ralph Sampson. "That was back in young days," he said, admitting that he had no idea he could make the block. "I surprised myself. That was the beauty of my game, and it has propelled me to my career to some degree. No one could sit there and tell you that I could do anything. I couldn't tell you what I couldn't do and what I could. And that was the beauty of everything. Even today, you can't sit here and tell me what I can do and what I can't."

"The surprises of your athletic feats aren't gone yet?" he was asked.

"That's my whole point," he said. "That's the beauty of the game. Even I don't know what I can do. If I knew, why would I play?"

His favorite Bulls championship was 1996, he said. "That's the first time I really came back and focused on my career without my father. That was probably my best."

Even that, however, didn't outrank the 1981 NCAA championship team he played on at North Carolina. "It's hard to outrank Carolina," he explained, "because that started everything. The confidence, the knowledge, and everything I gained from that, is without question the beginning of Michael Jordan as a whole. So the beginning is always going to outweigh everything else that has happened since."

Yet he also acknowledged that his favorite championship could be ahead of him. "It's not resolved until I say, 'I'm done.' Until I accept it," he said. "Until I accept it, that's all that matters."

He also held plenty of sweet feelings about the thousands of hours of practice over the years, another factor that set him apart. "It becomes such a routine for me that I don't view it as hard," he said. "I guess the hard thing about it is when you think about other players who should have those same feelings but yet they don't. That's the hard part. And that's probably why I'd never be able to coach, because I have a whole different perception about how you should do things and how you shouldn't. I could easily get frustrated watching other people not take advantage of an opportunity given to them.

"It's not necessarily younger players," he added. "It's older players, too. Older players have bad habits, bad preparations for games and things like that. You could say it's predominantly young players, because they're young and have their future ahead of them. But some of the older players, veteran players, have bad habits, too."

When he came to the Bulls in 1984, he found a team held hostage by drug abusers and slackers, people with deeply negative attitudes. "I found bad habits that were multiplied because of bad things surrounding the team," he recalled. "I'm not saying I had the perfect approach, but I had good habits. I was taught good habits. And I was able to utilize them for what was most important to me — basketball. I prepared myself. I practiced hard. I did all the necessary things to make myself a better basketball player. I'm not saying everybody should be like Michael Jordan in this situation. You can be your own person. But you've got the have the same outlook in terms of what you're productivity's going to be on the basketball court and how you want that to happen. It doesn't happen just in games. It starts in practice, and that's the way I approach it."

His experience had left him concerned about the future of the league. "One person can't solve a multitude of problems, a multitude of concerns," he said. "As a member of the NBA, I'm concerned that this league can be marketed to be, or misunderstood to be, spoiled kids with a lot of money, with no effort, no motivation, paid off of their potential, never reaching their highest potential because of the spoiling of athletes. I don't want that attitude.

"A long time ago," he said, "people spoke of the league as no defense, just a lot of scoring and no fun to watch. Teams scoring 150 points or whatever. The league has worked on that image to where it's very competitive. You can see the challenge, you can see the strategizing going on during an NBA game. But we're certainly on the verge of losing that perception because of a lot of the things that have happened within the game. Once you get a crack in the armor, believe me, the whole armor is in danger because it becomes magnified and starts to spread and people start to look at the littlest things in the largest ways. For years they've done a great job of keeping things nice and tight, where other leagues have had their problems. Now as you look at it, baseball has come back to a certain degree. Football has certainly come back from their strike. And basketball now is showing cracks, and it's gonna start to spread if you don't take care of it."

One way to take care of basketball was to share the game's immense wealth, he said. "Some of the money should go back into the communities. The player's association should step forward. So should the league. It's a very profitable situation. They should give back to the community in some form, if it's the Team-Up situation, the Stay In School program, or some other expanded program, what they should do as well is support the ex NBA players, the guys who pioneered this whole process. That's one of the points that should be talked about."

As a player he had obviously been a guardian of the game, which led to questions about his interest in becoming a team executive, like Jerry West of the Lakers.

"When I walk away from the game, I'm separated, other than being a fan," he said. "I have total admiration for what the game gave to me and certainly will have interest in seeing that other players maintain the success of the Chicago Bulls as well as the league.

"I think I could make a pretty good GM," he added. "If you tell me to manage my money, I could manage the dollars in terms of who I paid. But if the public's perception of who deserves what interferes with that, then I couldn't be a very good GM."

"Would you borrow from the Jerry Krause school of management?" he was asked.

"Never," he replied quickly. "It would be totally independent of the Jerry Krause school of management. I wouldn't sneak around. I wouldn't be the Sleuth. That's one thing you wouldn't call me."

"Your clothing line won't have the Krause hat and coat?" he was asked.

Jordan laughed. "Or the . . . Nothing." He obviously started to say crumbs and thought better of it. "I almost slipped," he said, still smiling. It was obvious he wanted to turn loose his full sense of humor, but this wasn't the team bus.

Did he see anything positive in Krause's relationship with the team? "He works hard," Jordan said after a moment's thought. "I give him credit. He works hard to make things successful, or he works hard to get you to like him, one of the two. He works hard. But really I don't try to figure it out. I would rather save my energy."

Asked if there was anything in basketball he hadn't done, he replied, "I haven't won six championships."

TEXAS

From their win in New York, the Bulls jetted back home briefly to notch a big win over the Heat before heading south for a two-game trip to Texas. First up were the Dallas Mavericks, a team stumbling through yet another misguided season. "I think we're jelling now," Jordan said, sitting in the locker room at Reunion Arena before the March 12h game. "I think we're focused now. I think we're trying to finish off the season right."

David Moore of the *Dallas Morning News* asked him if he had seen Kevin Garnett's comment on national TV that he didn't want to be one of the people coming into Chicago to play for the Bulls in the wake of Jordan's acrimonious departure.

Jordan laughed, fully enjoying the anecdote. "I think a lot of things have to be considered," he said. "What do you say to the next team, the next stars that come in, from a management standpoint? You show a sense of loyalty to us, we'll show a sense of loyalty to you? And do you believe that? Or do you just hear it? That's the danger of what's happening with this organization. What can you tell the next group of guys who come in to pursue a championship? Do you tell them the same things they told us? Or do you tell them something else that may have the same effect? That's the key."

From there, the Bulls went out and ran up a decent lead against the struggling Mavericks. Chicago was up by 18 with about five minutes to go, and the fans were leaving in droves. But then the Bulls lost focus and watched the Mavs stage a strange comeback, aided by a succession of Bulls miscues and questionable calls, to tie it in regulation and win it in overtime. It was only the Bulls' second loss since the All-Star break, but later they would look back on it as the place where they lost homecourt advantage against the Jazz. In the waning seconds of overtime, a disgusted Jackson sat on the bench, clipping his fingernails.

"Sometimes you give 'em away in this game," the coach said afterward, "and we certainly gave that away. We had some help. The referees helped us give it away, but that'll happen sometimes on the road."

"We played giveaway," Tex Winter fumed. "It was ridiculous. In the long-term it'll be good for us. This team's had too much success."

"It's about as stunning a loss as you can imagine," Kerr said.

Getting dressed afterward to head out for good times in his home town, Rodman complained, "We gave it to 'em. If we had had the starting five in there, that game wouldn't have been close at all."

He wore a Sly and the Family Stone look, with a lime green paisley shirt, sunglasses tinted bright yellow, a leopard skin cap, and a thick necklace, which Jackson had commented before the game was heavy enough to use on a tow truck. Rodman began criticizing Jackson and stopped. "I don't want to say nothing wrong," he told the gathering of Dallas media in the locker room. "When you fuck around the whole fourth quarter and don't put a team like that away, any team in the league can beat you. It was pathetic."

Told that Winter had said the Bulls would learn from the loss, Rodman scoffed, "Man, we too old for this shit. What can we learn that we don't already know? That's kinda stupid, isn't it? We been in this league for 50 years. Fuck. We know what the fuck we should do, just let us play."

Asked where he was headed in his outfit, he said, "I'm gonna go out, have a couple of beers and party my ass off. I think it hurts worse when you lose a game like this. Go out have a couple of beers, and your girl says she's not gonna have sex with you. That hurts. That means you're double-fucked."

Flanked by two body guards, Rodman strolled out of the arena past rows of fans chirping for an autograph. At the security entrance, he hopped into a limo. A few feet away the rest of the Bulls had gotten onto the team bus. Jordan, in the very back seat, was sitting quietly, his face resting in his palm. There would be no noise this night.

The next day, after watching the game film, Winter had an even darker concern. It looked as if the Bulls had quit down the stretch. "We had a complete collapse, the worst I've seen in all the time I've been with the Bulls," the assistant coach said. "That's 13 years. I've seen a couple of other collapses, but not like that. We've had games where I've felt like we've given up, where we were down and didn't really come back, more so this year than any time in the past."

The big loss in Miami earlier in the year had been one of those games, he said. "That's concerned me. And then to see a world-championship ball club with all the experience we have collapse like we did. . . . We just weren't very smart. I think the guys feel badly about it. But this team has had too much success. They need to be humbled a little bit."

It was pointed out that Jackson seemed to be the kind of poor sport who never took losing well. "I don't think any of us do," Winter said. "Winning is nice, but losing is just awful. There's a big difference. Sometimes when you win, you're still not happy because of the way you played. But, boy, when you lose, it's just devastating. We've never lost much. It's so hard to take losing when you're not used to it. Once you get the habit of losing, it doesn't bother you quite so much."

"There's some anger and disappointment," Jackson agreed. "Most of the guys went out in Dallas and blew it off. They got rid of it that night and slept it off. We looked at the tape and put it to bed, buried it. It's past."

The Bulls assured that two nights later by playing what Winter would call their most energetic game of the season in rainy San Antonio. Jackson surprised nearly everyone by starting Kukoc against Spurs center David Robinson. An even bigger surprise was that it worked. Although Kukoc lacked the bulk, he had the quickness to give Robinson some problems, and the Bulls hopped out to a 10-2 lead.

The other Chicago concern was outstanding Spurs rookie Tim Duncan, but Jordan answered that on an early Duncan drive by swatting the rookie's shot away. At the other end, Duncan returned the favor with a block of Jordan's shot that sent the Alamodome crowd into a frenzy.

Undeterred, the Bulls closed the first period leading 27-17, having made up for their 35 percent shooting with nine offensive rebounds, including four by Rodman.

The Spurs used the second period to close the gap and pulled to 40-39 by intermission. But Kukoc opened the third by flashing in lane, taking a pass from Harper and dropping in a soft eight foot hook. With that momentum, the Bulls pushed their lead back to 51-41

Kukoc again opened the fourth with a whirligig finish in traffic that looked like it had been copied from a Jordan highlight reel. The Spurs pushed hard, but the Bulls shoved right back. Having learned his lesson two nights earlier, Jackson worked the officials furiously, prompting a fan to yell, "Forget it, Phil, they won't let you come back."

After outdistancing the Spurs by 10, the Bulls continued their burn through March, returning home to buzz New Jersey, then dipping down to win a big game in Indiana. They got a Friday night home win against Vancouver, then headed north into a snowstorm that left them circling for an hour over Toronto and reminded equipment manager John Ligmanowski of a few seasons back when the team jet nearly got flipped by wind shear in Detroit.

Once they landed, the Bulls found the young Raptors as problematic as the snow. Jordan shook hands with Toronto team captains Doug Christie and Dee Brown, then grinned broadly and hopped around during layup drills trying to awaken his legs. There were bags under Jordan's eyes, the weariness weighing on his smile.

Just before tipoff Johnny Ligmanowski dispensed the gum which is so important to this team and even tossed a few pieces to press row. After the introductions, the Bulls lined up to slap hands and began their jumping, Watusi-like, while waiting to go on the floor. Pippen came over to the press table to get one final stretch while casting furtive looks at the Raptor dancers.

"Scottie, Toronto next year," one fan yelled hopefully.

Pippen smiled and turned back to the gyrating dancers. Then the men in red circled Jackson for last-minute instructions, all of them chomping their gum in unison.

Kukoc opened the game with a rebound, and Jackson wasted no time before barking at him. At the offensive end Kukoc held ball on the perimeter.

"Here, here," Jackson shouted hoarsely, motioning to Pippen inside.

Kukoc delivered the pass, "Now to the goal," Jackson yelled. But Kukoc had anticipated and already cut, and Pippen hit him with the return pass for a nice two-handed jam.

Things were right in the Bulls' world, at least for the moment. But that was all that Jackson wanted, for each moment to unfold in timeless beauty and simplicity. On the next possession, Jordan scored and danced away from the goal with the trademark Jordan swagger, that mix of elegance and gameliness.

Moments later, Kukoc would miscommunicate with Jordan on a pass, and the star's anger would flash. He stood with palms up and open, questioning with frustration. Where was the ball? Then Jordan turned away, and Kukoc decided to pass. A turnover. Jordan answered with a daggerlike look and frowned darkly at Kukoc during an ensuing timeout.

The Raptors took advantage of Chicago's confusion to forge a lead, but in the second period Rodman's energy pumped the Bulls back on top. Later, when Rodman returned to the bench, Tex Winter followed him to his seat, to bend and tell him how fine the effort was. Rodman took the compliment without speaking, but his face showed the satisfaction.

In the third period, the Bulls expanded the lead to a dozen, but then came the loss of focus, just as it had in Dallas. Somehow, Jordan and his teammates managed to just hold on at the end, allowing the younger Raptors to make the final mistakes. Jackson smiled. The Bulls were living on the edge, but Pippen was back, and they were winning. And best of all, they were alive in the moment. Right where Jackson hoped they would be.

"It was a nice run. Had to close out someday.
Nobody wins 'em all."

— *The Devil's Advocate*

11/ Keeping the Faith

Dennis Rodman missed the free throw. That was nothing new. Since his earliest days in the league, his efforts at the line had always produced an adventurous array of bricks, clangers and airballs. As his misses went, this one wasn't all that ugly, just a tad long, striking the back of the iron and coming back his way. He rebounded and punched the ball with a flick of his tattooed wrist, almost like he was serving a volleyball. It soared straight up, high into the rafters, where it reached the height of its ellipse and then dropped, right back beside him with a slam.

"That's good," Tex Winter explained later. "I like to see that. He loses his poise, so I call a technical on him."

They were playing a game. Rodman was working on free throws after practice and had hit nine out of 10. "All right, the next one wins it," Winter had told him, simulating a late-game situation.

Rodman missed.

He gazed off into an emptiness of despair.

"You're one down," Winter said, bringing him back to the moment. "Now you gotta get two."

Rodman set his right toe on the line and squared up with his left a half step back. He hit the first, then came another miss, the one that had prompted him to launch the ball to the rafters. Winter stepped up, took Rodman's hand and talked to him soothingly, calming his frustration. As he had done so often over his three seasons with the Bulls, Rodman bowed his head and listened.

On the fourth try, Rodman hit two in a row with Winter jumping spryly across the lane to retrieve the ball and toss it back.

"We keep doing that until he hits two in a row with the pressure on," Winter explained.

The free throws finished, Winter directed Rodman over to the "Toss Back," a target on a large stand. The forward threw the ball at the target, which consisted of webbing tautly stretched over a metal frame, and the target tossed the ball back. Winter invented the "Toss Back" years ago with the help of a machinist, for the express purpose of drilling players on passing fundamentals. Rodman was intimately familiar with it. He crouched and fired picture perfect chest passes at the target, picking up speed as the target fired the ball back. Then Rodman began using his muscled biceps to send the ball back to the target, working it almost like a speed bag.

It was a sweet scene. A Saturday morning in April. Practice was over. A 76-year-old assistant coach and a soon-to-be 37-year-old forward putting in extra work. On free throws. And chest passes, of all things. Youth league coaches around the country can't get 12-year-olds to work on chest passes. It's beneath their dignity, yet here was the dyed and tattooed eighth wonder of the hip world, snapping and stepping like the team captain of the junior varsity.

Winter stepped back and admired the form. Like many of his skills, Rodman's chest passes were fundamentally pure. Even the forward's free throw technique was perfect in practice, so good, Winter boasted, that you could use it for an instructional video. But in the games Rodman would get nervous and his right arm, supposed to be perpendicular to the floor, would flap out wide like a wing, and the shots would turn ugly. Winter's entire efforts were aimed at quieting Rodman's raging anxiety over shooting.

Bill Sharman, the great Celtic guard and free throw purist, had once worked with Wilt Chamblerlain, another horrific free thrower. Chamberlain, like Rodman, became an excellent practice shooter, but he never could quell the performance anxiety in games.

Finally even Sharman gave up on Chamberlain.

"I could never do anything with his free throws," Sharman admitted later.

Winter, though, wasn't about to give up on Rodman.

Forget the fact that they were both perhaps closing in on the final games of their lengthy careers. Winter lived to coach, and Rodman craved the work.

"He wants to be coached," Winter said. "That's the one good thing about Dennis. He likes the attention. If you ignore him, then that's what bothers him. Sometimes I ignore him purposefully because I want him bothered a little bit. But generally I'll talk to him and work with him.

"I work with him every day for about five minutes, particularly on his free throw shooting. I'm trying to get him a little more comfortable, a little more involved in part of the offense, in being part of the offense, as opposed to just kind of taking his eye off the ball, kind of being a spectator, just going into the rebound position and not worrying about where he is. Sometimes he goes into the rebound position, which is what we want him to do, but not when he's supposed to be in some other spot to keep the offense flowing."

The Bulls' coaches knew that Rodman's offensive involvement would be a key in the playoffs' big games. Rodman, of course, wasn't alone in this effort. Nearly every player on the roster put in the extra hours at virtually all of the little things. Their combined efforts made the team atmosphere a supreme competitive environment. If there was anything for Winter and the coaches to mourn about the end of the Jordan era, it would be the eventual dissolution of this competitive environment. "The practice sessions I like," Winter explained, "working with them, as good as they are, as professional as they are, and the kind of money and notoriety they have, yet still seeing a willingness on their part to learn."

The mix of toughness and integrity and grandfatherly charm had made Winter a favorite of many Bulls players and staff members. Nothing better illustrated that than the coach's relationship with Rodman.

"Dennis will listen to Tex," equipment manager John Ligmanowski said. "When Dennis got thrown out of the game the other night and wouldn't get off the floor, Tex got up there and said, 'Hey, you better get off the floor.' He'll listen to Tex, because here's a guy 76-years old still working for a living."

"Tex is a few years younger than my parents and a product of that Depression era," Chip Schaefer explained. "To say that he is frugal would be an understatement. Johnny Bach used to call him penurious. I think that's a very apt description of him. But I think Tex in a lot of ways is the way we all should be. He doesn't like to see things get wasted. He takes that attitude at the dinner table, too. If there's a little bit of meat on your bone, he may just pick up your steak bone and finish it off for you."

"Tex saves shoe boxes, he's so tight," Ligmanowski said, laughing. "We had a meal one time when we were bringing in Larry Krystowiak. I think it was the first time we ever met Larry. Jerry Krause was there. Tex was there. Larry wasn't finished with his food, and Tex goes, 'You gonna finish that?' Larry goes, 'Yeah, I'm gonna finish that!' That was funny. Tex thought he was gonna get a few scraps. Jimmy Rodgers one time got Tex this fork that he could put in his pocket and it extends out like an antennae."

"Basketball is his absolute passion in life," Schaefer observed. "That's what keeps him going. There's times when he'll look tired, and I'll wonder if he has the energy for it. Then all of a sudden practice will start, and he's out here barking at these guys like he's coaching the K-State freshman team and it's 1948.

"Tex has three or four real passions in life. One of them's basketball. Certainly one of them's food. He really enjoys his finances. He pores over the business section of the paper as intensely as he does the sports section. He's a real joy. I hope he keeps on going."

"He's an innovator," explained Bill Cartwright, who had worked with Winter first as a player, then as a fellow Bulls assistant. "He's a really unique person in this sport. He absolutely loves basketball. And it's really fun to be around him, because whatever situation you see on the floor he can talk to you about it, because he's seen them all.

"You recall that everyone used to wear those Chuck Taylors, those canvas Converse shoes," Cartwright said, "and you talk to Tex, and he'll tell you, 'Oh yeah, I knew Chuck Taylor.'"

Over his 51 seasons on the bench, Winter had been the head coach at five colleges—Marquette, Kansas State, Washington, Northwestern and Long Beach State—and had served as head coach of the San Diego/Houston Rockets.

It was at Kansas State in the late 1950s and early 1960s that Winter first got to know Jerry Krause. Winter's teams were among the best in college basketball and even ranked at the top of the polls, and Krause was among the scouts who showed up to watch. "He was just a youngster out of college," Winter recalled, "just working as a gopher really with the Baltimore Bullets. First he was just a statistician. Then he finally sort of got into the scouting phase of it. So it was his first scouting experience. I spent quite a bit of time with him, befriended him. I'd go over the games with him on the old 16 mm analyst projector and point out things and talk terms and talk the triangle, and so forth. He just liked the concepts involved. I was at Northwestern later, and I spent a lot of time with him. He'd come up to practice, and we'd go to lunch once a week. He said that he'd be a general manager some day, and when he was, I'd have to come and help him. When it finally came about, he said that I'd promised him I'd come and help him, which I didn't. But I said, 'Make it worth my while.'"

Krause pulled Winter to Chicago with a handsome salary, but he couldn't find a head coach willing to listen to Winter's advice. First, Stan Albeck declined to buy into Winter's view of the game. Then came Doug Collins, who saw the triangle as unworkable in the modern NBA. In fact, Collins found himself with two assistants, Winter and

Jackson, who had been hired by Krause, assistants he really didn't want.

Discord on the coaching staff mounted to the point that Collins blocked Winter from coming to practice during the 1988-89 season. "Tex was basically out of the picture at that time," Jackson recalled. "He did some scouting for Jerry Krause and took some road trips. He didn't go on all of our game trips. When he was with us, he sat in a corner and kept notes on practice and didn't participate in the coaching. He was out of it."

"I was upset," Krause once admitted, "because Doug basically wasn't listening to Tex, and he wasn't listening to Phil Jackson. Doug did a great job for us for a couple or years. He took the heat off me from a public relations standpoint. Doug was great with the media. But he learned to coach on the fly, and he didn't listen to his assistants as much as he should have. Doug had a thing with Phil, too. As time went on, he was like Stan in that he got away from what we wanted to do."

The Bulls made it all the way to the conference finals before losing to the Detroit Pistons that season, but in the aftermath Krause decided to fire Collins and promote Jackson. "We brought Doug into the office," Krause once recalled, "and I think Doug thought he was going to talk about a contract extension. He had his agent with him. I said, 'Doug, we're going to have to let you go.' The look on his face was shocking. We had our conversation with him, and I called Phil, who was fishing out in Montana. I told him, 'I just let Doug go.' He said, 'What!?!?' And I said, 'Doug's gone, and I want you to be the head coach. You need to get your ass in here on a flight today. Soon as you can. I got to talk to you.' I brought Phil in and we talked philosophy. The first thing he said was, 'I've always been a defensive oriented guy, as a player with Red Holtzman, and as a coach. That's what you want me for?' I said, 'Yeah.' He said, 'I'm going to turn the offense over to Tex, and I'm going to run the triple-post.'

"I think some people who know me thought that I had set that all up, that I'd brought Phil in because he'd run Tex's stuff," Krause said. "I wish I'd been that smart, but I wasn't. It was all his idea. But I said, 'Great. That's super.' Because I knew the damn stuff would work. But I couldn't impose that on Doug. You couldn't impose anything on Doug. I would never impose what a coach runs on them anyway."

Without question, Winter said, it was the rise of Jackson to the position of head coach that made the use of his triangle offense possible. It was not, however, an easy transition.

Winter had spent years developing the triangle, or triple-post offense. It was an old college system that involved all five players shar ing the ball and moving. But it was totally foreign to the pro players of the 1990s, and many of them found it difficult to learn. Where for years the pro game had worked on isolation plays and one-on-one set ups, the triple-post used very little in the way of set plays. Instead the players learned to react to situations and to allow their ball movement to create weaknesses in defenses.

Among the offenses strongest questioners was Jordan.

"I've always been very much impressed with Michael as well as everyone else has been," Winter once explained. "I've never been a hero worshipper. I saw his strong points, but I also saw some weaknesses. I felt like there was a lot of things that we could do as a coaching staff to blend Michael in with the team a little bit better. I thought he was a great player, but I did not feel that we wanted to go with him exclusively. We wanted to try and get him to involve his teammates more. Until he was convinced that that was what he wanted to do, I don't think we had the chance to have the program that we had later down the line."

"Tex's offense emulated the offense I had played in with New York," Jackson said. "The ball dropped into the post a lot. You ran cuts. You did things off the ball. People were cutting and passing and moving the basketball. And it took the focus away from Michael, who had the ball in his hands a lot, who had been a great scorer. That had made the defenses all turn and face him. Suddenly he was on the back side of the defenses, and Michael saw the value in having an offense like that. He'd been in an offense like that at North Carolina. It didn't happen all at once. He started to see that over a period of time, as the concepts built up."

"It was different for different types of players," recalled former Bulls guard John Paxson. "For me it was great. A system offense is made for someone who doesn't have the athletic skills that a lot of guys in the league have. It played to my strengths. But it tightened the reins on guys like Michael and Scottie from the standpoint that we stopped coming down and isolating them on the side. There were subtleties involved, teamwork involved. But that was the job of Phil to sell us on the fact we could win playing that way."

"Everything was geared toward the middle, toward the post play," Jordan said, explaining his opposition. "We were totally changing our outlook . . . and I disagreed with that to a certain extent. I felt that was putting too much pressure on the people inside."

"What Michael had trouble with," Jackson said, "was when the ball went to one of the big guys like Bill Cartwright or Horace Grant or some of the other players who weren't tuned in to handling and pass-

ing the ball. They now had the ball. Could they be counted on to make
the right passes, the right choices? I brought Michael in my office and
told him basically, 'The ball is like a spotlight. And when it's in your
hands, the spotlight is on you. And you've gotta share that spotlight
with some of your teammates by having them do things with the basketball, too.' He said, 'I know that. It's just that when it comes down to
getting the job done, a lot of times they don't want to take the initia-
tive. Sometimes it's up to me to take it, and sometimes that's a tough
balance.'

   "All along the way it was a compromise of efforts," Jackson said.
"Everybody made such a big issue of the triple-post offense. We just
said, 'It's a format out of which to play. You can play any way you
want out of the triangle.' Because if it's a sound offense, you should be
able to do that. One of the concepts is to hit the open man."

   Jordan's presence also stretched the flexibility of Winter's concepts and challenged the older coach's thinking. "There were times
when Michael knew he was going to get 40 points," Jackson said. "He
was just hot those nights. He was going to go on his own, and he would
just take over a ball game. We had to understand that that was just part
of his magnitude, that was something he could do that nobody else in
this game could do. And it was going to be okay. Those weren't always
the easiest nights for us to win as a team. But they were certainly spectacular nights for him as a showman and a scorer."

   "It took some time," Paxson recalled. "Michael was out there
playing with these guys, and unless he had a great deal of respect for
them as players, I think he figured, 'Why should I pass them the ball
when I have the ability to score myself or do the job myself? I'd rather
rely on myself to succeed or fail than some of these other guys.' The
thing I like about Michael is that he finally came to understand that if
we were going to win championships he had to make some sacrifices
individually. He had to go about the task of involving his teammates
more."

   "A lot of times," Jackson said, "my convincing story to Michael
was, 'We want you to get your thirty-some points, and we want you to
do whatever is necessary. It's great for us if you get 12 or 14 points by
halftime, and you have 18 points at the end of the third quarter. Then
get your 14 or 18 points in the fourth quarter. That's great. If it works
out that way, that's exactly what it'll be.' Who could argue with that?
We'd tell him, 'Just play your cards. Make them play everybody during the course of the game and then finish it out for us.' I think that's
why sometimes Michael has downplayed the triangle. He says it's a
good offense for three quarters, but it's not great for the fourth quarter.

That's because he took over in the fourth quarter. He can perform."

"Phil was definitely set on what we were going to do and he wouldn't waiver," Winter recalled. "Even though the triple-post offense evolved through my many, many years of coaching, Phil was sold on it even more than I was at times. There's times when I would say, 'We should get away from this. Let Michael have more one-on-one opportunities.' And Phil was persistent in not doing so. It's to his credit that we stayed to his basic philosophy of basketball."

The team's effort with the offense intensified over the early months of the 1990-91 season, and by February the players and Jordan clicked in their understanding, which resulted in impressive displays of execution. They finished that February with an 11-1 record that included a host of road wins during a West Coast trip. "We had been on the road for something like two weeks," Jordan recalled, "and it just came together. I could feel it⁻ then."

"I remember we were on a West Coast swing before we really started kicking it in and getting some really nice action off of it," recalled Bill Cartwright. "It was fun. People started seeing that. We were getting dunks and wide-open jump shots. But before that, it took a lot of time and patience for us to grow."

The Bulls won the Eastern Conference with a 61-21 record in 1991, and Jordan claimed his fifth straight scoring title with a 31.5 average. During the playoffs, he was named the league's MVP for the second time. Best of all, the Bulls won the first of their titles, soon to be followed by two more consecutive championships.

"It may sound sort of self-serving," Winter said, "but I think the offense has very definitely been one of the Chicago Bulls' strengths. Because the program has perpetuated itself. Even when Jordan left us, I think people were amazed—and we were too—that we could win 55 games."

Jordan had never discussed the offense with Winter, and had never acknowledged its importance. When the superstar returned to the Bulls in 1995 after his 18-month retirement, both he and the team struggled in the playoffs that spring, leading to speculation among the media that perhaps it was time for Chicago to find a new offensive system. Even Winter himself had doubts. In the wake of the loss to Orlando in the 1995 playoffs, Winter pushed Jackson to discuss the issue with Jordan in the season-ending conference Jackson held privately with each player.

"With his impulsiveness, Tex said, 'Phil, I'd like you to ask him, does he think we need to change the offense,'" Jackson recalled. "'Is it something we should plan on using next year? I want you to ask him just for me.' So I did, and Michael said, 'The triple-post offense is the backbone of this team. It's our system, something that everybody can hang their hat on, so that they can know where to go and how to operate.'"

Indeed, the offense played a key role in Chicago's success for the next two seasons, but that didn't mean the debate ended. If anything, the issue seemed to become more pronounced with the passing of each NBA season.

In 1958, Winter's Kansas State team defeated Wilt Chamberlain and the Kansas Jayhawks in the Big Eight Conference tournament, preventing the dominant giant from returning to the NCAA tournament his junior season. Chamberlain was so disappointed by the loss that he withdrew from school and spent a year touring with the Harlem Globetrotters.

Decades later, Winter would joke facetiously that he "drove" Chamberlain from the college game. Still, his team's victory over Kansas in the basketball-crazy Midwest was one of the great upsets of that era. In some ways, the success of his team play against the individual brilliance of Chamberlain was a theme that still resonated every game night for the Chicago Bulls. There was Jordan's individual mastery, and there was Winter, extolling his triangle offense and the purity of team play. Their careers had evolved to a nightly give-and-take on the issue.

"It's a balancing act, is what it is," Winter said in 1998. "Every game is a thin line, it's a thin line as to how much freedom you want to give a player who has as much talent as Michael has. And how much do you want him to sacrifice his own individual talents to score to involve his teammates more?"

Asked if Jordan and his coaches ever actually debated the issue, Winter replied, "I think he understands, but Michael wants to score when he touches the ball. And he feels like he's got the ability to. So, consequently why should he give up the ball? He probably doesn't have the trust in a lot of his teammates he should. He'd rather put it on his own shoulders to bare that load."

Jordan's teammates often felt that lack of trust, Winter said. In fact, Jackson's film sessions and post-season preachings about togetherness were often meant primarily for Jordan, Winter said. "Michael understands. He's a very smart basketball player. It's just that he's such a competitor that he likes challenges. And when he catches that ball, if he feels like he can, he's gonna try to score. And often times he does.

Even when he goes one on one, most of it comes out of the concept of the offense. He's not going off on his own and completely abandoning our principles. We won't let him do that."

If Jordan's competitiveness raged to the point that he bordered on killing chemistry, Jackson would usually caution him that he was trying to do too much. "That's usually about all it takes," Winter said. "Phil will remind him to involve his teammates. Phil will let him know that he missed a teammate that was open. He'll penetrate, for example, to the middle, and Kerr's man will fly in to attack him. And Kerr's wide open, and Michael may try to beat the two people rather than hit Kerr."

The triangle offense was still the apparatus that provided for the ball movement necessary to defuse Jordan's competitiveness when it reached toxic levels. As Jordan book collaborator Mark Vancil pointed out, most fans would have never heard of the triangle offense if not for Jordan's individual mastery. That certainly was true. On the other hand, there was a strong argument that Jordan would never have realized his potential as the leader of a championship team if he hadn't molded his game to fit within Winter's team approach.

Jackson synthesized the argument. Oftentimes the team struggled in executing the offense, he pointed out, but "we were still philosophically in tune with one another because of it. And it shows.

"A lot of times," Jackson said, "it's all right to say from a coaching standpoint, 'You know we executed offensively in these games, and it's really a matter great function of the team.' But the reality is that the triangle offense works great because Michael Jordan has an ability to move between five different positions and sail by double-teams and knows how to function in this thing so that he can always bail out the offense in the last five seconds. That's made it really a great offense for a superstar."

The Bulls would often use the offense for the first 20 seconds of a possession, then turn the ball over to Jordan to execute one-on-one moves as the shot clock wound down. The friction between the individual and the system brought still more innovation. But there was little question that Winter had been one of the people to stand up to Jordan, the result of which was Jordan's begrudging respect. It hadn't been earned without a price.

"Michael's sort of his own man," Winter explained in 1995. "I think he's talked to Phil occasionally about what we do offensively and how he fits into the scheme of things. I let Phil handle that. My basic job is of teacher. When we step out on that floor at a practice session, I'm going to coach whoever shows up. And I'm going to coach them the way I coach, whether it's Michael Jordan, Scottie Pippen, or whoever it is. It doesn't make any difference. They know that. If I see Michael making a mistake, I'll correct him as fast as I will anyone else. On the other hand, he's such a great athlete you have to handle him a little differently than you do the other players. I don't think you can come down on him hard in a very critical way, whereas some younger guy or some other guy you feel you might be able to motivate by coming down on them pretty tough."

Winter pointed out in 1998 that only in the last few seasons had Jordan himself actually gotten the real hang of the chest pass. The coach added that he didn't think Scottie Pippen would ever quite get the technique down. "There's something with Pippen's wrist," Winter said. "He just throw a correct chest pass."

Told this comment later, Jordan smiled. "I have tremendous respect for Tex Winter," he said. "His nitpicking over the years has been important in the building up of my game. I couldn't have been as fundamentally sound without him."

The use of the word "nitpicking" gave the compliment Jordan's trademark backhanded edge. "He's appreciative of the little things," Winter said, "but at the same time, even though he says that, he still has a hard time being a real fundamental basketball player. He accepts the coaching, but he just doesn't play that way. He's more of a high-wire act, you know. He's into degree of difficulty instead of just working, just trying to be real fundamentally sound. You can't fault him for that because that's one of the reasons he's been effective. I think he's more appreciative now of the basic fundamental skills necessary to make our offense function than he was earlier."

Still, you didn't have to spend much time around the Bulls to sense the underlying conflict between player and coach. Sometimes it surfaced in strange ways.

For example, during the 1996 playoffs Jordan walked out of the training room and into the Chicago Bulls locker room at the United Center and stopped suddenly. There, sitting in Jordan's locker space was Winter, quietly conducting a pre-game interview with a reporter.

Apparently annoyed that someone was sitting in his locker space before a game, Jordan eyed Winter, then turned and walked a few steps to the center of the locker room, where he paused and turned back around.

"Tex, you want this?" Jordan said gruffly, holding up the shoe box that had held his brand new pair of Air Jordans for the evening. Jordan knew Winter would want the box. Winter wanted everything. If he passed a drink machine, he instinctively reached into the change receptacle to see if anyone had left a little silver. Some days after practice, when the reporters cleared out of the Berto Center, Winter would venture down to the press room to pick up any newspapers left there so that he could read them without having to buy his own.

Winter looked up at Jordan holding the box and nodded that, yes, he wanted it.

Jordan could have walked four feet and handed it to him. Instead, he turned it over in his hand, looked at it a moment, curled his lip just a bit and dropped the box at his own feet. If Winter wanted it, he would have to get up and pick it up off the floor.

Perhaps Jordan didn't mean it as an insult. But at the very least it was a gesture of thoughtless disrespect, certainly not the kind of behavior fans would expect from His Airness.

Winter ignored it, and went back to his interview.

The incident only proved that, contrary to reports, Jordan was indeed quite human and fallible. As *Sports Illustrated* writer Rick Reilly had pointed out in an essay published in May 1998, Jordan performed great deeds of charity in privacy, neither seeking or wanting publicity for his actions. As befitting a role model and public figure of his immense stature, Jordan tried to save his worst moments for privacy, too. As Phil Jackson had explained, living with the master competitor could be trying at times.

At times the issue was merely a matter of Jordan's playfulness.

"Tex is like a grandpa to all of us," former Bulls trainer Mark Pfeil once pointed out. "But the players would mock him. Michael used to tease him and stuff. Over everything. One time in practice, Michael sneaked up behind him and pulled Tex's shorts all the way down to his knees, and there was Tex's bare butt sticking out."

Winter smiled at recounting of Jordan's prank and the star's occasional testiness. They were small prices to pay for the privilege of working with the game's ultimate competitor. "I've been with Michael now 12 or 13 years," Winter pointed out. "I've been his coach longer than anybody. He's only three years at North Carolina, four years in high school. The rest of it's been with the Bulls, and I've been with him all but his first year. I really didn't get very well acquainted with him at first. I just observed him more than anything else. Made kind of a study of him. I'd never seen anyone with such tremendous physical talents, the reflexes particularly. Catlike actions and moves. Alertness."

All of it, the competitive nature, the physical talent, the leadership skills, the sense of humor, the drive, added up to a package that had fascinated the planet for more than a decade. Jordan was obviously bigger than basketball itself, except perhaps in the eyes of Winter. "I don't think there's anybody bigger than the team itself, than the five men functioning on the floor at the same time," the coach said. "And that includes Michael. I think oftentimes where we might get in trouble is that too many people might think that's the case, that one player might be bigger than the system or the program, the franchise. And he's not. Even Michael. I don't know that he realizes it. It's probably just as well that he doesn't. But we're all dispensable. He would be hard to replace, there's no question about that. But on the other hand, if the system is sound, the program is sound, the franchise is sound throughout, then it could continue to succeed."

Having said that, Winter acknowledged that his triangle offense might not last past Jordan's career itself, at least not in the NBA. In the women's college game, the offense was thriving. Coach Pat Summitt had successfully incorporated it into her approach at the University of Tennessee, the game's dominant program. The University of Connecticut, another top women's program, also made use of the triangle, which Winter attributed to the dedication of female athletes and their coaches and their drive to teach and learn the fundamentals of the game. The NBA, however, seemed to be another story, with both Phoenix and Dallas having tried the offense and failing miserably.

The issue raised questions about the legacy of this great Bulls team. Certainly Jordan and his team had brought vast changes in the economics of the game, but in many ways the prosperity he brought to the game also threatened it. As far as his individual style, there were legitimate questions about the ability of Kobe Bryant and other young players to duplicate it successfully. More important was the style of the team itself. Had the Bulls brought any lasting changes as a group? Would the team's style of play eventually force other teams to change?

Ron Harper was one of many Bulls who had struggled mightily to adapt to the offense after coming to Chicago. "If I was a coach, there would be some part of this I would try, I think," Harper said. "But it's a challenge. On this team you've got to know the spots for all five guys. I can go to the five man spot and be a center. I can be a four, a two, a point guard. You have to have guys who are interchangeable, more complete players. If your player is a good isolation guy, if that's what his skills are meant for, that's what you're gonna need to do. But in this game, where the defenses are very solid, you need to get things that change up here and there. The way we play is a new kind of style. It's old school, too. But it's so old it's new. The Bulls have been seen all over. People are seeing how we do things. But what Jim Cleamons tried to do in Dallas, it didn't work. What they tried to do in Phoenix, it didn't work. It worked sometimes, but they didn't have enough success. Some teams have some players who've gotta have the ball all the time.

On our team, guys don't have to have the basketball all the time. Here, you very seldom see a guy hold the ball all the time. You have to pass and move yourself. You got to learn that you won't have the basketball on this team here."

Scott Burrell, who had also struggled with the triangle, said learning the system required immense patience because it left new players feeling out of synch. "It just makes you off balance and not ready to go out and play," he said. "It drops your confidence 'cause you can't really go out there and play like you could. I think players lose with it because they don't have faith in it. You gotta have faith in it. It's hard to sell. You gotta have faith that it's gonna work.

Jud Buechler was one of those players who had taken a quick liking to Winter's offense. "Are you kidding me?" Buechler said when asked about it. "The triangle has given me a chance to play in this league. All the offenses in the NBA now, everything is so one-on-one, get the ball in isolation. As a player, it's not a very fun style to play, because if you're not that guy with the ball then you're just standing around out there. I was the guy standing in the parking lot on the other side of the floor going, 'Illegal defense!' the whole time to the referee. I came to Chicago, and all that changed. The way the triangle is set up, you pass, you move, you make decisions. It's more of a team game; it gets everybody involved. And that was my style of play. It's definitely helped me.

"If you talk to anybody who knows anything about the game of basketball, they'll tell you that they love to watch the Bulls play first of all because of Michael and Dennis and Scottie and the talent we have," Buechler said. "But they also like the style and the way we play ball. Everyone touches the ball. You share it. It's an exciting way to play. It's the way every player would like to have it. Who wants to turn on a game and watch the ball go into the post and watch a guy back a guy down, a guy spaced out on the other side standing around? Those games aren't very fun to watch."

Buechler said he understood that Phoenix and Dallas failed in using the triangle, "but they didn't give it any time. It's not something you can throw out there for half a season. It takes years. It took this team two or three years to get it down and figure it out."

"It is the type of offense where you need time," agreed Bulls assistant Bill Cartwright, a Winter disciple. "You need time with it. You need people to run the offense at maximum speed. They must be able to recognize the cuts, who's open and who's not. They must be able to read defenses, and all of that takes time. We've been fortunate to have guys here for years running this offense."

And that, in itself, helped explain why so many NBA teams opted to run isolation offenses. They were put together with quick assembly, while the triangle required many hours of intricate work. It's the age of McDonald's, of fast food, of quick turnaround. The isolation offense was quick process in an age of quick processes. The circumstances presented a question: How would the NBA sustain a sense of quality once Michael Jordan's Bulls ceased to run?

"It's a very valid question," Buechler said. "I'm not quite sure. Maybe they could change some of the rules of the game. Most of the offense are set up because of what the NBA has made for rules, particularly illegal defense. They want one-on-one play, they want exciting play. But it's kind of backfired in terms of the types of offenses teams are running out there right now."

"I think it's a problem that the NBA needs to address," Winter agreed. "What's happening is that the NBA is a superstar league. It features the players, which it should. But in so doing, then the superstars are the ones who make the money and get the recognition. Consequently, they're the ones who set the example for everyone who comes along in the league. What happens is, you don't get team play.

"You see," he said, "I think this offense is very simple, but it's so basic that these players with these great individual talents and skills that they've developed on the playground don't want it that simple. They want to make it their contest one on one against somebody, and that's the thing the NBA is going to have to guard against. Showmanship is important. There's no question that people come to see Michael Jordan play and to see him score. It's a superstar league, but I think it has to get back to where the team becomes more important than the individual."

Michael Jordan's Bulls had discovered that even though they were a house divided, they could still win, playing against whatever obstacles that happened into their path. Entering April, they defeated the Timberwolves in Chicago, then zipped to Texas for a quick win over Houston before returning home to finish off Washington in the United Center, which had begun to earn a term of affection among Chicago sports fans — "the UC" — much like they might speak of the Eisenhower or the Kennedy.

The early April wins pushed Chicago's win streak to a season-high 13, and the outburst gave them a nice pad over the Eastern Conference's second place team, Larry Bird's Indiana Pacers. In the Western Conference, however, the Utah Jazz hummed along, just ahead of Chicago in the race for homecourt advantage if the teams made it to the championship series.

Utah stumbled first, with a key road loss in Minnesota, opening the way for Chicago to take the best record in the league. The Bulls, however, experienced their own bit of faltering. They lost in Cleveland, then defeated Orlando and became the first team in the league to win 60 games. But then the Pacers came to the UC and met the Bulls with a physical challenge aimed at sending Jordan and his teammates to the line, where they stumbled. The Pacers won handily in Chicago, 114-105, a tremendous confidence booster for Bird's team. In the aftermath, the Bulls lost again, this time on the road in Detroit, the outgrowth of which was a 62-20 finish to the season. That left them tied with Utah, except that the Jazz had won both games against Chicago during the regular season, meaning they, not the Bulls, would hold the homecourt advantage if the two teams met in the NBA Finals. Some observers continued to believe the Bulls would be vulnerable in the playoffs. After all, Longley was still troubled by aching knees, and the core of the roster showed substantial age. Most of the coaches and players seemed to worry little about that, except perhaps for Tex Winter, who worried about everything.

Instead, the Bulls turned to more important matters, the clashing of words and swords behind the scenes. The public relations struggle between the two sides continued at a feverish pace, with the competitors hoping to influence the thinking of various columnists in Chicago. Krause and Reinsdorf remained quite cautious, while Jackson, perhaps sensing his team's success on the floor, became emboldened. The coach turned up the tempo of the the struggle by speaking publicly on the issue. If nothing else, the situation taught that in the late stages of a struggle, one needed to choose his words very carefully. In retrospect, Jackson would see that the prudent thing would have been just to let the Bulls' play do most of the talking. But he didn't do that, and it would cost him.

"And magnificently we will float into the mystic."
— Van Morrison

12/ The Devil's Advocate

Phil Jackson's final weeks as coach of the Chicago Bulls were marked by more turbulence. But it was nothing that Michael Jordan couldn't overcome. After all, the star lived for the playoff season, that time when every synapse in his competitive spirit was fused to every twitch of his muscle fiber, when his will was fully wired and hypercharged. Each spring, it seemed, Jackson and his staff would work on subtle means of reining in that immense force. Each spring, they knew the ultimate futility of their efforts. Their best hope was to preach togetherness, constantly reminding Jordan to include his teammates, to pull them along just enough so that when he needed them, they would be there to help.

Jordan knew this and complied whenever and wherever possible. He was gracious and diplomatic and respectful. Yet that took him just so far. In the end, he was the only one who really understood his attack mentality. Only he could sense when to unleash it. And he would be the first to admit that it wasn't perfect. But it was damn near close, eerily close some nights, when he would slip into his terminator mode late in a key game with important things on the line. "He's just so damn confident," Tex Winter said one playoff night after Jordan had teetered between success and failure, what Winter referred to as the "high-wire act."

The suspense had never been greater, with the future of his team and his career on the line. In reality, the public relations campaigning of the regular season had been only fun and games, a diversion. In the end, Jordan's play would send the one single message that trumped all others.

It began in late April with the very first playoff game in the first round against the New Jersey Nets. The Bulls played sluggishly, blew a late, 14-point lead and allowed the young Nets to take them to overtime, where Jordan stole the ball from Kerry Kittles with 90 seconds to play, sped upcourt, tongue out, and dunked. Then he growled.

New Jersey's Kendall Gill had fouled him going to the basket, and Jordan made the free throw, propelling Chicago to a 96-93 win.

The growl was a tad uncharacteristic, but these were emotional times.

"We walk away feeling lucky more than anything," said Jordan, who finished with 39 points.

Chicago had opened the playoffs without Luc Longley, who had missed 23 of the previous 25 games with a bad knee. The Bulls had been outrebounded by the Nets in Game 1 and obviously missed his size on the boards. "It's been incredibly frustrating," said the 7-foot-2 Longley, the frustration obvious in his voice. "Originally we thought it would be something that wasn't a big deal." Yet days had become weeks from March into April, and the Bulls were already thin in the frontcourt.

"With Luc, he's a very sensitive guy about the way things feel, and you just can't push him before he's ready to go," Chip Schaefer said of the public pressure on Longley to get back into uniform. "I think it's weighed on him a little bit. He's had his toughness questioned a number of times, and I think that's wearing on him, too, to have his toughness questioned."

Longley would return for the second round of the playoffs, but the speculation hadn't been fun. Part of the pressure on the center came from the exceptional standard set by Jordan, Schaefer said. "He hasn't missed a game in the last three seasons, since he came back in 1995. That's just really extraordinary. That's just his determination. To me, that's just his way of saying he refuses to give in. Michael hates to be beholding. He doesn't want to owe you a favor. If he owes you a favor, it's like, 'What can I do to get the favor out of the way?' There have been times, have been games the past couple of years, where he's been sick enough or ill enough where he probably shouldn't have played and probably another guy wouldn't have played. But to me, that's him saying, 'I'm not gonna give these guys a chance to say I didn't earn my $33 million. I'm gonna be damn sure of that. I'm not gonna give these guys any ammunition when I sit down with them at the end of the season.' He's not gonna give them that chance."

Actually, trainer controversy had engulfed the New Jersey series almost from the outset, but it didn't involve player availability. When NBC reported that the Bulls had interviewed New Orleans

Saints trainer Dean Kleinschmidt to replace Schaefer, the news touched off speculation that Krause was preparing to name Iowa State's Tim Floyd to replace Jackson as coach for 1998-99. The report, attributed to Saints coach Mike Ditka, suggested that Floyd, a former Saints ball boy, was pulling his staff together to form the new Bulls regime. Floyd denied the account, and Ditka later issued a retraction.

Kleinschmidt told reporters he had talked with the Bulls but that Floyd had not contacted him on behalf of the team.

"In my search to find the finest possible trainer to carry on the excellent work of Chip Schaefer, I have interviewed Dean Kleinschmidt along with numerous others for that position," Krause said in a prepared statement before Game 2, trying to quell speculation that the change was another sign of Jackson being pushed out the door. "Nobody else in our organization, or anyone acting on behalf of our organization, has interviewed any of our candidates. We have not hired anybody for any job, including that of head coach."

Actually, Schaefer had learned in February from someone in his field that Krause was shopping around for another trainer. Each season Schaefer had struggled with the idea of returning to the Bulls because his wife had strong family ties in California and wanted to move back home, but he had assumed the decision to leave would always be his.

"It's like knowing you're gonna get a divorce and finding out after the fact that your spouse cheated on you," he said of the tip from a friend in the business that Krause was looking for his replacement. Schaefer had planned to go to Krause in March and tell him of his decision not to return. He admitted that the circumstances shouldn't have bothered him, but they did.

"For a couple of weeks, I didn't know how to react to it," he said.

He was crestfallen the day he learned the news. That night he ran into assistant coach Jimmy Rodgers at a movie theater and told him what he had learned. "Jimmy kind of soothed me a little bit," Schaefer said. "He's a guy who's been around the NBA for 20 some years. He said, 'You know, this whole league comes down to whose guy are you.' My intent over all these years was never to be anybody's guy."

Schaefer had a reputation around the team of taking a measured, balanced approach between Krause and Jackson. "I have always felt that I was," he said in explaining what was disappointing about Krause's move.

Some employees even said that, like Winter, Schaefer was part of the glue that allowed Krause and Jackson to keep working together after their relationship deteriorated. "I think I would like to have been more of a glue for them," Schaefer said. "But if that's one of my responsibilities, then I've failed."

Krause's move to replace him had left Schaefer with intensely mixed emotions. "I feel loyalty to Jerry, too," he said of Krause. "That was one of the things that was troubling about getting caught up in the rift between these two guys. I consider myself and my story of how I came to the Bulls as a fairly decent example of what's good about Jerry. Jerry's reputation scoutingwise is for finding people, finding baseball players and basketball players and coaches. He'll tell you how he found Tony LaRussa in Iowa and how he found Phil in the CBA, how he does these things."

Schaefer, too, was one of Krause's "finds" and maybe more of a reach than others because he was the head trainer at Loyola Marymount University in 1990 when star Hank Gathers dropped dead of a heart ailment. "I was embroiled in one of the biggest controversies, one of the hottest things in sports litigation," Schaefer said. "I'm in the middle of this Hank Gathers thing. If I were him and I got my resume, I would have looked at it like, 'This guy's done pretty well for himself, but I'm just not gonna touch this,' and tossed the file in the garbage can. But here Jerry looked at it and somehow waded through the bullshit and saw my master's degree in counseling, saw that I was from Deerfield, Illinois, saw that I had worked the NBA summer leagues and worked with the Lakers, did these things. All those things came out to him. Jerry's very good about sorting through things and kind of finding the ugly duckling. To me, I've told my wife many times, 'As much as I get upset at things that have happened over the years that Jerry's been involved with I'm very grateful for the opportunity he gave me.' I never want to lose sight of that."

It seemed obvious that Schaefer had no culpability in the Gathers issue. But a less-informed executive would have erred on the side of caution. The investigative nature in Krause had led him to find out that Schaefer was an excellent trainer who had done nothing but the best work in caring for Gathers and the other Loyola athletes. Krause hired Schaefer long before the litigation in the issue was resolved. Ultimately Schaefer was cleared completely of any wrongdoing in the matter and was left with a strong sense of obligation to Krause.

Yet, like many Bulls players, Schaefer sensed his feelings

toward Krause diminishing over his eight years with the team under the weight of the general manager's brusque approach. Sadly, Krause should have enjoyed substantial loyalty from the many players and employees he assembled, but he often seemed to find a way of angering them. "Once I was led to feel that I wasn't wanted or appreciated that killed any fire that I had," Schaefer said. "When I heard the things that I heard, I felt like Scottie felt in November. I mean I love the players and coaches, but it extinguished whatever flame I ever had for the organization. It had been going down over the years, but he put it out. You can look at it and say, 'Don't let it bother you.' But when it happens to you, you say, 'Damn, that bothers me.'"

Part of the conflict between Schaefer and Krause was the result of the conflict over the team's doctors, which left medical issues with the team "pretty inflamed," Schaefer said. "Things could have been handled differently or better. Hindsight being 20-20, I could think of things I might have done differently over the years. Again all the people involved are all good people. There's no bad people here. It was just a matter of circumstance. John Hefferon was the team physician when I came here in 1990. He was a guy that I certainly connected well with. . . . We had a nice relationship built up, and then Jerry over time soured on his opinion of him. For a long time, he had wanted to involve Jeff Weinberg (Krause's personal doctor) as the team physician."

Part of the problem was the location of Hefferon's downtown office, on good days an hour's commute from the Berto Center. If a player had a sprained ankle from practice or a sore throat or whatever it often meant getting on the Kennedy Expressway at 2 p.m. and heading into Chicago's snarl.

"Guys loved him," Schaefer said of Hefferon, "but they'd roll their eyes. It was a pain in the butt to go down there."

Another part of Hefferon's difficulty came in 1994-95, the second season Jordan was out of the game, after Krause had signed Ron Harper and Larry Krystkowiak for the Bulls. In a series of columns for the *Sun Times*, Krause implied that perhaps the team's medical staff hadn't inspected the players' health closely enough before they were signed. "To me what happened is that Dr. Hefferon became kind of a scapegoat for things that happened that were not his fault or were really fair," Schaefer said. "Jerry was under a lot of pressure. At that time, neither the Harper signing nor the Krystkowiak signing was going very well. Neither was playing very well. Clearly, Jerry was pointing the finger of blame at Dr.

Hefferon for passing these guys in physicals. In fact, Ron didn't miss one practice all year long because of injury. It was a weird thing. It was like, 'Why are you blaming him?'"

The outgrowth of Krause's decision to replace Hefferon with Weinberg was an image in the media that the general manager was tinkering with player availability issues. Although it may have appeared that way to the media, that was really more image than reality, the trainer said. For example, there was Game 5 of the 1997 Eastern Conference finals versus Miami. Pippen injured his foot in the first half. "He hurt the ball of his foot, the juncture where the foot meets the toe, the joint there," Schaefer said. "The thinking was that he partially dislocated that joint, spraining that capsule and injuring some of the soft tissue around the joint. There was a little bit of a scene there on ESPN with Jeff Weinberg going up into the stands and talking to Jerry Krause, and everybody saw Jerry shaking his head no. I got put in the middle again of a situation between Phil and Jerry. It appeared that Jerry would not allow Scottie to play in that game."

Pippen sat out the rest of the game while the Bulls won and advanced to the NBA Finals. "As a competitor he did want to give it a try," Schaefer said. "The doctors felt that without benefit of further diagnostic tests that there was a risk of damaging it further and being at risk for the Finals. That created a situation where Dr. Weinberg went to Jerry, and all of a sudden Jerry appeared to be making a medical decision, or what appeared to be a medical decision but was in fact a management decision. Phil got kind of upset that that happened, and I got stuck in the middle of that. He was upset that somehow his perception was that Jerry was making a decision regarding whether an athlete should play or not. There appeared to be some indecisiveness on the part of the doctors. That's what doctors are there for. Doctors have a lot more training and education. That's what they're qualified for. At that time Dr. Weinberg was trying to act in good faith, as a good liaison, and as a person who has been a friend of Jerry's for a long time."

However, television cameras followed his trek up to see Krause, which was replayed on an ESPN news broadcast. To some observers, the scene resonated all the way back to the issue of control in 1986 when Jordan wanted to return from his foot injury and management questioned his decision.

"In analysis, everybody's a little bit right," Schaefer said. "Teams have huge dollars invested in these guys, and they are a commodity, if you will."

Nothing illustrated the issue better than Patrick Ewing returning to the Knicks during the 1998 playoffs despite doctors' concerns that his injured wrist had not healed. Or even worse, Jerry Rice returning to the San Francisco 49ers too soon after a serious knee injury and reinjuring the knee. "Certainly any team wants an athlete who wants to play to be out there playing," Schaefer said. "But on the other hand, you can take that too far and put the athlete or yourself in jeopardy. You have to keep your eye on the big picture all the time. If Ewing fell again and hit his wrist just right, or if he tried to come back too soon, the Knicks are still going to owe him $80 million or whatever. You have to see the big picture. That's where management probably has a wider focus on things than the player or the coach. In the middle of a game, the coach wants to win that game. Again, it goes back to where it's kind of good to have two opinions sometimes and maybe have the coach and general manager be separate people.

"It's a lot easier on medical issues to say a guy can't play," Schaefer said. "It's the coach who wants his best team on the floor, the athlete who wants to play. Most times whether a guy should play or not is a fairly obvious thing. It's not a complex thing. You're looking at the schedule, you're looking at the game, you're looking at the injury and the severity of it. It's pretty obvious. There are very few times that it's really gray. Most of the time the player makes the call."

While Schaefer could defend Krause on many medical controversies, the contacts with Saints trainer Dean Kleinschmidt left him wondering. "I don't know what truth there is to his desire to hire Tim Floyd, or to the Tim Floyd/Dean Kleinschmidt thing," Schaefer said. "But it almost appeared like he had the attitude, 'I don't care about professionalism. I'm gonna get my friend the coach in, and I'm gonna let my friend, the coach, hire his friend the trainer. We can all sit around and talk about bass lures or something. Forget that Phil Jackson was a great basketball coach, I want to get this batch of friends together.' Well, what does that have to do with running a professional organization?"

"That's baloney," Krause said. "Chip is very wrong in his opinions. He doesn't have a clue what my intentions were."

Schaefer "aligned himself with people who treated Doc Weinberg like a dog," Krause said. "Whether he resigned or not I had decided Chip was not going to be here next year. He and Al (strength coach Al Vermeil) had had a continual (disagreement). I had decided Chip was not going to be here under any circumstances.

When we brought him back (for 1997-98) I had told him then it was just going to be a one-year contract. No more than that. As for his commenting on moves by management, he had very little knowledge of the things we did. Chip has always been a person who believed he was more than a trainer. He was nothing more than that."

When Schaefer informed Krause in March that he was resigning, he was struck by Krause's urgency to accept his decision and announce it with a press release. It was almost as if Krause was "trying to get everyone out the door that he can," the trainer said. "I think they're trying to set themselves up with flexibility at the end of the year, but what you wind up doing is creating anxiety."

There was anxiety for the players, anxiety for the coaching staff. And certainly anxiety for Bulls fans. To Schaefer, though, the key was Jordan. "I see him being awfully close in similarity to the way he was when he left the game the first time in 1993," the trainer said. "In the early '90s, he would talk. We would have moments where we were alone while I was treating an injury of his, and he would speak of his frustrations. He would say, 'I don't think I can take this much longer.' I always thought he was just sort of venting. I was shocked when he retired the first time. But there are some things that are similar to that now. You can see the intrusions onto what he likes to do. Just a look of weariness on his face sometimes that he didn't have two years ago, or even last year. I don't know what he's going to do, I really don't. I think there's part of him that wants to stay. If it is winding down, it's almost like these guys don't want to let go, whereas months ago they spoke of wanting to end it and wanting to leave. Now, it's like you're ready to get that divorce and you think, 'One more time. Let's try it again, babe.' They're almost afraid to move on out and do something different."

On the other hand, Schaefer had a perfect read on Jackson. The coach was clearly ready to move on, despite Jordan's statements that he would quit if Jackson didn't come back. The statements pressured both Krause and Jackson. "I can't see Phil doing it again," the trainer said. "They'd have to have a thing where Jimmy Rodgers signed on as coach, and they'd go back and try to do it again. But if that happens, you lose a big part of it, You lose a huge part of what makes the thing successful and makes it go."

"I think Phil's just had enough," Krause agreed. "He's got family problems. I know that's part of it."

"I'm not even sure of the best way for it to end," Schaefer said. "To me, people in Chicago are a little weird about it, too. No one's gonna play forever. If we both agree Michael is a human being and not gonna play forever, then it only becomes a matter of when. At some point in time, he'll have his last year. It might not be this year. It might not be next year. It might be two years from now. But it seems like people aren't willing to accept that, and that's weird to me."

Part of the anxiety was expressed in the hopes of fans and editorialists that Reinsdorf would somehow send Krause on a sabbatical while Jackson, Jordan and Pippen finished out their careers. It would "almost be a shame if Krause took a sabbatical," Schaefer said. "To me, there doesn't need to be a winner and a loser. It would almost be a shame if it came to a thing in this battle of wills with the Jackson/Jordan side defeating the Reinsdorf/Krause side."

The Bulls had been a situation where everything worked. The spirit, camaraderie, emotion — all those elements had come together at a very special level for this team. Yet there was no question that the conflict had the potential to extinguish whatever had been achieved, just as it extinguished Schaefer's joy at working with the team. That could be seen in the looks on Jordan's and Pippen's faces whenever Krause was mentioned. The situation had much potential for long-term hatred.

Even Krause and Reinsdorf showed some signs of recognizing that. Yet it was too late. Krause's hopes of rebuilding the team in the future had cast a deep shadow over the present.

"Sometimes it just seems that these guys get themselves in trouble by almost trying to do too much," Schaefer said of Krause and Reinsdorf. "Sometimes you just need to let it happen. They got a great coaching staff in place. They got a great roster of players. It's been made so much more complex in a lot of ways than it has to be. There's a lot of axioms about simplicity in life. It's all gotten so complicated. I don't understand how it got this way."

Once again the Bulls faltered against the Nets in the fourth quarter In Game 2, Chicago missed seven of 13 free throws. Once again, the Bulls somehow managed to hang on for a win, with 32 points from Jordan, 19 from Toni Kukoc and 16 rebounds from Rodman. Several newspaper accounts described them as vulnerable and perhaps even distracted by the internal conflict. "I'm pretty sure that's what people have been writing," Jordan said after the second game. "Some teams probably feel that way, too. But until they actually come in and do it (beat the Bulls), it's just conversation."

He emphasized that for Game 3 in New Jersey by hitting 15 of his first 18 shots and scoring 38 points as the Bulls swept the Nets with a 116-101 victory. It was the third straight first-round sweep for Chicago. The Bulls had run up a 24-1 record in first round games since 1991.

Scott Burrell did his part by hitting 9 of 11 shots from the field to finish with 23 points, including 11 in the third quarter as the Bulls stretched the lead to 93-76. Afterward, Jordan was glowing in his comments about Burrell, "his project." Burrell had averaged 13.7 minutes and 5.2 points while playing in 80 games during the regular season. Even he admitted he was still struggling to learn the offense, evidenced by his 42 percent shooting from the floor.

"For one thing he doesn't play consistent minutes and when you only play five or six minutes, it's hard to be a consistent shooter," Kerr told reporters. As for Jordan's tutelage, Burrell revealed in private that his Airness still hadn't eased up on treating him like a rookie. "That's just the way he is, I guess," Burrell said. "That's just the way he motivates people. I'm too old to be motivated. If I don't know what I have to do. . . . I just try not to pay attention to it. It's not really irritating. That's just the way he is. That's just part of the price."

DIARY DAYS

The opening of the playoffs also had coincided with the first issues of *ESPN* magazine. As a highlight, the magazine published excerpts from Jackson's diary put together by *Sun Times* columnist Rick Telander. At first, Jackson and Telander had been under contract to write a book based on the diary, but Jackson said he had decided to kill the book deal as the season began. The publishers prevailed upon Jackson to at least do the magazine story, and he agreed. The coach presented his diary with the understanding that he would be able to see any parts excerpted before publication. Unfortunately, there was a time squeeze, and Jackson never got the opportunity to approve what was published. It would prove perhaps to be the worst mistake of Jackson's career.

There were references to his marital difficulties with longtime wife June, plus snide and unkind remarks about Krause (Jackson said he considered giving him the book *Any Idiot Can Manage*. "But in the end I didn't give him anything because I couldn't find it in myself to give him something of value.") The passages also included what came across as egotistical ramblings about other teams.

Jackson seemed to be blatantly campaigning to take over as coach of the Lakers and Knicks, teams that already had coaches. It was quite outrageous. Even worse, the comments provided the first real opening for Krause to attack Jackson.

The next issue of *ESPN* magazine bore a second installment of the Jackson diaries which proved mostly to be an apology and retraction of things said in the first installment. Even the magazine itself lampooned Jackson in a subsequent spoof comparing the Last Run of the Bulls to the final episode of the long-running "Seinfeld" series. Each of the Bulls' primary figures was projected as a member of the TV cast, with Jackson designated as the strange and daffy Kramer.

Krause was understandably angry about the publishing of the diary but kept his anger behind the scenes. "As far as me being sensitive to this issue, I don't know that I've been overly sensitive," the GM said in a private interview for this book. "I think I know where things are coming from. When you know where the gun's being aimed from, you really don't worry about the result of the bullet."

Krause also met with new *Tribune* columnist Skip Bayless and outlined his complaints against Jackson, according to one team source. Days later, Jackson sat down with Bayless in what the coach thought was a courtesy introduction. But the columnist launched into a series of inflammatory questions about Jackson's relationship with Krause. "Bayless used Krause's comments to get Phil going," said the source.

Jackson responded to Krause's comments. "I'm not gonna let that be the final word," the coach explained at the time. Yet when Bayless' column appeared, there was little use of Krause's comments, only Jackson's angry response on issues, another situation where the coach appeared to be on the attack.

Bayless subsequently weighed in on Jackson during the playoffs as an egotist desperately seeking to take control of the team and maintain his image of being vital to the Bulls' success. "You have to wonder about Phil Jackson's motives," Bayless wrote. "You have to question why he says he'll suggest to Michael Jordan that No. 23 retire. Love and respect? Or revenge and insecurity? Has a vial of self-importance transformed Dr. Jackson into a wild-haired coach Hyde? Zen Master or Spin Master?

"Is Jackson trying to influence Jordan to retire prematurely in order to wreak revenge on Jerrys Reinsdorf and Krause?" the columnist asked. "Jackson despises General Manager Krause. Jackson blames Chairman Reinsdorf for sticking with Krause, who has stuck it to Jackson during contract negotiations."

The net result of the *ESPN* article and the Bayless columns left Jackson despondent and played a major role in his ultimate decision to leave the team. "It has not been healthy for me to be here because I have gotten a reputation now as being a backbiter, as being devious, as being ungrateful," the coach said in a private interview as the season wound down. "There have been a lot of things that I've had to suffer about my character that I've been very upset about. It's not right. I think it's a spin on the other side to portray me as that, or as worthy of being let go. I went to Mr. Reinsdorf and said I won't have my character blotted. You know this is a situation that's changing, and we can go through this without having to spoil a person's being or character or reputation. That's been my feeling, and yet it's been allowed to happen. I don't know if people seeded it.

"I may be responsible for seeding some bad things about Jerry Krause in the *ESPN* article, which I am sorry ever came out," Jackson said. "It wasn't supposed to be like that, although I did write it down, and it was in my diary. The diary was in the hands of a writer. His responsibility was to let me edit it, which he didn't. It got out of my control. So there has been some rebuttal because of that. As a result, it has been a situation in which to come back would be almost unthinkable, almost an impossibility."

Tex Winter said he didn't in any form believe Jackson was the egotist portrayed by Bayless, "but I can see from the way things have come down that some people might read it that way. It's unfortunate that things came down the way they did. On the other hand, when you come out in a story, particularly one that's taken out of a diary . . . I think the mistake was that he allowed somebody to be privy to his situation and thoughts. And Phil didn't really intend that at all. That's what really hurt Phil. But those were his personal thoughts."

The assistant coach acknowledged that Jackson's *ESPN* comments had hurt and angered Krause. "I like 'em both, sure," Winter said. "I ride the fence. I'm a double agent. I find out what one side's thinking. Then I'm on the other side, find out what they're thinking. And I still don't know what either one of them is thinking."

A GREAT PUSS

In the wake of the New Jersey series, Krause granted an interview in his Berto Center office. His lung infections had given him fits all season, necessitating treatment with steroids. The steroids, in turn, had kept him awake most nights coming and going to the bathroom. The illness had combined with the fan anger over the impending breakup of the team to make it a very difficult year. Was it the worst of all his years in Chicago? he was asked.

"On me personally? Oh yeah, this year's been the toughest," the GM said. "The first year (1985) was so damn tough because I didn't know. I knew we were gonna do some things, but I didn't know how we were gonna do 'em. The first year was pretty bad. Jesus. We had Quintin (Dailey) go off in a drunk tank, and had all those injuries."

Asked if he could envision a day where Pippen's number would be retired by the team, Krause replied, "I don't know. First of all, I don't retire numbers. Scottie Pippen has been a great player here. I have no complaints with him. Obviously we've had some contractual things, and some of that comes from other people who are involved with it. Not Scottie or not me. But those people have inflamed both sides."

Told that Jackson had said Pippen would be the linchpin in keeping the dynasty going, Krause said, "We'll see what happens. I'm not gonna make any decisions until the end of the season. But this thing has gotten so big that it's been overblown unbelievably. Unbelievably. This is not the end of the earth. We're not having the end of the earth. The mountains will not come down on us. We'll all live tomorrow, no matter what happens. When Auerbach lost Russell, it wasn't the end of the earth, either. He found a way to somehow get back up there. Teams can be rebuilt in this league.

"There's a point here where we're just gonna have to make some decisions about this team," he said. "And we will. But what I'm saying to you is, that I don't want to break up this team. Nature, nature breaks up teams. Nature and the monetary nature of things in the sense that there are certain guys that you just say, 'Well, at this age and at this point in his career, we can't do that.' And nature makes guys older. Guys don't stay young."

Krause was asked to envision another title, more champagne, another moment with Jordan at the microphone. "That would be great with me," he said. "I got no problem with that. Six is important to me. We kept it together to win six."

Indeed, after the season he had suffered through, to not win another title would have been misery. As with the Bulls' other key figures, Krause's competitiveness was one of the elements of their success. His credo was to "hire good people, step back, let 'em do their jobs.

"The game for me is the game of scouting, the game of evaluation," he said. "The things that I do best. The building, that's the fun. The fun is putting it together, putting an organization together. That's what it's all about for me. That's different. They get their nuts off out there playing. I get my nuts off out here." He pointed to the administrative setting around him, the charts for player evaluations, the mountains of game tape, the personnel craft that Freddie Hassleman, that old Yankee scout, had taught him years before.

"Freddie was a beautiful little man," Krause said. "I would be driving a car for him later on in his life. He was so old he couldn't drive, and we'd go scouting.

"Freddie used to see things. He'd say, 'That guy's got a good face.' He'd call it 'a good puss. That guy's got a good puss.' 'What's a good pus, Freddie?' 'I can't tell you. But you'll know when you see one.' A few years later, one day I called him. I was in a ballpark someplace, and I said, 'Freddie, I saw a good puss. I know what you're talking about now. That guy's got the face. You couldn't tell me what it was. I had to see it.' When you sit at the feet of guys like that. . ."

An interviewer pointed out Jerry West's wisdom that a scout can see what players can do athletically, but a scout can't read players' hearts, can't see what they're made of.

"You better get to know their hearts," Krause replied. He said that he later did a study of Hasselman's puss theory. Krause asked himself, who was the best competitor in baseball? Pete Rose. In basketball? Jerry Sloan. In football? Dick Butkus. It occurred to him the puss might have something to do with it. He said he went into a newspaper reference room and looked into back issues to find profile shots of Rose, Butkus and Sloan at age 22. "Same face," he said. "Same chin. Same nose. Jaw out. Same profile face. Then I walked in a ballpark in Kalamazoo, Michigan, and I took one look and I said, 'Oh shit, number 4.' It was Kirk Gibson. So you can't tell me that there ain't certain kinds of faces."

Did all the master competitors make a habit of teasing and humiliating their general managers on the team bus? Jordan had only done that to him three or four times, Krause said. "Who cares? He's drunk every time. He hadn't been sober yet when he's done it. It's a young man's mistakes. He was drunk. I can live with that fine. I can live with what Scottie did. I know why he did it. It doesn't bother me."

He said he once sat on the bus with a championship baseball

team and watched that team's star and general manager go at each other.

Experience suggested Krause was right. Great competitors weren't always the nicest of guys, or the friendliest. George Mikan and Jim Pollard won six pro basketball titles together (one in the old National League, five in the NBA) as the core of the old Minneapolis Lakers, and they endured icy relations with one another to accomplish it. Kareem Abdul-Jabbar and Magic Johnson also endured their strained relationship with the newer version of the Lakers. As did West and Showtime coach Pat Riley.

"Do you think Riley and West liked each other about the last four years they worked together?" Krause asked. "They hated one another. Hate. There's nothing like that hatred. Out and out hatred."

Riley, in fact, told associates that West had a "toxic" envy for him.

Kevin McHale and Larry Bird rarely spoke off the court, yet on it they won three championships together as the heart of the `80s Celtics. In the NBA, it seemed, success often bred envy, dislike and distrust.

"People's true character is tested as much by winning as it is by losing," the general manager observed.

Krause said he thought of Karen Stack, his assistant, like a daughter and also had strong feelings for his other two assistants, Jim Stack and Clarence Gaines. The GM said that if anyone tried to harm Karen Stack, he'd go after them. "But there's certain people in this organization I wouldn't do that for," he said. "We'll leave it at that."

Asked about the comment of a Bulls staff member that the friction between the coach and general manager had actually benefited the team, Krause said, "Phil and I think very differently in a lot of ways. We go at each other. It's competitive all the time. I want the scouts to stand up and fight. I want the coaches to stand up and fight. I don't mind that. I'm gonna sit and make a decision on what people tell me and what my own instincts tell me. But I'm gonna listen to everybody and try to think every thought they express in a meeting. Somebody has to pull the trigger."

Despite their difficulties, Krause said Jackson had never tried to take his power or oust him as general manager. Instead, a turf war developed over smaller chores. "I let Phil handle the plane arrangements and hotel rooms," Krause said. "Phil got crazy about it. The more I gave him to do, the more he wanted."

"There's never been a power struggle," Reinsdorf agreed later. "Phil never asked for Krause to be removed. It never happened. Phil never told me he thought we were a house divided. He said it was difficult to work with Jerry Krause but not impossible. Phil never ever said that. He did express the fact that it was very strained."

If it was a house divided, it was Jackson who divided it, Krause said. "It was always 'us' and 'they.' Jerry and I were always 'they.'"

Krause blamed much of the strife on agent Todd Musburger. "That guy had a lot to do with it," the GM said. "The next coach we have here will never have an agent."

Of Jackson, Krause said, "I think we've had a professional relationship that's been basically good. We've been very successful as a team. There haven't been too many other combinations that have been that successful. I respect Phil as a good basketball coach. We have our differences. We will probably have our differences the rest of our lives. But that's life, that's gonna happen."

Krause and former Bulls coach Dick Motta had long hated each other, Krause pointed out. "I didn't ever think I could sit down with Dick Motta, but I did. At a surprise birthday party for Brad Davis. Brad's wife and I threw a party for him."

The party was held in a downtown Chicago restaurant. "I wound up sitting next to Motta, and we kind of hashed it out some things," Krause said. "For years we didn't speak to one another. I couldn't stand the man."

As for the current Bulls team, Krause said, "I'm not sure that we realize what we've done. It doesn't hit you right away first of all. It hits you later in life. With me, I've been so busy doing it that I haven't had the chance to sit back and smell the roses. Jerry (Reinsdorf) always tells me, 'C'mon and sit back and smell the roses. They're blooming.' I think as I get older I will, but I gotta figure out a way to win next year.

"I've got great family. This game has been very good to me. Very good. Not a beef in the world. I've come to a place in my life where I can pretty much live the way I want to," Krause said, pointing out that his parents had needed to work their entire lives.

"I think I have a pretty good idea of what we've accomplished. But you know something? I'm gonna be working for a while now. So I've gotta figure out a way to do it again."

His phone rang. It was St. Louis Cardinals manager Tony LaRussa, in town for a series with the Cubs. They chatted, and upon hanging up, Krause said, "The good life is right here, with a call from Tony from the clubhouse at Wrigley Field. That's what the good life is. Tony LaRussa calls me. We're gonna get together. I knew he'd call me. Here's a guy, Tony's ego has not changed one bit since I met him in 1978. He was a kid working in the White Sox organization, a double A manager. Tony is one of the best people I've ever met in my life."

In regards to his career, Krause acknowledged that his toughest days could well be ahead of him. "Obviously the team has to be rebuilt one time or another," he said. "That's a necessity. As the years go on, Jerry will make decisions. And I'll make decisions, and we'll see where we are. I've had some thoughts about what I want to do with my life. And there'll come a point where I'll walk away too. Jerry and I've discussed where we want to finish some day."

He was asked again about his relationship with Pippen. "No question" he's come a long way, the GM said.

He was asked again if he would retire Pippen's jersey number. He responded by mentioning Bulls great Chet Walker, like Krause a Bradley alum. Walker and Krause had a history of feuding, including the Bulls 1991 championship party where Walker claimed that Krause denied him admittance. "I get people who send me stuff about Chet Walker's number being retired, and all that crap," Krause said. "The numbers don't mean anything."

"It does to Scottie," his interviewer said.

"I shouldn't say it doesn't mean anything," Krause said. "It doesn't mean as much to me as it does to those players, okay? That's fine. I've gotta be concerned about the next team!

"Besides, we put all the numbers on the banners," he said, pointing out that the numbers of all the players are on the team's championship banners. And the team does more important things for players after they leave, he said, citing the fact that the Bulls had found throat surgeons to correct Bill Cartwright's voice problems.

It was mentioned that his role model, Red Auerbach, had made a point of retiring his players' numbers, of honoring them as special contributors to the team's championships, a situation that helped create the Celtic Pride spirit.

"I hope eventually we'll have that here," he replied. "But you gotta remember, too, it's a different breed of athlete than it was when the Boston group was in. It's a different breed of cat. You're talking about guys who made $100,000 a year. And they couldn't have free agency. And there were no agents. It was much easier to do it then, believe me. Obviously there's a difference."

And a much different breed of general managers, it would seem.

He was asked if the differences between him and Pippen and Jackson and Jordan would ever be settled. "Who knows in future years what's gonna happen here?" he replied. "We will try to do what we have to do. There's a challenge here."

As the playoffs progressed, Krause would recruit an unidentified Bulls assistant coach to go to Pippen as a private emissary with the hopes of arranging a meeting between the general manager and star player. The coach told Pippen, "You really need to talk to Jerry." "I wanted Scottie to come up and we could talk like two grown men," Krause revealed. "We could get our feelings out on the table. Even if he left, we could hash it out man to man, and if he had to leave he could leave like a man. We asked him several times. But he never responded."

Later, in the glorious aftermath of the season, Krause would again approach Pippen. "Look, if you don't want to come up to the office we could meet somewhere," the GM said. Pippen's answer was to stare at him blankly, Krause said.

What Krause said he wanted to tell Pippen was that there were misconceptions about the team's efforts to trade him. "I didn't shop him," Krause said. "He was never shopped. We did talk to teams that expressed an interest." The Bulls came closest to trading Pippen in 1995 to Seattle and in 1997 to Boston, Krause said. "Those teams made serious offers that we had to consider, but we turned them down. Teams have called and asked, 'Is he available?' And I always say everybody's available, except Michael.' Teams have called us. When four teams call us expressing an interest in Scottie, I'm gonna find out who else is interested."

As Michael Jordan liked to say, the playoffs never really started until you lost a game at home. If that was the case, then the playoffs started for the Bulls after the second game of the second round against the Charlotte Hornets.

The Bulls had used their trademark defense to hold the Hornets to 32 second-half points while claiming Game 1 of the series. But late in Game 2 former Bull B.J. Armstrong found the groove with his jumper and propelled the Hornets to the 78-76 upset. Charlotte forward Anthony Mason also did a nice job on Jordan defensively, using his size to take away some of Jordan's effectiveness in the post.

"It's probably been three weeks since we played a real good

game," Jackson told reporters. "I thought that some of us are going through the motions and just letting everybody else take the responsibility, letting Michael take the responsibility for scoring and not carrying their own weight."

In the wake of the loss, Reinsdorf finally broke his silence with an interview with the *Chicago Tribune*'s Sam Smith. The chairman denied that he planned to break up the team. "If we win the championship, I would be inclined to invite everyone back," Reinsdorf told Smith. "Neither I nor Jerry Krause has ever said — anywhere — that we want to break up the team. We get accused of saying it. I read it all the time. I hear Spike Lee saying it on the Jay Leno show."

Jackson's agent, Todd Musburger, countered Reinsdorf's claims by telling Chicago's WMAQ radio that he wasn't convinced of the chairman's sincerity. "They are trying to put the responsibility on the players for not coming back, not the team," Musburger said. "The Bulls are having a hard time taking the responsibility for what might happen. They told us loud and clear (during the previous summer's contract talks) this would be the last year of Phil's duties as coach of the team. They have had ample time to display what they want to do."

Reinsdorf's message was that it was Jackson, not Krause, breaking up the team. Jackson himself admitted that he had been eager to leave for the past two years. "But as it gets into the playoffs, it's going to be harder and harder to say goodbye to this team," he said, adding that he had no intention of coming back. "It's being wanted back," Jackson explained. "That's the whole thing."

Jordan admitted being confused by Reinsdorf's timing. "I think all of it's been a pretty trying season," Jordan said. "We've still been able to get on the basketball court and play the game, and that's what we're going to be remembered for, not all this conversation that's going on now."

Asked if Reinsdorf was trying to put the blame for the breakup on Jackson and himself, Jordan replied, "If that's the case, it's a bad time, but it's a lot of things that have been bad timing that have happened to us thus far. But I don't know. It kind of caught us off guard because we never really expected it. We didn't expect any more conversation about next year until this year was over and done with. So his reasoning I really don't know. But he certainly has the prerogative to make a decision like that."

"I was a little bit surprised about the timing of it," Pippen told reporters. "If it was something he wanted to get out, I felt like he could have come out way before the playoffs. But I'm sure he wanted to get you guys off his back about running Michael out of the game."

"That's how out of touch things are," Chip Schaefer observed, "when you have to win a title to have the owner be 'inclined' to ask everybody back. You know how hard it is to win 62 games?"

Privately, Reinsdorf expressed exasperation over the circumstances, so much so that the team chairman wanted to establish a chronology to his talks with Jackson. Reinsdorf said that he first met with Jackson in Phoenix in November 1994 to discuss the coach's future with the team. "Michael was off playing baseball, and I never thought he was coming back," Reinsdorf said. "I told Phil we were gonna have to rebuild and asked did he want to see us through the rebuilding. He said he wanted to think about it. Then lo and behold Michael came back."

That changed everything, Reinsdorf said, and the discussions over Jackson's future with the team took on a new tenor. It was obvious by June 1995 that Jackson had warmed to the idea of coming back to coach Jordan for another run at more championships. His contract with the team ended in 1996, which left the parties negotiating over the 1995-96 season. By March of 1996, "Todd Musburger and Krause were going at each other," Reinsdorf said, necessitating the chairman's involvement. "Phil and I met at the United Center after the first game of the Orlando series that year. I told Phil I thought he was the best coach in the NBA. He said I was the best owner in the NBA. I said, 'If that's the case, we ought to be smart enough to figure out how to stay together.' We agreed to agree on that and went on to win our fourth title."

Reinsdorf said that within days after the championship they resumed negotiations. The team chairman said he first mentioned a five-year deal to Jackson. "He said he was tired of being an NBA coach," Reinsdorf recalled. "Look at him now as compared to what he looked like when he started. He said it was too bad that coaches couldn't take sabbaticals and come back to their jobs after a year or two off."

Reinsdorf said that after Jackson declined a five-year extension, they concentrated on a two-year deal. When they reached a stalemate over money, Reinsdorf suggested a one-year contract. "Phil said, 'Great. That's what I wanted to do all along,'" Reinsdorf recalled.

Then the team produced a 69-win season and was rolling toward the 1997 league championship. "During the '97 Finals, Phil and I met in Park City in Utah and he told me, 'I don't know if I want to coach next year. I don't know if I ever want to walk into a gym again,'" Reinsdorf said. "I told him that it wasn't the right time to decide his future. He said, 'If I do come back, I just want to come back one more year.'"

What followed was another round of charged negotiations between Krause and Musburger, which produced no agreement. Instead, Reinsdorf and Jackson met in Montana to complete the negotiations. "I flew out to Montana," Reinsdorf said. "We talked at length. Phil said at the most he wanted to coach one more year. Phil and I have never had a cross word between us. We had nice conversations in Montana. Within a day or two, Phil told me positively this was his last year."

Then came Krause's obviously gleeful announcement that Jackson would not be back with the team after the 1997-98 season, which left Reinsdorf to endure a year of media speculation and criticism over Jackson's status with the team. The chairman said the circumstances led him to meet with Jackson during the playoffs. He told the coach that he'd been reading how management was pushing Jackson out. "I asked him, 'Has anything changed? Do you want to coach another season?' He said, 'No,'" Reinsdorf recalled. "Then two days later, Skip Bayless wrote an article quoting Phil that made it sound like we were pushing him out."

It was the Bayless column that prompted Reinsdorf to step forward and address the issue with the *Tribune*'s Smith. Reinsdorf was clearly frustrated with the circumstances after the Bayless column. (If Reinsdorf, Krause and Jackson could agree on anything, it was that Bayless was a nightmare of a media personality, what Reinsdorf called the *Tribune*'s answer to acerbic *Sun Times* columnist Jay Mariotti. Hired in March, Bayless had immediately targeted the Bulls, slamming first one side then the other. "The guy hasn't been here long enough to know where State Street is," Krause said testily.)

"I told Phil, 'I really have to go public to set the record straight.' The reason I picked that moment was I felt enough had been said," Reinsdorf said privately. "The world was getting the wrong impression. Nobody was pushing Phil out."

What could account for the vastly different accounts of the circumstances? Some observers suggested that Jackson had mixed feelings about leaving. Other observers pointed to Jackson's dislike for Krause. Was Jackson, long a master of mind games, using the circumstances as a way of tormenting the GM? as Bayless suggested.

"Probably Phil didn't know what he wanted," Reinsdorf said.

There was no question that Jackson had second thoughts about leaving the team, regardless of whether he felt comfortable expressing those to feelings to Reinsdorf. And the coach clearly felt he had worn out his welcome. In March, Jackson had likened the situation with the Bulls to the end of the New York Knicks' dynasty in the 1970s. "I was in New York," Jackson said. "We had 11 great years of a run. I was there for 10 of those great years. The eleventh year things started to turn. Fortunately I got off before the landslide hit in the late '70s. But when it turned, the town turned against the Knicks, and it took them almost 10 years to get it back."

"The people were against them," Jackson said of Knicks management, "because they were overcharging, the were abusing their position for power. They were being brusque and intrusive in the press. They said things like the bottom line is the figure that really counts now, not wins and losses."

The parallels between the Knicks and Bulls were disturbing, Jackson said. "It draws a pattern that's scary, because the people in Chicago are going to have a long memory and they're going to remember this stuff later on down the line. I hope it doesn't happen, because I think this town deserves winners. They're good sports fans."

Yet just a few weeks later, after being told that Reinsdorf again said he was the best coach in the NBA, Jackson said, "Jerry has a real good feel for what is organizational stuff and what makes good sense. He's always been first to say that I'm the best coach in the NBA, which is great. I know I'm the best coach for this group in the NBA. That's the only thing I can say. With this group, we've developed a style that's worked extremely well. With another group, who knows if I could build this relationship or not? This has taken a long period of time to really integrate it into this kind of a situation. But, be that as it may, Jerry knows — and he and I have talked about this before — we don't want anything to dull the sheen on what we've done. We really don't. Even this little pecking that goes back and forth. If I leave, it's a good time to leave. I've had a wonderful stay here. I've been blessed by the fact that I've had the chance to work with these guys in this organization in this time in the history of the game. For whatever reason it all came together."

Shrugging off the controversy of Reinsdorf's comments, the Bulls rolled over the Hornets in Game 3 of the Eastern Conference semifinals, a contest that had the home fans heading for the exits early. At the next day's practice in the Charlotte Coliseum, Ron Harper explained the mood of the players: "On our team we got some older guys, and we know we aren't going to be around for a long period of time. We know this is our chance now to go out and to just show folk what a good basketball team we have."

Pippen had produced a line of "Last Dance" hats and T-shirts for sale to the public. Harper was asked when he planned to start wearing his. "My Last Dance hat ain't coming out till we get to the championship, the final round," he replied, laughing.

Just as Pat Riley had trademarked the "threepeat" slogan when he was coach of the Lakers, Pippen had made his move on the "Last Dance" phrase.

"It was just something fun to do. We're always trying to have some fun," Harper explained, adding that actually getting the hats manufactured and into stores for public sale had been difficult.

"I'll buy one," offered the *Tribune's* Skip Mylenski. "I'll contribute to your pension fund."

"It's Scottie's pension fund," Harper corrected.

Harper was asked if his hesitation in wearing the hat was a sign he was holding out hope that the cavalry would ride in and keep the team together. "No. No. No. Believe me," he said. "Let me tell you what I hope the cavalry do. Let it go. It's been fun."

As one of the few Bulls under contract for next season what were Harper's plans? If he had to spend one more year in Chicago, wouldn't he rather do it on a championship team again? "If it was my choice?" he said. "I would do this until we say we had to stop. But I think the key part is that everybody has to be happy. Everybody's deals have to be the deals that they get. Phil's gotta have the deal that he wants. MJ don't care about no cash. SP needs to get his cash, I think."

A reporter asked if money was the key to happiness. "Money's not the key to happiness all the time," Harper said. "It's how you treat and respect the guys on your team. I think the reason we play well is because we respect what our skills are. If we had a boss that came down every day and said, 'Hi, how ya doin'?' and smiled a little bit . . . He don't have to come in and hold anybody's hand. Just come in, you know, and speak. That's why (Scottie's) not a happy camper. It's how you treat people. Growing up as a kid I always learned you treat people the way you want them to treat you. So if you respect them, they will respect you back."

Terry Armour of the *Tribune* posed this question: "I'm pretty sure Reinsdorf is gonna say for Scottie to get the money he wants

Michael is gonna have to take a pay cut. Do you think Michael will take a pay cut?"

"I think he will," Harper said. "MJ ain't worrying about no cash. That's the least of his problems."

"Should Michael have to take a pay cut?" another reporter asked.

"I don't think MJ should have to take a pay cut. I think my boy Scottie should get his cash," Harper said. "He should get his just due for all the hard work and time he put in for this team. He's only got five championship rings, on the all-Defensive team, all-NBA team, All-Star, all-world team, the Dream Team, the beam team, on my team.

"They've made a lot of cash since Michael Jordan and Scottie Pippen have been on this team," Harper observed. "They've sold out how many games? Five hundred and some games? Consecutive? They got two of the best players on this team, and they sell out every building they go into."

Another reporter pointed out that the Bulls' current owners paid less than $20 million for the team, meaning they had hundreds of millions in equity in the francise. "They should give some of that up," Harper said, "to some of the guys like Scottie who should get his just due."

Over their seasons of success, the Bulls had acquired quite an entourage, so much so that they began using two buses for playoff travel. And to avoid trouble, Jackson and Jordan would sometimes hang back, waiting to see which bus Krause got on, so they could get on the other.

"Jud Buechler was on the floor stretching," Chip Schaefer said, "and he looked around at all the people we have now in this traveling circus, and he said, 'God, we're like Noah's Ark now. We have two of everything.'

"The staff has just grown and grown and grown," Schaefer said. "We have more players, more coaches, more strength coaches, more massage therapists. I have an assistant trainer that I didn't even particularly ask for. We got more doctors, more media people. We got more everything. It's unbelievable."

The trainer's favorite year was 1991, the first championship season. "We had the same 12 players that we'd had all year long," he said. "Phil had three assistants and myself. We only had two broadcasters because of the simulcast for radio and TV. Most of the year we traveled with this little special forces hit squad of just 24 people. So there was a lot of more intimacy about it. Over the years, we've added three more players to the roster and another coach, and the broadcasters are up to five with TV and radio and a Spanish broadcaster. It's just grown and grown and grown."

Schaefer pointed out that the growth went to the very heart of the philosophical debate concerning the team versus the organization. It was embodied in the wrangling Jordan and Reinsdorf did over championship rings. "It's something they've had a big debate about over the years," Schaefer said. "Jerry Reinsdorf's philosophy is that it's the whole organization. The person who answers the telephones and licks the stamps in the office is as deserving of a ring as Michael Jordan. I can see the merits of that. Michael, of course, feels there's this smaller group, mainly the players and coaches, who should get something different and unique, maybe just a ring with one more diamond in it or something. Jerry has just the opposite philosophy. It's worthy of debate."

Reinsdorf had usually addressed the matter by giving the players something beyond their championship rings. One year it was an especially fancy money clip, something that your average NBA player certainly needed.

The Bulls' blowout win in Game 3 had left the Hornets in tatters with Anthony Mason on the bench at the end of the game screaming profanities at coach Dave Cowens. That, in turn, set the stage for the Bulls to breeze in Game 4, 94-80, followed by a tighter win in Game 5 back in Chicago to close out the series.

In Chicago's 93-84 win in Game 5, Jordan finished with 33 points while Rodman, playing on his 37th birthday, had 21 rebounds. Jordan scored 11 of his points in the fourth-quarter. With less than a minute left, the crowd at the United Center began chanting "MVP, MVP."

Indeed, word had already begun circulating that he had outpolled Utah's Karl Malone in the balloting for the award.

That same week, *Fortune* magazine reported that Jordan had the most earnings of any sports endorser in 1997 with $ 47 million dollars, almost twice as much as the $24 million earned by golfer Tiger Woods. And another poll of advertising executives found that far and away Jordan continued to be the sports celebrity most coveted as a product pitchman.

FILM CLIPS

As usual, Jackson had prepared his team for the playoffs by splicing pieces of a popular film around cuts from the game tapes. That way he kept them from being bored by all the basketball while exposing them to a new or overlooked feature film. Each year during the Bulls' run of championships he had come up with something unique. One year it was "Apocalypse Now." In 1996, he had used "Pulp Fiction," and in 1997 the selection was "Silverado."

For the Indiana and Utah series in the 1998 playoffs, Jackson used "The Devil's Advocate," a dark Taylor Hackford film starring Al Pacino and Keanu Reeves. Pacino was literally the devil, disguised as a New York law firm executive who specialized in finding and recruiting the best talent.

Asked if the central antagonist in the film was a thinly disguised reference to Krause, Jud Buechler laughed and said, "Don't go there. Don't even go there."

"It's a little far out," Tex Winter said of Jackson's decision to select a film in which the devil was a talent-scouting executive.

It wasn't a message lost on the players.

"Who is the Devil?" forward Dickey Simpkins said with a smile. "I can't answer that question. That might be trouble. I got to wait until after I sign another contract before I answer that."

The film also had ties to Jackson's circumstances. Reeves played a young Florida lawyer who had been raised in a fundamentalist home and was later recruited by the devil's New York firm because he had never lost a case. In fact, Reeves was so intent on winning that he seemed willing to sacrifice his marriage in the name of competition. Jackson had made it no secret that his own marriage to wife June had suffered because of his intense commitment to the Bulls.

"It's a very disturbing movie," Buechler said. "I don' know. Phil usually has a hidden meaning in all those things, but this year I'm not quite sure what the meaning is. It involves the devil, some pretty gory stuff in there, that's for sure."

Buechler, whose wife was pregnant and about to deliver during the playoffs, said he had to cover his eyes during disturbing scenes involving birth issues.

Jackson said the film had many applications, including several for Rodman. In the film, Reeves' wife kept changing hair colors trying to find her identity as she sank deeper and deeper into madness. "It has applications where needed," Jackson said, "and I try not to make a big distinction about who the applications are for. There are some things that are obviously for Dennis in 'The Devil's Advocate,' dealing with the darker side of life. He loves movies so much. There are just some basic statements about free will and about self determination, that, regardless of what you believe, you are a determinator of your own life. There's other things that are about being possessed or losing control of your own life. It makes some sense to me that can be played around with."

Played around with indeed. In some scenes, certain characters' faces turn grotesquely ugly, and in another, Reeves' wife uses a broken window pane to cut her own throat while in a mental hospital. Jackson spliced these scenes into sections of game tape that showed bouts of ugly play by the Bulls. "We had a couple of cuts of the guy's wife when she looked in the mirror and turned real ugly," Winter said. "He had that in at a time when we had a couple of real ugly plays. Finally, when we did something really bad, it showed her slitting her throat. Committed suicide. The thing of it is, this devil's advocate makes them do all these things, causes it all."

These scenes were particularly useful to Jackson if Jordan seemed too intent on one-on-one play, Winter explained. "Sometimes when there was too much one on one, he'd maybe get the ugly scene in there, or he'd suggest we're cutting our own throat. You know?"

Jordan and his teammates laughed at the ways Jackson presented these notions to them, Winter said. "It's a good way to get across points without your having to say much."

Winter saw it as Jackson's special way of speaking to Jordan, of reminding the superstar about the need to include teammates and to avoid trying to win games by himself. "These guys, Michael and Scottie in particular, these guys have been with Phil just that long," Winter said. "They've begun to interpret a lot of things now that they didn't understand at all at first. But they've been there so long they can practically read his mind on it now."

"Phil does a lot of stuff that if you just let it pass, you don't really understand," Bill Wennington said. "But if you think about it, he's trying to get us motivated or thinking at a deeper level. Sometimes we catch on, and sometimes we don't. I think Phil's and Michael's relationship is very special. They communicate in their own way on their own level, and they do so very well. There are a lot of times when things aren't going well and we need to move the ball around, and it's in Michael's hands a lot. Phil relates that to Michael by saying, 'Hey, you know, we gotta move the ball around a little bit,' without demeaning him or saying, 'You did it wrong.'"

The other members of the Bulls sensed that Jackson could say those things to Jordan while maybe no other coach could, Wennington said.

Asked if the film could be applied to the larger issues that the Bulls faced this season, Jackson said, "A lot of it is. The thing about being strangers in a strange land. And little stuff, like there's a statement, 'Behold. I send you as a sheep before the wolves.' I've got the crowd in Indiana and Utah (Chicago's final foes of the season) both and the referees' calls, and all those kind of little distractions that go on when you're out there playing on the road. Both of those teams are involved in this movie, how you have to be self-reliant as a basketball team."

Each game's scouting tape brought another group of segments from the film. Asked what he drew from the viewing, Steve Kerr answered quickly, "Nothing, except that it's a sick movie. That's all. Phil told us there's no redeeming value. He's just doing it for entertainment."

It was easily the strangest movie Jackson had shown the team, Buechler said. "It's been his worst selection out of all the selections he's made. I think maybe Phil would agree to that."

"I'm not sure what the message is supposed to be," Tex Winter said. "But there's scenes in there that are very disturbing."

HOOSIERS

The Indiana Pacers, coached by Larry Bird, stepped up as the Bulls' foes in the Eastern Conference finals, but in the first two games Chicago promptly smothered the Pacers in pressure. Scottie Pippen, in particular, so hounded and harassed Pacer point guard Mark Jackson that he had Bird pleading for the officials to bring some relief. Harper, too, played his role by shutting down Reggie Miller.

The Pacers' pain was measured in their 26 turnovers in Game 1.

"Pippen was hyped up and they let him hang on Mark to bring the ball up," Bird fussed.

In the midst of it all, Bird still had to pause and pay homage to Jordan. "No question since I've been round, he and Magic are the best I've seen," the Indiana coach told reporters. "Believe it or not, every year in this league you learn a little bit more. He might not have the skills like he did when he was young. He might not shoot as high a percentage. But you become a better player as you get older."

The league acknowledged as much by naming Jordan the MVP before Game 2 of the series, making him, at 35, the oldest to claim the award. It was his fifth time to earn the honor.

"It's a cheap 35," Jordan said. "I didn't play much of my second year (foot injury) and I sat out 18 months (retirement and baseball). I don't really have the time on the court a normal 35 would have if they played each and every game. To win it at this age means I made the right choice to still play the game because I can still play it at the highest level."

The day before Game 2, Bill Russell had presented Jordan the award, followed by a second ceremony right before tipoff featuring commissioner David Stern and a 40-second standing ovation from the United Center crowd. Afterward, Jordan was confronted with the need to prove he deserved it. "I've always said that getting that type of trophy is added pressure — you have to go out and live up to it at some particular time," he told reporters. "Tonight was no different — I felt pressure to go out and prove that you guys didn't make any mistakes in your voting."

Clearly there was no mistake.

The Bulls were up 98-91 late in the fourth when Indiana scored four points in less than 10 seconds to pull to 98-95. When Jordan answered with a drive, he slipped but somehow managed to keep his dribble, get back up and cut his way through a scrum of defenders to hit a runner that bounced around and in.

Next he nailed a 14-foot fallaway on the baseline to kill the Pacer resurgence. He finished with 41 points, the 35th postseason game of his career in which he had scored 40 or more points. He shot 13-for-22 from the field and 15-for-18 from the line with five assists, four of Chicago's 15 steals and four rebounds.

Rodman, on the other hand, had only two points and six rebounds in 24 minutes after being held out of the starting lineup for the second straight game. He had spent a good portion of the night in the locker room riding an exercise bike. When Jackson wanted to insert him into the game, an assistant trainer had to fetch him. "It was irritating having to send for him," Jackson admitted. "I will have a talk with him in the next couple days to see if we can set him straight."

Jordan's main help came from Pippen, who had 21 points, six rebounds, five steals, five assists and three blocked shots, and Toni

Kukoc, who scored 16 points.

For some reason, Krause chose Game 2 as the time to approach Jordan in his private room in the Bulls' locker room to discuss the star's comments critical of team management in a recent *New Yorker* article. The result was a heated exchange between the star and GM. "For some reason Jerry wanted to do this," a team employee revealed. "Jerry was representing Reinsdorf in saying they were really upset about what Michael said. Jerry tried to reason with him about the *New Yorker* article. Apparently Michael went right back in his face, saying, 'Don't you dare try to challenge me about it, not with all the manipulating of the press you guys do.' He's not putting up with any of that shit."

Another team official heard about the incident and remarked, "Oh, gee, that's real smart, Jerry trying to go in there and smooth things over. He's the wrong person to do that."

Jordan emerged from the exchange on his way to the postgame media interview session. He looked at a team employee and said, "Fuck your two bosses."

"I don't think Michael and I raised our voices," Krause said of the incident. ""There was something in the *New Yorker* article that had pissed Jerry off, something that made Jerry very mad."

Reinsdorf was angry because Jordan had told writer Henry Louis Gates, Jr., about the team chairman's comment that he would "live to regret" giving Jordan the $30 million contract in 1996. Actually, during their 1997 contract negotiations in Las Vegas, Reinsdorf raised the issue, telling Jordan that he had heard the star was upset by something he had said during the 1996 negotiations. He and Jordan discussed the issue, Reinsdorf said, and they made up and agreed to put it behind them. Or so the chairman thought until he read Jordan's angry words published in the June 1 issue of the *New Yorker*. "I went to Michael myself," Reinsdorf said of his anger. "I went down after a game we won in the Indian series, I said, 'What's this shit in the *New Yorker*? I thought we had put this behind us.' He said, 'I gave that interview out a year ago. That interview is a year old!'"

Reinsdorf then recalled that the article indicated Jordan was interviewed in Michael Jordan's Restaurant in Chicago, and suddenly Jordan's explanation made sense. "Michael hasn't been in that restaurant in a year," the team chairman said. "He got in a fight with his partners. They're in litigation. So I realized he was right. The *New Yorker* interview was done in June 1997 before we cleared the air in Las Vegas."

It almost seemed as if some media grinch was conspiring to deepen the Bulls' woes, as if the team's key figures weren't struggling enough in their relationships. A huge part of the problem was the lack of personal communication between the key parties, which left them hanging on every media message, sometimes taking humbrage even at the turn of phrase.

The media, unaware of the *New Yorker* confrontation, focused instead on Rodman's behavior during Game 2. "Dennis is fine, he don't have no problem with anybody," Harper told reporters. "He was late to a game. He's late to every game. Who cares? We know Dennis as a team, and the guys let him do what he wants to do as long as he steps on the basketball court and plays basketball."

"I think Dennis has had to compromise his principles more than I have had to compromise mine," Jackson joked, adding, "Dennis has given up his whole life — wrestling, movies, MTV. Think of the things he's had to give up to play basketball."

Yes, Jackson told reporters, Rodman came late to games and was tardy for virtually every practice. "He doesn't like his money. We take it from him and find ways to give it back to him," the coach quipped.

Following Game 2, Bird was even more incensed about the free rein officials had given Pippen on defense. "I'd like to see Scottie Pippen guard Michael Jordan fullcourt like Scottie guards Mark Jackson and see how long he stays in the game," Bird said. "I tell my guys, 'You're not going to get the calls in this series. You've just got to try to play through it,' which they have been. I thought Scottie got away with a lot more than he did the other night."

The comment brought a smile from Jordan and this reply: "Scottie and I have had some great battles in practice, and he didn't get those calls, either."

On Thursday, before heading to Indiana, the Bulls players had declined to speak with the media, which netted a $50,000 fine for the team from the NBA. In playoffs past, the players had sometimes made such refusals, and the team quietly paid the fine. But this time, Krause was incensed and lit into Jackson on the team plane in front of the players. "It's your fault," the GM yelled.

Later, on the tarmac at the Indiana airport, the two exchanged angry words as the players and support personnel watched from a waiting bus, unable to hear exactly what they were saying to each other.

"We got fine $50,000 for not showing up at the media session," Krause said, adding that in the past he'd gotten information that "our coach said, 'Hey, guys, let's fuck management. Don't show up at the media session.'" Krause's allegation seemed to support Jackson's concerns that the general manager had a spy among the players who would pass information to management. That was nonsense, Krause said, adding that Jackson "had his own spies."

In fact, Krause said, he had been forced to downplay his friendship with Toni Kukoc because of Jackson's paranoia. "We couldn't be friends because of Phil's craziness, because Phil takes it out on Toni," the GM said. "I never even talked to Toni about basketball."

Krause also questioned the accuracy of a Kukoc quote in which the Croatian forward claimed to be closer to Jackson than to Krause (the quote was tape recorded in a private locker room interview in Toronto in March). As for the confrontation on the plane and on the tarmac in Indianapolis, Krause said, "I was really mad. When I left the airplane Phil was waiting for me at the bottom of the steps. He said, 'Why couldn't you have done that in private?'"

Some staff members figured Krause was simply using the opportunity to vent his frustrations with Jackson. Asked about it later, Jackson said, "I did approach him in a private moment, because I thought in a private moment we could address it. I said, 'There was a better way to handle this than that (berating him in front of the team).' And he didn't want to hear it. He just wanted to go ahead and proceed down the same path he had chosen, which has the tendency to make me rigid. Especially when I had come over to try and get him back on the right page.

"I realize Jerry's a . . .," Jackson said, then hesitated. "I don't want to get into ethnic slander, but from what I've known of all my encounters living with Jewish society most of my life, when the kaddish is said, that person becomes a nonentity. And Jerry basically said the kaddish (a Hebrew death prayer) over me. And the funeral was said, and I've become a nonentity to him in his life. So it had become very difficult for him to talk to me, to address me personally, and I understood that. He is not going to address me personally again. That's basically his feeling about it in some form or fashion. I've recognized that for the last couple of months. So I understood a little bit about his mentality, because he couldn't really look me in the face when he was trying to get his piece said. I understood that he was doing something he felt he had to do. He didn't want to have a personal contact with me. He still had to do this on some organizational level."

"The kaddish thing is hilarious," Krause said, adding that the reason he didn't want to speak to Jackson alone was because he didn't trust the coach not to lie. Krause's answer was a resolution to have a witness each time he spoke with Jackson.

Asked if he thought Krause had also said the *kaddish* over Pippen, Jackson again hesitated, then said, "Yes. He hates Scottie. Scottie has become a nonperson in his life because Scottie called him a liar. And that's the worst thing you could do. Jerry won't admit that he lies. It's very difficult because the owner, Jerry Reinsdorf, doesn't lie. And Jerry Krause also doesn't want to be thought of as a liar. But when you're a general manager, almost by virtue of your job, you have to tell lies. It's unfortunate.

"You have to recuse yourself, is what you have to do," Jackson said. "In this job, I've tried to make it an issue not to lie, although Jerry has accused me face to face of lying. To which I said, 'Well, you know, Jerry, there are times I go to speak and I'm caught in situations,' particularly in front of the press, where they ask, 'Is Dennis at practice today,' or something which we're trying to avoid. I choose not to say something, or I choose not to recuse myself."

Jackson suggested that Krause's *kaddish* over Pippen had been in place for some time. Apparently, Pippen felt slighted when Krause talked to Jordan in the spring of 1997 about signing free agent Brian Williams but didn't seek Pippen's opinion (Krause said he spoke with Pippen about the move). "Scottie basically felt like the Brian Williams thing was cut and dried, and he wasn't talked to," Jackson said. "Michael was talked to. By virtue of Michael being talked to, it was assumed that Scottie had been talked to. And Scottie was not addressed as an individual, he felt, which again was another symbolic thing where Scottie doesn't have the same kind of status as Michael, which he deserves as a co-captain."

Asked if he thought Krause had said the *kaddish* over Jackson, Tex Winter said, "Yes, he probably has."

With their internal conflicts flaming up before their eyes, the Bulls found a way to lose two spectacular games in Indiana over the Memorial Day weekend. Each time, Chicago had a solid lead in the fourth quarter only to see the Pacers take control in the closing minutes. In Game 3, Indiana won 107-105 to cut the series lead to 2-1. The Pacers' bench, led by forward Jalen Rose and guard Travis Best, had helped sink the Bulls. Reporters asked Jackson about his opponent's bench and he answered gamely "Wait until we get to Utah," suggesting that the Bulls were indeed headed to the Finals and that the Jazz subs would be even tougher.

Jackson created further controversy on the eve of Game 4 by telling the press that Chicago's dynasty was on its last legs. "Right now, it's an end of a basketball team that had a great run," he said.

Certainly the Pacers were trying their best to make that happen. Game 4 came down to an unusual series of events that left Jackson fuming about the officiating and countering that Bird's politicking in the media was turning the tide with the referees.

For the packed house at Market Square Arena, the officiating only boosted the drama. Miller hit a 3-pointer with 0.7 seconds remaining to give the Pacers a 96-94 win that tied the series at two games apiece.

Jordan got one last shot, but his 26-footer at the buzzer hit the backboard, rolled around the rim and out, bringing a thunderous celebration. "There were so many debatable calls late in the game, but Reggie still had to make that shot," Jackson told the gathered media. He blasted the officiating by likening it to the 1972 Olympic gold medal game when the United States lost to the Soviet Union on a bad call.

The Pacers had fought the whole game to catch the Bulls and finally took the lead, 88-87, with just over four minutes left when Derrick McKey hit a 3-pointer.

The Bulls, however, led 94-91 and seemed in control until Travis Best scored on a drive with 33 seconds to go. Then Rodman was whistled for an illegal offensive pick, sending the ball back to the Pacers. "The offensive foul by Dennis was an awful call," Jackson said. What angered the Bulls coaches were the illegal down screens the Pacers had set all day long trying to free Miller from Harper's cloying defense. The Pacer big men were constantly stepping out and giving Harper a forearm, which had Winter fussing. The officials, however, made no illegal pick calls until the one on Rodman in the final seconds.

Chicago was still leading 94-93 when Jordan blocked a jumper by McKey with 6.4 seconds left. Indiana retained possession, but Pippen then stole the inbounds pass after Harper tipped it. The Pacers quickly fouled Pippen, and there was an extended debate over whether Miller threw a punch at Harper.

No technical was called, leading Jackson to say the officials "backed off, acted like they were afraid," words that would bring the coach a fine from the league.

Pippen went to the line to shoot his free throws and promptly missed both, a dreadful lapse in the clutch. He squeezed his head in anguish frustration as he came off the floor for the ensuing timeout.

The Pacer coaches then called for Miller to come off yet another down screen, which he did. He ran to the top of the key and shoved Jordan backward and out of the play to get open for the winning three. The Bulls coaches screamed for yet another offensive foul, but the arena was already awash in pandemonium.

The Bulls returned to Chicago and responded with a 106-87 blowout victory to regain the lead in the series, 3-2. Jordan scored 29 in the rout, which pushed his career totals to 35,000 points, including regular season and playoffs, third behind Kareem Abdul-Jabbar and Wilt Chamberlain.

That week, the Chicagoland Chamber of Commerce estimated that with each game the Bulls added $10.5 million to the area economy. The estimate included about $1 million spent directly on tickets, food, souvenirs and such; a $1.5 million payroll at the arena; and an $8 million "induced" from local residents watching TV, patronizing sports bars and making Bulls-related purchases. And none of that even addressed Chicago's growing international image, fueled by Bulls memorabilia sold globally. Diane Swonk, deputy chief economist at First Chicago, told *The Financial Times*: "Chicago is now known for Michael Jordan rather than Al Capone, so it's positive that way."

The net result was only more pressure on the two Jerrys.

Unfortunately, the Bulls couldn't enjoy such glowing reports. They had to return to Indiana for Game 6, where somehow the Pacers again managed to win with a late-game turnaround. This time the drama came when Jordan tripped on his way to the basket in the final seconds. There was no call, and the Pacers scooped up the ball and headed off with a 3-3 tie in the series.

"It was an obvious foul at the end," Jordan said afterward. "People may think I tripped over my feet, but I'm not that clumsy."

The turn of events only brought more debate about the officiating, which Bird tempered with a bit of levity. "If I see David Falk reffing the next game, I know we're in trouble," he told reporters.

"All teams are just kind of tired of all the things Chicago has done," Indiana's Antonio Davis said before Game 7. "They've beaten a lot of people — embarrassed a lot of people — so I'm sure there are a lot of teams out there that would like to see them lose."

Past embarrassments, though, had little to do with it. The key factor would prove to be Chicago's homecourt advantage. They were 27-2 in playoff games in the United Center dating back to 1996. That didn't stop the Pacers from pressing the issue. Indiana took an early 13-point lead, which prompted Jackson to abandon the six-man rotation he had used for most of the series. First he inserted Rodman for Kukoc, which produced a 7-0 Chicago run. Then Jackson turned to Steve Kerr and Jud Buechler. Kerr would finish with 11 points and Buechler with five key rebounds and plenty of scrambling hustle.

"We were behind, so he wanted some offense. He kind of took a chance because Best outplayed me this series," Kerr said of Jackson. "Then he went on a hunch and went with Jud, who had a great game. It says he trusts us, he trusts his bench."

"I learned something about our bench: To stick with our bench and not back away from it," Jackson acknowledged. "I think that's what I have to consider and keep considering that we can still find ways to win ballgames, even though sometimes we feel a little short-handed."

By halftime, the Bulls had eased back in front, 48-45. Then Kukoc took over in the third quarter as Jordan continued to struggle offensively. The Croatian would finish with 21 points, shooting 7-of-11, including 3-of-4 three pointers. In the third period when Jordan had sunk to the bottom of a 9-for-25 shooting performance, Kukoc hit all five of his shots, including three triples, for 14 points.

Chicago opened the fourth with a 69-65 lead, yet even when Jordan returned with under 10 minutes to play he continued to miss shots. Finally, he began attacking the basket, driving into the Pacer defense and drawing fouls. "His jump shot didn't work but his free throws did," Bird said after Jordan's show of will in the final minutes pushed the Bulls to the win. "He put his head down, went into traffic and drew fouls."

"It's about heart," Jordan said, "and you saw a lot of heart out there on the basketball court."

His first five points of the game had pushed him past Kareem Abdul-Jabbar as the leading scorer in playoff history, with nearly 5,800 points. He finished the night with 28 points, nine rebounds, eight assists and two steals, enough to seal Chicago's 88-83 win. "That's why he's the best player in the league and probably the greatest player ever," Bird said.

"I'm pretty sure people are going to say that some of the swagger is gone," Jordan said of his team's narrow playoff escape. "Maybe. But nobody has taken anything away from us so far."

Their next stop was the NBA Finals against the Utah Jazz, who had swept the Los Angeles Lakers in the Western Conference championship series and had been forced to wait 10 days for the Bulls to advance. "We may be a little tired, but our hearts are not tired," Jordan said when asked if his team would be ready to travel to Utah for the next round. "We haven't lost in the Finals, and that's a great confidence to have. Sure, it was a battle to get there. But we're there. Now let's just do the job."

UTAH

At the NBA Finals, time always seemed elastic for the Chicago Bulls. "This time of year each game is like a season in itself," Tex Winter observed. It was in this last championship series that the players finally seemed to gain a full understanding of what Jackson meant when he encouraged them to inhabit the moment. None of them, after all, wanted those moments to end. "There's 15 guys in that room who want this to go on forever, or as long as it can," said Bill Wennington, nodding toward the Bulls' locker room. "They all want to come back. No one wants this to end. It's a great thing. This unit of people gets along really, really well. So the chemistry is there. Whether we're at home or on the road, we're having fun together. And we're playing well."

If nothing else, the push of the Indiana series had left the Bulls feeling that they'd lifted their play to a higher level. While there was much media speculation that they might be too weary to take on the well-rested Jazz, Chicago's confidence was high. Utah had homecourt advantage in the Finals format, which called for the first two games in Salt Lake's Delta Center, the next three in Chicago, and the final two in Utah, if necessary.

Winter, however, was concerned about Chicago's matchup with the overpowering Karl Malone, at 6-9, 252 pounds. The Bulls assistant predicted that Longley would quickly get into foul trouble and the issue would fall to the mercurial Rodman, a shade under 6-7 and packing about 220 pounds. Malone had traditionally proved tough for Rodman to defend, Winter pointed out. "That's his big complaint all the time, that he's had to play guys who are 50 pounds heavier than he is. And my answer to him is, 'What do you think you're getting that fabulous salary for? No one told you it was gonna be easy.'"

Illegal screens were one of Winter's pet peeves, and he complained that Indiana had set plenty of them against the Bulls. "That was amazing. You'll see a lot of illegal screens here, too," he said, referring to Utah. "Backpicks. Stockton running up and running into you."

During the 1997 championship series against the Jazz, Winter had even gotten a rare technical for complaining about illegal screens and picks. "I kept hollering, 'Watch Stockton on the back picks. Watch Stockton on the back picks!' Finally," Winter recalled, "the official came over by the bench during a timeout, and I said, 'Watch the back picks!' He looked at me real sternly. I was gesturing. He said, 'That's enough out of you.' I said, 'Well, read page 44, section 3, of the rule book.' He said, 'That's a technical!'"

The league later rescinded the technical and Winter didn't have to pay the customary $500 fine. NBA vice president Rod Thorn explained that officials had to fill out reports explaining each technical and on rare occasions they would back off a call they made in the heat of a game. Winter figured that Thorn had told the officiating crew, "Just ignore that old guy. Hell. Don't pay any attention to him."

"Thorn knows I try to help the officials a great deal," the assistant said. "That's all I do. I don't cuss or anything like that."

After defeating Indiana on Sunday, May 31st, the Bulls practiced in Chicago on Monday, then jetted to Utah for Game 1, set for Wednesday the 3rd. The Jazz admitted they had been driven toward distraction by the 10 days off. The Bulls, meanwhile, were in game shape and figuring that they merely needed to win one of the first two games in Salt Lake City. The Finals format always seemed to put immense pressure on the home team to hold serve in the first two games.

To avoid much of the pre-game hype, the Bulls again waited in the visitors locker room at the Delta Center before Game 1, not wanting to take the floor until after the national anthem. Harper emerged first with a scowl. There to greet him were the ever-present camera crews with their kleig lights. Because this was the Finals, there were even more cameras, even more sound technicians lingering in the shadows, the various appendages of NBA Entertainment and the networks, all attempting to document the moment for prosperity and profit. Harper began stretching on the railing along the runway as the first rifts of the national anthem drifted in from the arena. Kukoc sauntered out behind Harper, pausing to squint at the lights. He, too, threw a leg up on the rail to stretch as the other Bulls emerged, all relatively calm. Jordan came out, clapping and juking, popping his hands together rhythmically. "This is fun," Jordan had told reporters earlier. "It could very well be the last one. So I'm enjoying it with that purpose in mind." He went over to Harper and clapped three times and began dancing again. The cameras and microphones moved in then, like giant plant pods hovering over the Bulls, feeding off their energy and aura, allowing millions across the globe to vicariously sample that Jordan air. The master on the verge of the moment. Loose. Smiling. Confident.

Rodman came out next, bringing his new playoff hair, a vibrant green with a grating of black, perhaps in acknowledgment of Jackson's splices of the green-haired wife in "The Devil's Advocate." The new color wasn't particularly menacing or bizarre. Just very different. He was the last out the door, which meant the Bulls could gather as a group and ask their usual question — "What time is it?" — and give their usual answer — "Game time! Hoo!"

They turned from there, with Randy Brown leading. Jordan, behind Burrell, reached up and began massaging his shoulders, as if to say, "Relax, fella, this is why I've given you all this shit. To be ready to play for the championship."

In the arena, the booing had already begun in anticipation of their appearance. In 1997, the Jazz had opened their Finals games with a spectacular celebration featuring thousands of balloons, fireworks and a rumbling motorcycle at center court. In anticipation this time around, Jackson strolled the sidelines wearing ear plugs, and the Jazz game operations crew didn't disappoint. First thousands of balloons rained from rafters, then came the fireworks and the snorting Harley, all of which had Burrell jamming his fingers in his ears and looking up in amazement.

Utah coach Jerry Sloan, who had been known as Mr. Chicago Bull as a hard-nosed guard in the 1960s and '70s, greeted team owner Larry Miller, then jammed his hands in his pockets, looking a bit pressed by the silliness and noise. He appeared to try to ignore the unfurling of the Western Conference Champions banner, a strange ceremony for the franchise to conduct in the moments before taking on the reigning five-time league champions.

As expected, the Jazz seemed tight and the Bulls a bit weary in battling through a 17-all first period. Then Jackson went to his bench in the second period and quickly found disaster and a brace of turnovers. The Jazz jumped to a seven-point lead, and the Bulls starters would spend most of the rest of the game trying to pull close enough to steal a victory at the end. They almost pulled it off.

The NBC broadcast crew featuring Doug Collins and Isiah Thomas picked up on a Jordan snit at the end of regulation, apparently because he wanted the ball, but his demanding nature was so much a part of the Bulls' routine that Pippen and the rest shook it off as business as usual.

Fortunately, Malone had struggled, hitting only one of his first nine shots in the second half, which allowed Chicago to stay close. But the big power forward found some confidence as the game tightened, beginning with a time-worn pick and roll executed with point guard John Stockton with just under five minutes left. The Malone bucket put the Jazz up by seven. The Bulls, though, answered with a run, beginning with two Longley free throws and a pair of Jordan jumpers. Then Pippen hit a three to tie it at 75, and Sloan, on the sideline, looked like somebody had just plunged a knife in his chest. Pippen clinched both fists as he walked off the floor, but the Bulls' huddle during the ensuing timeout was animated. They were only screaming over the crowd noise, the Bulls would insist later when asked if Jordan was fussing about not getting the ball.

Pippen responded after the timeout by taking a rushed trey that missed badly, and Malone hit two jumpers to put Utah up by four with 55.7 left. The Bulls, though, managed to tie it on two Pippen free throws and a Longley jumper with 14 seconds to go. From there, Chicago's defense forced overtime, but in the extra period Stockton victimized Kerr on a late shot in the lane to give the Jazz a 1-0 lead in the series.

The 1998 Finals was off to a great start and appeared headed toward a doozie of a finish. As was their trademark, the Bulls made their adjustments for Game 2, which involved spreading their triangle offense and opening the floor up for easy baskets by their cutters.

In the first half, the triangle had never worked better. "Tonight it really shined bright for us," Buechler said. "It's an offense designed for everyone to touch the ball, to pass and cut. And the guys did that tonight, instead of going to Michael every time and posting up. Early on everyone got involved, and that really helped out for later in the game."

"The first half was beautiful," Winter agreed. "We followed through with our principles a lot better. Got a lot of cutting to the basket. And Michael gave up the ball. He was looking to feed cutters."

Winter's face, though, showed his frustration. "The second half we abandoned it, aborted it," he said. "We tried to go way too much one on one. Michael especially forced a lot of things."

If the Bulls had stuck with their scheme they might have won by a dozen, the assistant coach figured. But Jordan had delivered a win against Indiana in Game 7 by going to the basket and drawing fouls. He attempted to do the same in Game 2 against Utah, but the officials weren't giving him the call. Instead, Jordan wound up on his back while the Jazz scooped up the ball and headed the way for easy transition baskets. Suddenly Chicago's seven-point edge had turned into an 86-85 Utah lead with less than two minutes to go. "I don't know what it is," Winter said, shaking his head. "Michael, he's got so damn much confidence."

As it turned out, it was Kerr who rescued the Bulls in the closing moments, with a rebound no less. "It's ironic," the guard agreed. "I think it was my first rebound of the series, wasn't it?"

Jordan knifed inside for a layup that pushed the Bulls back ahead 88-86 with 47.9 seconds left. But moments later with the series on the line, and the score tied at 88, Kerr got open for a transition three. "I missed the shot and the ball went right to me," said Kerr. "Lucky bounce. As soon as I got the ball, I saw Michael underneath and just flipped it to him."

Jordan's bucket and ensuing free throw propelled the Bulls to a 93-88 win, the victory they needed to wrest away homecourt advantage. The difference was clearly the Bulls' 18 offensive rebounds, five by Kukoc and five by Rodman. "They did a great job of rotating, hustling after plays," said Utah's Jeff Hornacek. "I think we got outhustled. They got the loose balls. We anticipate all the games being close. It's going to be a play here or there that wins the game. I thought that Steve Kerr play killed it."

"Even when we went down by one," said Kerr, "we went back to the huddle, everyone was quiet and focused, and we came back out and took control."

STATEMENTS

The series then shifted back to Chicago, where a swarm of media gathered at the Berto Center as the Bulls shot around before Sunday's Game 3. Jordan rushed off the floor after practice with a TV producer in tow pleading for some interview time.

"It's for NBC, Michael," the producer said.

"I don't give a damn," Jordan shot back as he ducked into the team's training room.

A few feet away, Winter was again drilling Rodman on pressure free throws. "Tie score," the coach said as the forward took aim. Across the gym, Randy Brown, who was getting no playing time, was feeding passes to Kerr, his rival for minutes who was practicing three-pointers.

"Good job, the rhythm is good," Winter said, grabbing Rodman's hand and shaking it as they finished yet another session. Winter paused to answer a few questions and admitted that where he once held out hope that the team might remain intact he now saw that as the remotest of possibilites. "I don't think it's necessarily a shame to break it up," he said. "It's too bad that has to be, but you have to have changes. And it could be well-timed."

Winter had figured the Bulls would struggle to win the title in '97, yet here they were a year later, in solid position again to rule the league. If the team returned, it would likely be too far past its prime to meet expectations in 1999, the coach reasoned.

Besides, keeping the key parties together would take some Jackson-inspired therapy. Perhaps Jordan and Pippen could be assigned to go fishing with Krause to relax and talk out their problems. The lake would have to be very shallow. The two stars could later sit with Reinsdorf and enjoy a good cigar.

But how would Winter heal the relationship between Jackson and Krause? Only Reinsdorf could do that, the assistant coach said. As it would turn out, the team chairman tried, but it just wasn't possible.

"Well, I think time heals all wounds, but time can also wound all heals," Jackson said, toying with a riddle when posed the question in a private interview. "In retrospect, at some point, we're going to back away from this so that we're not so close and say, 'You know, this was a collection of pretty talented people. The Bulls were very successful. Even though we were enmeshed in the midst of it, we really were enjoying it.' I've always felt that way.

"Perhaps we could have enjoyed it more if we could have appreciated it," Jackson said. "I've really enjoyed it a lot, and as a consequence, I've really revelled in it the most. Tex doesn't revel in it as much as I do. But the players do. The players have this association with it, and I have an association with that, too, because I was a player."

The coach admitted that no matter how hard their feelings he and Krause would always be bonded by their mutual success with the Bulls. In fact, their story was one destined to be told and retold.

Having acknowledged that, Jackson said there was virtually no chance of his return. He said he had tried to make it clear to

Reinsdorf in 1997 that it was impossible for Krause and him to keep working together. The implication was that the team chairman had faced a choice, the coach or the general manager, and had clearly sided with Krause.

"Last year I felt that coming back, even though the ground had been seeded, the groundwork wasn't good," Jackson said. "I felt like my message about how a house divided against itself cannot stand wasn't really listened to by Jerry Reinsdorf. I really like Jerry, and I have a tendency to like authority figures. And Jerry has been a good one as an owner for a coach to appreciate because he stays away and stays in the background and doesn't intrude and allows things to happen. And yet he's gotta coerce both of us to work together in this atmosphere. For this group to come back, I just don't see how it's gonna happen. Right now we're in the throes of saying, 'Look at the genius of this team. Look at the collective effort between the coaching staff and the team on the floor, all the strengths of the individuals.' But the reality is that while no one wants to back away from another championship or another two championships, going through another long period of 82 games in that respect is going to be difficult. It's not a good thought."

Even so, Jackson couldn't avoid leaving the door cracked. "If it comes down to a chance of Michael not playing, then my responsibility would be to him and to the continuation of his career, and I would have to consider it," he said. "I have to be a person that is loyal to the people who have been loyal to me. I feel that conviction. The only thing that would take me basically out of the mix would be my own personal well being, my own personal physical and emotional health in dealing with this."

Clearly, Jackson had been left emotionally frayed by the season and the struggle for control of the team.

The emotional health of the entire team got a boost in Game 3 as Pippen and Harper and Jordan took turns overpowering Utah's guards in the largest rout in NBA history. The performance established how absolutely dominant the Bulls could be as a team and Pippen could be as an individual defender. The conclusion itself turned into the kind of dunkfest for substitutes usually reserved for rec league blowouts. The game had opened with a blast of applause from the United Center crowd, followed by a brief scoring outburst from Malone. Then the Chicago defense closed out the proceedings and propelled the Bulls to a 96-54 victory. The margin was so great that a cross-country airlines flight that had radioed in for a game update for a Utah fan had to call back a second time to confirm the score. It was the worst point difference in league history, either playoff or regular season.

Jerry Sloan expressed surprise when he was handed a box score. "This is actually the score?" the Utah coach said. "I thought it was 196 (points). It sure seemed like they scored 196."

"It was one heck of an effort, defensively, for our team," Jackson said. "We were very quick to the basketball."

"I'm somewhat embarrassed for NBA basketball for the guys to come out and play at this level, with no more fight left in them than what we had," Sloan said. "(The Bulls) got all the loose balls, all the offensive rebounds, and we turned the ball over (26 times). I've never seen a team that quick defensively."

Pippen had roamed the floor, free to terrorize Utah's passing lanes. "It's a luxury to have a defender like Scottie," Jackson told reporters. "He can cover more than one situation at a time. He can play a man and play a play. He can hang tight on his man and he's also able to rotate like that."

"A lot of times Phil wants me to be a help defender, and that's pretty much what I'm doing in this series," Pippen said. "He wants me to limit their way to the basket, keep them out of their sets, things like that. I take pride in being able to do that."

In one game, the Bulls had sent a resounding rebuke to Krause's plans to rebuild because they were too old. Tacked on was the emphasis that Pippen was too special a player to consider tossing away in any trade.

"I almost feel sorry for them," Jackson said privately in discussing how Krause's and Reinsdorf's agenda had been shattered.

Pippen, in a private moment, addressed the issue with the tallest of grins. "Ain't nothing changed," he said, unable to suppress the smile. The day after Game 3 a team employee revealed that the Bulls had renewed all but four of their skybox leases, and those four would soon go, too. "Is that right?" Jackson said with surprise when informed of the news. Regardless, Jordan and Pippen had fun with the topic at practice that morning in the United Center. Jordan walked into the empty arena and stood looking around. Suddenly, he pretended to be speaking into a microphone: "Ladies and gentlemen, welcome to how your arena is going to look next season." Then the star pointed to the upper reaches of the vast building and said, "There are your choice seats." Strangely, one sole spectator was sitting in that nosebleed section, and when Jordan pointed, the man stood and began waving his arms wildly, leaving Jordan and his teammates to hoot at the oddity of the moment. In the other corner, a few feet away, Pippen performed a similar skit with an imaginary microphone. Actually, the building was safely sold out for 1998-99, but in the realest of senses the stars were right. No matter what happened, the magic would likely be gone.

Just when Chicago seemed to be soaring in the 1998 championship series, Rodman changed the flight pattern by missing practice to slip off to appear at a professional wrestling event in Detroit as "Rodzilla." Some accounts suggested he was paid as much as $250,000 for the appearance while others reported that he was paid nothing. Privately, Rodman said the appearance was part of an $8 million contract.

The media took great interest in delving into the strange turn of events, which cost Rodman $10,000 in fines. When Rodman returned to practice before Game 4, Winter was ready with a lecture. "I just asked him what he thought he was doing," the coach revealed. "He said, 'Well, if you had a chance to give up $10,000 to make $8 million would you do it?' That's what he told me. I said, 'Don't kid me. There's no way you made $8 million.' He said, 'Oh, yes, I did.'"

Behind his frown, Winter took the matter with a smile. "You know, Rodman's no dummy," he said. "Actually, he's beaten the system. You have to give somebody credit who can do that. And I'm not so sure that maybe the system shouldn't take a lickin' every once in a while."

MBA's from Harvard would have trouble figuring out how to earn the money that Rodman had in the past three seasons, Winter said. "It's a reflection a little bit on our society, though. Which is a shame, but that's part of the system, too." The coach had talked often with Rodman about taking better care of his money but didn't think his message had gotten through, especially when it came to his gambling. "Anybody that likes him and has some compassion for him is gonna be concerned about him," Winter explained, pointing out that the reason his teammates put up with Rodman was because they liked him. "He's a very likable guy. Very generous. Generous to a fault, really. Wants attention. He's a contradiction, really. He's a very shy guy in a lot of ways. Very withdrawn. And yet he calls attention to himself on every turn. That's a contradicting personality. I think Phil's got a better read on him than the rest of us. Phil was somewhat a maverick himself. He wrote that book, *The Maverick*, which he's still embarrassed about. I didn't read it. He asked me not to, so I didn't. He said, 'You don't want to read that.' Phil is more sympathetic toward Rodman than I am by a long shot."

As the plot would turn in Rodman's strange world, Game 4 of the Finals came down to his ability at the free throw line. He responded by hitting four free throws in the closing seconds to go with his 14 rebounds to seal an 86-82 Chicago win and a virtually insurmountable 3-1 lead in the series.

"The much-maligned Dennis Rodman had a wonderful game for us," admitted Jackson, who had blasted the forward's behavior just a day earlier. "As usual, he takes himself out of a hole and plays well enough to redeem himself."

On a night when the Jazz responded to their Game 3 blowout with a show of fire, the Bulls managed to stay ahead by hitting 17 of 24 free throws in the fourth period. Rodman, a 55-percent shooter during the season, rolled in two for 78-75 lead with 1:38 left. Then, with under a minute left and Chicago ahead by two, he added two more.

"How 'bout that?" Winter asked afterward as he was about to slip out of the United Center. "The last two especially. He bounced those two in. I just told him to stay on the line. 'Shoot 'em the way we shoot 'em in practice. You know how you shoot in practice. You shoot 80 to 90 percent. Shoot the same shot.'"

Winter said he had figured the season might come down to Rodman free throws. "If he's in the ball game late, he's probably the guy they're gonna try to foul. That's why we didn't neglect to work it with him all the time," the coach said. "Sometimes it seems like it's worthless because he doesn't get very many free throws, but if he's gonna be in the ball game late in the game, he's gonna get fouled. So he's at least gotta have a chance to hit 'em. He's not gonna make 'em all, but he'll make a good percentage of 'em."

As the coach talked, he held yet another of Jordan's empty shoe boxes under his arm. Asked what he did with all the empty boxes he collected, he replied, "Well, I use 'em for file cabinets. I label 'em and put different things in 'em, investments or whatever."

It was pointed out that Jordan's shoe boxes were probably worth more than Winter's investments, what with the mania over collecting items from the star's era in the league. "Well they probably are," Winter agreed. "Maybe I'll sell 'em one of these days."

After Game 4, Jordan had told the media that he and his teammates were in great shape to claim their sixth title, if only they kept focused. Winter, though, figured it was very hard to beat a solid team four straight games, which proved to be solid thinking. It wasn't like the Bulls hadn't stumbled here before. They lost Game 5 of the 1993 Finals to Phoenix and had to travel back to the southwest to defeat the Suns. "Unfortunately, we have to go back to Utah, and it's a duplicate situation of 1993," Jordan said after Chicago lost Game 5 to Utah and saw their series lead narrowed to 3-2. "So when you get on the plane headed to Utah, you have to be very positive, you have to be ready to play. It's one loss, and you can't let it eat at you to the point where it becomes two losses."

It had clearly been a case of celebrating too early, too many laughs at their good fortune, and the result was an 83-81 Utah win. Even Jordan admitted getting caught up in the fallacy. "I really didn't have a tee time," he told reporters, "because I anticipated drinking so much champagne that I wouldn't be able to get up." As poorly as the Bulls played (Jordan was 9 for 26 from the floor and Pippen 2 for 16), they still had a shot to win it at the end. Kukoc's 30 points on 11-of-13 shooting had kept them close, despite Malone's 39 points.

The Bulls got the ball back with 1.1 seconds to go, and during the ensuing timeout, Jordan sat there enjoying the circumstances. If ever there was a moment to inhabit, as Jackson had encouraged him to do, this was it. Moments later Jordan missed the falling-out-of-bounds shot, which sealed Chicago's loss, but that didn't prevent his treasuring the moment. "I'm pretty sure people were hoping I would make that shot. Except people from Utah," he said. "For 1.1 seconds, everyone was holding their breath, which was kind of cute.

"No one knew what was going to happen," he said. "Me, you, no one who was watching the game. And that was the cute part about it. And I love those moments. Great players thrive on that in some respects because they have an opportunity to decide happiness and sadness. That's what you live for. That's the fun part about it."

The real breath-holding, however, came in Game 6 back in Utah, where the Jazz charged out early and Pippen came up with horrendous back spasms. The pain sent him to the locker room where a massage therapist literally pounded on his back trying to drive the spasms out. One team employee reported Krause standing back in a corner of the room, almost transfixed, watching Pippen absorb the blows, eager to get back in the game to help Jordan. The GM didn't intrude upon the scene, but afterward, after Pippen had returned to the game and winced his way through the proceedings, giving Jordan just enough support to get to the end, some observers said that Krause seemed dramatically and genuinely changed in his opinion of Pippen.

"I just tried to gut it out," Pippen said. "I felt my presence on the floor would mean more than just sitting in the locker room. I knew I was going to come back in the second half, but I just didn't know how much I was going to be able to give."

He returned to the game to run the offense as Jordan scored a magnificent 45 points, including the final jumper from the key after which Jordan stood poised, his arm draped in a follow through, savoring the moment, inhabiting the moment, frozen in that moment. Photos of the shot would show in the soft focus a number of Utah fans suspended there in agony with him, their hands covering eyes and ears, the ball hanging there in air, ready to swish for an 87-86 Chicago win. Cute.

"Things start to move very slowly and you start to see the court very well," said Jordan, explaining the last play. "You start reading what the defense is trying to do. And I saw that. I saw the moment."

The Jazz would get a final Stockton shot, but Ron Harper hustled to help him miss. When the ball had bounded away and the buzzer sounded, Jordan produced yet another of those moments to inhabit, this time with he and Jackson together in a prolonged embrace.

The emotion would carry them away from there, first on a peaceful plane ride home, shared with Krause and Reinsdorf and free of acrimony. Reinsdorf, known for his needling of others, liked to think that he was one of the few people in the organization who could trade barbs with Jordan and not come out a loser. He recalled that during the 1993 championship series Jordan was dealing blackjack on the plane and had instituted a rule that he won all ties, which for some reason his teammates accepted. "These guys were dumb enough to do it," the team chairman recalled with a chuckle. In 1998, as the team headed back home after yet another championship, there was Jordan, enjoying perhaps his last card game in the sweet privacy of the team plane. The mood was light, and Reinsdorf couldn't resist a needle. This time Jordan was dealing tonk. "You making up your own rules again so you can take advantage of these guys?" the chairman asked.

"That's the way to stay on top," Jordan replied.

He played his fill, squeezing every last drop from the moment, but with an hour still to go in the flight he could do no more, and an exhausted Jordan found a quiet place to curl up in deep sleep.

He would awaken, of course, from the dream to find that Jackson had ridden off on his motorcycle after turning down Reinsdorf's late offer to stay with the team. Another year trading insults and hard lines with Krause just wasn't worth it, no matter how exhilarating the finishes. "I told Phil we wanted him back the Wednesday night after we won the title during our office celebration," Reinsdorf insisted. "I sat down with Phil and told him, 'If you've changed your mind, we want you back, no conditions, whether Scottie and Michael come back or not.' He said, 'That's very generous.' I told him, 'Generosity has nothing to do with it. You've earned it.'

"He took a deep breath," Reinsdorf said, "and then he said, 'No, I have to step back.'"

As for the rest of them, the players, their futures would be frozen in another summer of charged NBA labor deliberations. Who knew where it would end up?

All they really had, as Jackson had told them, was the moment. The sweet, sad, wonderful moment. And that was more than enough.

EPILOG

It almost didn't happen, Jerry Reinsdorf would admit later. The Bulls came very close in the summer of 1997 to giving up on their hopes for a sixth championship. He and Jerry Krause doubted that they would be good enough to win another title, and there was an enticing offer from the Boston Celtics for Pippen.

"We considered giving up a shot at the sixth title to begin rebuilding, and we would have given it up if we could have made the right deal," Reinsdorf said. "The reason we considered breaking the team up is that we wanted to minimize the period of time between winning the last championship and getting back into contention with the next team."

Pippen was going into the last year of his contract, and if they didn't trade him they would get nothing for him in a trade.

Krause kept upping the ante with the Celtics. Ultimately, the Bulls didn't get what they wanted, so they kept the team together.

The reward for that, Reinsdorf said, was the franchise's unexpected sixth title in 1998.

Both he and Krause figured the price for that title was steep. "We now have very little to trade, very little to work with in rebuilding," Reinsdorf said.

Their other option, of course, would have been to offer Pippen a nice fat contract extension before the 1997-98 season. But that wasn't their history. In the past, they could have signed key players for lesser sums, but many times they had waited, had found some means of offending those players, and had then been forced to sign them for much more. Or they had watched those players walk away, as Horace Grant did in 1994. Chip Schaefer pointed out that if they'd been just a bit nicer, the Bulls could have probably re-signed Grant with no more effort than a good steak dinner.

As it was, the Bulls somehow found a way to anger and insult their key players.

Suddenly, in the aftermath of the 1998 playoffs, they found themselves needing Pippen very badly. They needed Pippen back on the roster for 1999 to entice Jordan to stay. And they needed Jordan to keep from plunging into the abyss of miserable losing, the fate they had dreaded for years.

"I really admired what he did," Krause said of Pippen's insistence on playing with a bad back in Game 6. "At halftime I didn't think there was any way he was gonna play. He was hurtin'."

But Pippen's response to the new appreciation management expressed for him would have to wait until the league's labor problems were settled, which left both Krause and Reinsdorf hanging in doubt as the columnists for Chicago's newspapers took turns whacking them for chasing away the greatest team in NBA history.

Reindorf assured Jordan that he could take the entire summer of 1998 before deciding his future. "I told him the money would be there under the salary cap," the chairman pointed out. Because he owned 100 percent of the corporation that managed the Bulls as general partner for the team's limited partnership, the power was Reinsdorf's alone to wield. How much did he want to pay?

Players and coaches think only about the present, never about the future, Reinsdorf said. "Michael couldn't care less about what happens after he leaves."

The chairman did sense that Jordan wanted to keep playing but only if Pippen returned.

The first sign of danger had actually come with Jackson's indifference to Resindorf's late offer to return. "Jerry and I talked about making the offer to him," Krause said. "Could I have lived with Phil another year? Yeah. For the good of the franchise. My personal relationship with Phil did not hurt the franchise. It got crazy. That's true. There was no love lost between Phil and I. But we could have done it. We could have worked together for another year. No one can say I'm not an organization man."

Jackson told Rick Telander that he might have stayed if management had asked him to hang around until after Jordan finished his career. "But they never suggested that," Jackson said.

For Jackson's replacement, Krause gathered a list of a half dozen candidates with his only declaration being that the next Bulls coach would definitely not be represented by an agent.

Did Krause actually think that he could go back and start all over again? Conjure up all this magic again?

The answer to that lay in a simple, hubris-filled comment the GM made after Jordan hit the shot in Salt Lake City to win the sixth championship. "Jerry and I have done it six times now," Krause told Phil Rosenthal of the *Sun Times*.

It was one final sour note on his theme from October. Organizations do win championships.

He was wrong, of course. These were and are Michael Jordan's Chicago Bulls. Always have been. Always will be.

Acknowedgments

I would like to thank the following for answering my questions: Terry Armour, Marty Burns, Jud Buechler, Scott Burrell, Bill Cartwright, Horace Grant, Ron Harper, John Jackson, Phil Jackson, Michael Jordan, Steve Kerr, Joe Kleine, Jerry Krause, Toni Kukoc, Rusty LaRue, Bruce Levine, John Ligmanowski, Luc Longley, Kent McDill, Scottie Pippen, Jerry Reinsdorf, Dennis Rodman, Jim Rose, Chip Schaefer, Sam Smith, Rick Telander, Rod Thorn, Mark Vancil, Bill Wennington, Tex Winter and numerous others (you know who you are).

For their friendship and guidance, I would like to thank L.J. Beaty, George Mumford, Bill Kovarik, David Halberstam, Mike Hudson, Mike Shank, Lindy Davis, Billy Packer, Kay Kuhn, Susan Storey, Heather Lowhorn, Greg and Lindy Boeck, Marty Burns, Jeff Joniak, Steve Kashul, Scott McCoy, Cheryl Raye, Mark Vancil, Rick Telander, Joe Austin, Ron Anderson and Mark Morrison.

I have a number of people to thank for making this project possible. First, Bob Snodgrass, the publisher at Addax, and his assistants Darcie Kidson, Sharon Snodgrass, and Michelle Washington, all helped guide it through the publishing process. Then, of course, there's my wife Karen and children Jenna, Henry and Morgan, who somehow manage to cope with the crazy nature of my work.

I want to acknowledge the work of the dozens of writers and reporters who have covered the NBA, including Mitch Albom, Terry Armour, Lacy J. Banks, Jesse Barkin, Terry Boers, Gary Seymour, Mike Nadel, Jim O'Donnell, Cheryl Raye, Mitch Chortkoff, Robert Falkoff, Bill Gleason, Scott Howard-Cooper, Mike Imrem, Melissa Isaacson, John Jackson, Paul Ladewski, Bernie Lincicome, Bob Logan, Jay Mariotti, Kent McDill, Corky Meinecke, Mike Mulligan, Fred Mitchell, Skip Myslenski, Glenn Rogers, Steve Rosenbloom, Phil Rosenthal, Skip Bayless, Eddie Sefko, Gene Seymour, Sam Smith, Ray Sons, Paul Sullivan, Mike Tulumello, Mark Vancil, Bob Verdi, Scoop Jackson, Kerry Eggers, Michael Bradley, Terry Pluto, Tourre, Mike Kahn, Michael Hunt, Martin Frank and many, many others. Their work has been invaluable. Extensive use was made of a variety of publications, including the

ESPN Magazine, Sports Illustrated, Slam, Toronto Globe and Mail, Waterbury Republican, Milwaukee Journal Sentinel, Inside Stuff, Lindy's Pro Basketball Annual, the Akron Beacon Journal, Baltimore Sun, Basketball Times, Boston Globe, Chicago Defender, Chicago Tribune, Chicago Sun-Times, Copley Newspapers, Daily Southtown, The Detroit News, The Detroit Free Press, The Daily Herald, Hoop Magazine, Houston Post, Houston Chronicle, Inside Sports, Los Angeles Times, The National, New York Daily News, The New York Times, New York Post, The Charlotte Observer, USA Today, The Oregonian, Philadelphia Inquirer, San Antonio Express-News, Sport, Sports Illustrated, The Sporting News, Street & Smith's Pro Basketball Yearbook, and *The Washington Post.*

Also vital were several books, including:

And Now, Your Chicago Bulls! by Roland Lazenby

Bull Run! by Roland Lazenby

Bull Session by Johnny Kerr and Terry Pluto

Michael Jordan by Mitchell Krugel

Rare Air by Michael Jordan with Mark Vancil

Sportswit by Lee Green

The Bob Verdi Collection by Bob Verdi

The Glory and the Dream by William Manchester

The Jordan Rules by Sam Smith

The Sporting News NBA Official Guide and Register

DATE DUE

Demco, Inc. 38-293